"THE REGULATIONS OF ROBBERS"

"THE REGULATIONS OF ROBBERS"

*Legal Fictions of Slavery
and Resistance*

Christina Accomando

The Ohio State University Press
Columbus

Library of Congress Cataloging-in-Publication Data

Accomando, Christina.
    The regulations of robbers : legal fictions of slavery and resistance / Christina Accomando.
        p. cm.
    Includes bibliographical references (p.) and index.
    Contents: Legal fictions of slavery and resistance — "Further deponent sayeth not": multiple consciousness and suppressed narratives in tellings of slave revolt — Part two: "I want it root and branch destroyed": the radical politics and shifting voices of Sojourner Truth — A woman among the pettifoggers: truth as legal actor — Framing truth and resisting frames — Part three: The regulations of robbers: Harriet Jacobs's legal critique — "We could have told them a different story": slave law and slave voices — Reframing legal fictions of womanhood — Epilogue — Confronting the legacies: decoding modern rhetorics of race
    ISBN 0-8142-0883-5 (cloth : alk. paper) — ISBN 0-8142-5081-5 (pbk. : alk. paper)
    1. American prose literature—African American authors—History and criticism. 2. American prose literature—Women authors—History and criticism. 3. American prose literature—19th century—History and criticism. 4. Feminism and literature—United States—History—19th century. 5. Slaves—United States—Biography—History and criticism. 6. African American women—Biography—History and criticism. 7. African Americans—Biography—History and criticism. 8. Slaves' writings, American—History and criticism. 9. Autobiography—African American authors. 10. Slavery in literature. 11. Law and literature. 12. Race in literature. I. Title.

PS366.A35 A28 2001
306.3'62'0973–dc21
                                                                    2001002939

Cover design by Jennifer Carr.
Text design by BN Typographics West.
Type set in Adobe Garamond by BN Typographics West.
Printed by Thomson-Shore, Inc.

The paper used in this publication meets the minimum requirements of the American National Standard for Information Sciences— Permanence of Paper for Printed Library Materials. ANSI Z39.48-1992.

9 8 7 6 5 4 3 2 1

To the memory of my grandmother,
Nicolette Laloy Hsu,
a passionate teacher
and fighter for justice.

"I regarded such laws as the regulations of robbers, who had no rights that I was bound to respect."

—HARRIET JACOBS, 1861

contents

acknowledgments

This book emerges from several years of research, teaching and activism. I am grateful for the contributions of many advisors, colleagues, and friends over the years. Nicole Tonkovich helped to shape this effort from its beginnings. I thank her for her friendship, her intellectual rigor, and her pragmatic advice. Stephanie Jed's insights have been vital to my approach to legal documents and texts in general, ever since her seminar on "The Aesthetics of Quotidian Writing" many years ago expanded the boundaries of literary analysis for me. I am indebted to Frances Smith Foster's groundbreaking scholarship, her reading of my early drafts, and her continuing support. I greatly appreciate Peggy Cooper Davis's interest in my work and her careful reading of the book manuscript.

In the earliest stages of this project, Megan Matchinske, José van Dijck, and Kim Dillon provided invaluable encouragement and friendship. Anne Shea, Judith Coker, Scott Bentley, and Kristin Anderson have continued to be heroic readers, valued colleagues, and supportive friends. I am also grateful to Grace Hong, Démian Pritchard, Ramie Tateishi, Emily Rogers, writing group members Jennifer Eichstedt and Mary Scoggin, and HSU colleagues Barbara Curiel, Eleanor Castleberry, Betsy Boone, Kim Berry, Wurlig Bao, and David Boxer. In addition to my academic alliances, I also am indebted to the political organizations that simultaneously drained and sustained me over the years. I particularly want to thank Jane Patton, my friend and mentor who first encouraged and facilitated my activism more than twenty years ago.

I have presented parts of this research at the MELUS Conference on

Literature and the Idea of Social Justice, NEH Summer Institute on American Literature, Modern Language Association Convention, American Literature Association Conference, National Women's Studies Association Conference, and the University of Pennsylvania Afro-American Studies Conference, which have provided fertile ground for discussion of many of these ideas. I also have been fortunate to be able to bring much of this material into my courses in literature and ethnic studies at the University of California San Diego, San Diego State University, and Humboldt State University. Over the years my students have provided stimulating discussions and have reminded me why I am in academia.

The Humboldt State University Faculty Development Diversity Award, HSU Research, Scholarship and Creative Activity Grant, and HSU Foundation Award helped enable me to complete the book project. A UCSD Department of Literature Dissertation Fellowship facilitated completion of the first version of this project. The University of California President's Washington Scholarship provided me with funds to conduct research in Washington, D.C., at the Library of Congress, Howard University's Moorland-Spingarn Research Center, and the Mary McLeod Bethune Museum and Archives. I especially thank Mary Lou Hultgren of Hampton University for her help in securing the cover image of Sojourner Truth. The Women's Research and Education Institute awarded me a WREI Congressional Fellowship, enabling me to spend a year working on race discrimination, reproductive rights, and religious freedom issues in the House Judiciary Subcommittee on Civil and Constitutional Rights. I thank WREI and my fellow Fellows, especially Susan Messina, for friendship and intellectual stimulation. I also want to acknowledge with respect and warmth Subcommittee Chair Don Edwards, whose humanity and genuine commitment to civil rights endured through his many years in Congress.

Finally, those closest to me have lived intimately with this project for more than ten years. David Berman has provided emotional support, critical feedback, and a vital vantage point from outside the halls of academia. My wonderful, incomparable family provided support in immeasurable ways. My parents, Claire Hsu Accomando and Allan Accomando, and my grandparents, Nicolette Laloy Hsu and Fuyun Hsu, have been my finest teachers and have served as models of intellect and compassion.

PART ONE

Introduction

chapter one

Legal Fictions of Slavery and Resistance

For one hour, he talked so bitterly against me and against my being in possession of my liberty that I was trembling, . . . for I certainly thought everybody must believe him; indeed I almost believed the dreadful things he said.

— LUCY DELANEY, on the opposing lawyer's arguments in her 1844 suit for freedom

In the era of the Boston Massacre and Declaration of Independence, Boston poet and Middle Passage survivor Phillis Wheatley addressed herself to British and American officials, as well as to a community of literate people of color, and engaged in debates over slavery and revolution. Toward the end of the war for independence, another Massachusetts slave, Elizabeth Freeman, used the state constitution to sue for her own independence and won. In a young United States, Lucy Terry—kidnapped from Africa decades earlier—lobbied the Vermont governor, made an antidiscrimination speech to the trustees of Williams College, and argued before the U.S. Supreme Court. In the 1820s, New York slave Sojourner Truth decided to override her owner's broken contract and the state emancipation act to take freedom into her own hands. She went on to initiate three successful court cases, petition the federal government, and attempt to vote a half-century before it was legal. North Carolina slave Harriet Jacobs also escaped slavery and on the eve of the Civil War published a legal critique of the institution that had rationalized her bondage. Missouri slave Polly Berry—born free and kidnapped not from Africa but from Illinois—successfully sued for her own freedom and that of her daughter, Lucy Delaney. Delaney published an account of the courtroom drama fifty years later, during the legal retrenchments of post-Reconstruction, and served in many public capacities, including president of the Female Union and secretary of Colonel Robert Shaw's Woman's Relief Corps.[1]

Like the opposing lawyer in Delaney's suit for freedom, American law has "talked . . . bitterly against" African American subjects (Delaney 40).

The laws and legal fictions of American slavery tell us that slaves and African Americans had no legal or political voice, and the suppression of those voices may have been largely effective, but the efforts of these women suggest that reality did not always fit those fictions. Slavery produced an inherently—and intentionally—incomplete and unstable record. The official records were not meant to register the voices and the agency of those subjected to the system. The perpetuation of slavery—and the interests of the many who benefitted from it, whether slaveholders or not—required that such voices be suppressed. These textual silencings make it difficult to study the history and legacies of U.S. slavery and resistance. How can we read or teach the contradictory and partial texts of slavery? How can we understand the workings of this institution and still resist the urge to believe all "the dreadful things" it says? To begin to read the story of American slavery, we need to develop different reading strategies and seek out different sorts of texts.

In a nation founded upon articulations of liberty and equality, human enslavement has been justified with complex and contradictory narratives. Slavery also has been resisted, physically and rhetorically, from its very beginnings. The legal and rhetorical fictions of American bondage, centuries in the making, still are embedded in law and culture and still are resisted and rewritten. This study examines legal, political, and literary discourses of slavery and resistance in order to take apart dominant texts and read the counternarratives of activism. I will consider poetry, oratory, slave narrative, and a range of legal critiques by former slaves (including Wheatley, Truth, and Jacobs) alongside and against statutes, court cases, and legal treatises. Drawing upon critical race theory, as well as feminist legal theory and black feminist thought, I advocate a methodology of "multiple consciousness" as a way to counter the false neutrality of the dominant discourses of slavery, particularly those of American law. Multiple voices and shifting perspectives can help displace the constructed univocality of legal discourse and turn attention to stories that have been suppressed. On the one hand, this focus on multiple voices is a theoretical or critical maneuver in the present—contemporary critics can and should step into the textual waters and enact that displacement today. At the same time, part of this project is to make visible how, in the eighteenth and nineteenth centuries, African American critics—slaves, former slaves, activists, orators, and writers—already were engaged in such work. Resisting slavery physically as well as discursively, as a practice and as a legal construct, these women and men worked to deconstruct slavery and its underlying ideologies. In this study, I examine those critiques of slavery and expose instabilities and contradictions within the law and other dominant narratives. Central to this effort is deconstructing the often invisible framing or packaging of legal and other documents. I seek to call attention to the multiple perspectives already embedded in the texts I examine, and I also generate multiple consciousness by juxtaposing different texts, discourses, and moments.

Selling Shadows and Framing Truth

The textually compromised record of slavery requires scholars to pay heightened attention to the textual details of how the "facts" of slavery come to us. A methodology of deconstructing the usually invisible framing around seemingly objective or official texts can help problematize the reading of those texts. The texts and myths surrounding Sojourner Truth will be analyzed in a later chapter, but an image from her textual history can help illustrate this argument for the analysis of framing.

Truth was aware of the value attached to her name and face, and to help support herself, she sold visiting cards that featured her photograph and the caption "I Sell the Shadow to Support the Substance." Many of these "shadows" still exist today, reproduced in scholarly works as well as on postage stamps, political buttons, feminist posters, and other products. One of the original cards is on display in the Smithsonian Institution's National Portrait Gallery. It is a small card, with a tiny photograph glued to its face. The photograph looks like many other "shadows" of Truth, depicting her seated, directly eyeing the camera, with white kerchief and shawl, knitting props in her lap, and a closed book by her arm. These details—which do not especially suggest her identity as an activist—serve to frame Truth in particular ways: the white yarn across her lap plants her in a domestic sphere; the kerchief and shawl help mark her class; the eyeglasses and book suggest intellect, though the book remains closed. Other details, such as the picture's frame and its location, also provide information and context to a present-day viewer. The photograph is attached to the calling card, which is mounted on white backing, surrounded by a huge white mat and bounded by a large frame. It hangs there, alone on a blank wall, authorized by its presence in the Smithsonian, and framed by an expanse of whiteness.[2]

The literal framing—the vast white mat and solid frame—suggests other ways that Sojourner Truth, or any subject, can be framed. While

Truth played a key role in shaping and selling her image,[3] her framed-by-white photograph also serves as a suggestive metaphor of what frequently happens in written versions of her words. Truth's "shadow" is surrounded here by a literally white expanse just as her words often are surrounded by various "white" expectations and representations. The small picture (about two by three inches) is easy to miss, especially compared to some of the larger-than-life images in the same area. The frame and mat take up more space than the photograph and encourage a viewer either to look away or perhaps to look more closely. Truth's repeated caption juxtaposing "shadow" and "substance" suggests a distinction between image and reality, packaging and content, representations of the body and the body itself. "Shadow" was a common metaphor at the time for photographs, as well as an image of darkness. The phrase "sell the shadow" denotes making money from the calling cards and also suggests the marketing of constructions of Truth's blackness.

Whether present-day viewers look at photographs, speeches, letters, or narratives, we are looking at "shadows" of Truth—representations, constructions, framings. It is impossible to study Sojourner Truth—or any subject—without being confronted by framing of one form or another. No historical figure can be restored or reconstituted, and such unrecoverability is particularly striking in Truth's case. As an African American and a former slave in a nation that justified slavery by dehumanizing blacks and that sought to keep literacy and education from slaves, Truth was never intended to have a voice in American letters. As an orator, preacher, and activist—not a writer—Truth's words were immediately captured and framed, and their preservation is highly mediated. Others—often white women—make choices about what is in the frame and how it is presented, but those choices are rarely announced. Truth herself was also very active in shaping and deploying representations of herself in speeches, photographs, and the narrative that she sold. The many layers of representation cannot be ignored in examining Truth or in any study relying on texts. Such issues are particularly relevant in studies of texts emerging from slavery, since its laws and practices produced records inevitably and intentionally rent with silences and gaps. Neither Truth nor "truth" can emerge unmediated in texts; since framing is inevitable, it is crucial to examine the nature of that framing.

The visual image of a frame serves as a metaphor and a theoretical model. To frame means to construct or enclose, to arrange and adjust for a particular purpose. It also can mean to incriminate falsely, to set up. A frame can refer to a physical structure, including a picture frame, a building, or the human body. The parts of these common dictionary definitions are suggestive: How are images and institutions, buildings and bodies, constructed? When something is enclosed, what is kept out? For whose particular purposes? Who has the power to incriminate? And if we fail to pursue these questions, are we the ones being set up? If our attention is on the apparent subject, the frame may seem invisible. That very invisibility makes it particularly important to pay attention to details and consequences of framing. To reveal the power relations embedded in such choices, it is key to ask not only what is inside the frame and what is outside its boundaries but also who places the framed subject there and with what agendas.

A viewer using this method must consider how the subject is represented and packaged, what it is next to, what is at the center and what is at the edges, and finally, how that framing is resisted. I examine here how various U.S. subjects—from slaves to the nation—are represented and depicted, and how underlying categories, particularly race and gender, are constructed, labeled, packaged, and classified, by authors, activists, and lawmakers. I also examine what happens when something or someone does not fit in the frames—how those representations and categories are rearranged, resisted, and rewritten. Given the interlocking contexts of racism and patriarchy, African American women resisting slavery and its constructions—Truth taking a new name and making herself an orator and a legal subject, for example, or Wheatley fashioning herself as a patriot and poet—pose a particularly radical challenge to the dominant framework, which denies African American women subjecthood and humanity.

Examining how subjects resist framing is crucial to avoid letting a focus on framing remove the subject from the picture. Part of my methodology is to make visible those aspects of framing and representation that often go unnoticed. This emphasis, however, must not duplicate the problems of erasure that I critique. Hence, I intend to keep marginalized voices at the center even as I analyze how those voices have been framed. The framers in these cases might be judges and lawmakers, writers and editors, or contemporary scholars and critics. The central figures in this study—Wheatley, Truth, and Jacobs—were slaves but also come to us today as authors and activists, as social and political critics, challenging these fictions in their lives and in the discourse they left behind. While dominant discourses, including the law, uphold and reproduce the state, the alternate stories generated by these African American women out of a context

of suppression and silencing necessarily have a different relationship to the
state, often an oppositional one, and reading their stories necessarily shifts
the frames.

In general terms, I will examine how facts and facticity are constructed.
The term *facticity*, "the property of being factual," highlights not so much
what is actually factual or "true" but rather how things are permitted to
have this property—what things count as "facts" (D. Smith 10). If, for
example, "facts" need to be documented—that is, need to be on paper to
be considered authentic or authoritative—then oral texts do not easily
attain the weight of facticity. Behind the recording of such facts are structures of power that determine, for instance, who learns to write and whose
writings are published. Literary scholar Stephanie Jed uses the term "f-act"
to identify how *acts* of fact-making can reveal power relations.[4] She writes
that "f-acts are always produced in the context of acts which affirm existing relations of rule. To ignore these relations in favor of the more objectified 'facts' is to perpetuate the conditions of domination and inequality
in which facts are always made" (7). Specifically, I want to examine the
acts that allow certain things to enter the "official" frame of historical documents, in particular the legal record.

Analyzing frames helps reveal who has the power to place "facts" in the
official record. I do not suggest that there is one official record, as there are
different ways that various "facts" come to be. Legal facts can be generated
through a statute, court transcript, or judicial ruling. Hence, it affects fact-
making procedures if women (of any race) cannot vote or hold office, if
African Americans (men and women) cannot testify.[5] Facts in the political
realm might be generated by which items make it into written political
records and what records endure. If nineteenth-century political action
includes giving speeches at conventions, for example, significant questions
include which versions of what speeches are transcribed into official proceedings, or printed in abolitionist newspapers, or reprinted in Elizabeth
Cady Stanton's *History of Woman Suffrage*. Whether and where such
speeches are printed affects how accessible they are to scholars today. For
example, the *Liberator* is easier to find in libraries than many other papers,
and items preserved in the *History of Woman Suffrage* tend to look like
official parts of the women's movement.

Dissecting fact-making procedures is not to say that nothing is true
but rather to question the procedures that place certain details into the
realm of facticity while omitting others. In critiquing a notion of "facts,"
I also use the term *fictions* to refer to literary as well as legal and other

constructed facts. This terminology is not meant to collapse all distinctions but to highlight the constructedness of these discourses and to break down a seeming binary (legal documents establish facts, literary documents create fiction; law is real, literature is constructed). There are significant differences, and there are not always clear lines between the categories.

I am particularly interested in legal, political, and literary framings of race, gender, and slavery. Race and gender have real effects in the real world, but as categories they are social and cultural constructions that encode various hierarchies and relations of power. During legalized human enslavement in the U.S., such categories and their intersections were not only constructed but also literally codified in particular ways. I examine constructions of race and gender in various discourses of slavery and resistance, including slave law, abolitionist rhetoric, and slave narratives. Especially key is how these categories appeared in the middle of the nineteenth century—during intense political activity in the abolition and suffrage movements, as slavery became increasingly controversial and at the same time increasingly federalized,[6] when former slaves were publishing accounts of their lives, in the midst of an explosion in white women's writing and sentimental fiction, and with the nation on the brink of the Civil War. In the nineteenth century, anxieties about defining race led to greater efforts at categorization as condition, color, or origin failed to provide simple dividing lines. The lines were never simple, of course, and grew increasingly problematic, blurred, and complex, particularly as mixed-race and free-black populations increased. Laws governing racial identity, miscegenation, rape, reproduction, literacy, testimony, and property framed African Americans in specific (and contradictory) ways—as nonhuman, with dangerous sexuality and nonexistent subjectivity.

To maintain both American "equality" and American slavery, slavery's defenders (and sometimes its opponents) often constructed the slave in opposition to the (white) American—as foreign, alien, other. The construction of slaves and African Americans more generally as not-American quickly slips into their construction as not-human. "All men" can be created equal only if "men" takes on a very narrow definition (even narrower than the obvious gender exclusion). In some configurations, the slave or African American as inferior is deemed (by Southern judges and lawmakers, for example) necessary to the existence of the white American with liberty and equality.

Constructions of slavery also clash with nineteenth-century notions of (white) gender roles, so that gender and sexuality are redefined as they intersect with race. The complex arrangement of slave law erases black subjectivity while it also constructs black sexuality as dangerous, aberrant, and illicit. In this contradictory configuration, African Americans are hence both nonexistent as subjects *and* threatening. Black womanhood—slave or free—is defined in opposition to ideals of white womanhood. Slave women are kept outside of "womanhood" when they are framed first and foremost as laborers. At the same time, certain tropes of African American womanhood emerge, such as the Mammy and the Jezebel, which contradict each other and white womanhood.[7] This study examines the application of these images and what happens when reality does not fit the frames. Frequently the stereotypes are then imposed all the more forcefully—erasing those women, making them foreign and other. At the same time, such women also refuse the framings and create new images. The dominant tropes are both invoked and resisted, reinscribed and subverted.

Multiple Consciousness and Critical Race Theory

My project is aligned with the efforts of critical race theory, an emerging body of scholarship that has restructured how we look at race, law, culture, and power. Articulated primarily by legal scholars of color over the last two decades, critical race theory operates with the premise that race and racism always have been embedded in U.S. law. No single doctrine or methodology defines critical race theory, but several features characterize this interdisciplinary body of work. Kimberlé Crenshaw writes that this school of thought "reflects a common skepticism toward dominant claims of . . . neutrality, objectivity, and color blindness. Critical race theory embraces a contextualized historical analysis of racial hierarchy as part of its challenge to the presumptive legitimacy of societal institutions" ("A Black Feminist Critique" 214). Racial hierarchy and racism are not aberrations or accidents but are instead systemic and institutionalized. Current laws and policies that treat racism and discrimination as only individual acts of prejudice ignore the widespread systemic racism that operates daily in U.S. society.

Critical race theorists argue that even as legal approaches have been used to fight racism, the law also has played a central role in upholding white supremacy and other forms of domination. While the law has the appearance of rationality, objectivity, and neutrality (presented, for example, as "color blindness"), in fact, laws are not neutral, and responsible scholarship about the law cannot be neutral. Critical race theorists, while identifying and analyzing the relationship between racism and law, also argue for resistance and change. In Mari Matsuda's words, "This new jurisprudence was born of scholars who were cynically hopeful" (*Where Is Your Body?* 48–49). These scholars often work in a context of contradiction or duality, for example, simultaneously using the law and critiquing it. "The dissonance of combining deep criticism of law with an aspirational view of law is part of the experience of people of color," writes Matsuda, who argues that mainstream legal scholarship can learn from those who have been traditionally silenced ("Looking to the Bottom" 65).

Because dominant narratives have left out the stories of those who have been subordinated, critical race theory often uses strategies of storytelling to recognize the need to relate narratives that are not usually heard.[8] Thus, while reading legal doctrine and documents carefully and critically, scholars also need to seek out alternate stories, voices that have been silenced or marginalized by the "official" voice of the law. While formed only in the late 1980s as a body of theory with a name, such ideas have been in circulation since much earlier.[9] I will argue that several thinkers during the period of U.S. slavery were already using some of the strategies now advocated by critical race theory.

Many aspects of critical race theory are applicable to the study of the law and literature of slavery. In particular, I use the notion of "multiple consciousness" as a means to bring alternate stories into the official record. Legal scholar Angela Harris advocates multiple consciousness as a mode of reading literature and law in order to introduce a dialogue of voices, resist disciplinary restrictions, and destabilize seeming neutralities.[10] While the law presents itself in a single, unified voice (the voice of "We, the People"), Harris seeks to displace that false "univocality" with multiple voices and shifting perspectives. In "Race and Essentialism in Feminist Legal Theory," Harris sets up the single "neutral" voice of law and the decontextualized voice of literature as two potential extremes. She discusses various literary and legal scholars[11] who "struggle against their discipline's grain," and she argues that "the aim is to understand both legal and literary discourse as the complex struggle and unending dialogue between these voices" (237). What she seeks is not a "golden mean or static equilibrium between two extremes, but rather a process in which propositions are constantly put forth, challenged, and subverted" (237). I want to use this strategy of multiple consciousness to destabilize the seemingly neutral language of law and policy, by critiquing those discourses and eventually shifting discussion to other narratives as well. "In order to energize legal theory," argues Harris, "we need to subvert it with narratives and stories, accounts of the particular, the different, and the hitherto silenced" (255). A focus on multiple voices and unstable categories can still be situated even as it refuses any single location.

In fact, this strategy requires us to pay attention to who is speaking, under what authority, and with what agendas. It also requires us to consider how certain voices are granted the authority to speak in the first place. While "official" or dominant discourses, such as the law, give more credence to those with more power, the approach of multiple consciousness questions assumptions of authority and gives credence to voices that speak the experiences of groups that have been silenced or marginalized. Of course no single voice can speak some "singular" experience of any group, which is precisely why it is important to seek out multiple perspectives.

In this study, I both deploy multiple consciousness as a critical strategy and reveal how it is already being used in many of the texts I examine. Depending on context, this method might take various forms, including juxtaposition and reading for silences. First, juxtaposition is a technique that calls for putting next to each other different items—perhaps things that we do not expect to examine alongside each other—in order to consider a variety of comparisons and contrasts. In this study I will juxtapose, among other things, different discourses, separate moments, and multiple versions of the same event. I examine a range of discourses here because legal, literary, political, and other discourses all play a role in constructing race, gender, and slavery in the U.S. Examining them together is one way to generate a multiplicity of voices. Law and literature are different discourses; at the same time, there is not a simple line to be drawn between them. Law often relies on tropes, imagery, metaphor; it constructs fictions. It also has state power behind it, a distinction not to be minimized. Literature often can reinforce or challenge legal, "nonfictional" issues. Simultaneously examining the narratives of law and literature can be a powerful counter to the rigid (if contradictory) stereotypes around race and gender and to the seeming neutrality of the "unified" voice of law.

Discrete disciplinary lines, narrow specializations, and traditional methodological approaches make it difficult to make such juxtapositions. Issues are sometimes framed (by the academy, for example, or by anthology selections, bookstore categories, library shelves, etc.) in such narrow ways that crossing the lines seems impossible. Law professor and scholar Patricia Williams deliberately breaks such rules and moves easily and strategically between periods, disciplines, and genres. In her theory and her imagery she breaks out of the frames of disciplines and texts. "I want to look at legal issues within a framework inscribed not just within the four corners of a document—be it contract or the Constitution—but by the disciplines of psychology, sociology, history, criticism, and philosophy," she writes in *The Alchemy of Race and Rights.* "This sort of analytic technique can serve to describe a community of context for those social actors whose traditional legal status has been the isolation of oxymoron, of oddity, of outsider" (7). Williams refuses the narrow and arbitrary frame of a legal document and of the legal discipline itself. Instead, she places legal issues in historical, political, and personal contexts. Her chapter "On Being the Object of Property," for example, juxtaposes slavery time and the twentieth century, legal and medical and social practices, reproduction in different moments and of different groups, slave contracts and surrogacy contracts, the impregnating of her great-great-grandmother as an eleven-year-old slave girl, and the modern sterilization of women of color. By comparing these diverse narratives, Williams displaces the seeming neutrality of the legal and social policies that would make property of the bodies of certain women. Her method provides a valuable strategy for legal criticism that is feminist and antiracist.

Next, reading for silences is a strategy made necessary by the inherently incomplete "official" record of slavery. Once we recognize that there are gaps and silences in the record, we need to look actively for omitted or marginalized stories. This strategy might mean reading carefully for subtext and multiple layers of meaning, including irony, indirection, or the directing of different messages to different readers (in Wheatley's poetry, for example). It might mean reading for contradictions, both intentional (when Truth simultaneously critiques and uses the law, for instance) and unintentional (as when a slave law says it will do one thing and does quite another). It might mean noticing whose testimony is privileged and looking for another version of that story, or paying special attention to something or someone appearing only in the margins (e.g. only in the footnotes, or mentioned without being quoted, or quoted in a highly compromised way). In her essay "When the First Quail Calls: Multiple Consciousness as Jurisprudential Method," Matsuda writes, "The multiple consciousness I urge lawyers to attain is not a random ability to see all points of view but a deliberate choice to see the world from the standpoint of the oppressed" (in *Where Is Your Body?* 8). Jacobs, describing how slaves would have responded to a question that was not posed to them, writes, "*We* could have told them a different story" (146–47). Reading for silences tells us to listen for that "different story," sometimes by probing a text more deeply and sometimes by seeking out another text altogether.

Analyzing dominant tropes and seeking out alternative narratives can highlight some of the erasures. Crenshaw argues that in legal doctrine and in politics, African American women are marginalized partly as a result of "the lack of available and widely comprehended narratives to communicate" the intersectional reality of their lives ("Whose Story" 404). She argues, for example, that pervasive "stereotypes and myths that justified the sexual abuse of black women in slavery continue to be played out in current society" (412), in the actual harassment of women as well as in legal and social responses to such treatment. Often those stereotypes make it nearly impossible to hear alternate stories (during Anita Hill's Senate testimony, for example). To read for silences, it is important to identify when such myths surface, to critique those narratives, and to introduce different stories in various forms.

Treating legal discourse as narrative can help provide tools for analyzing the impact of framing, including the consequences of leaving certain things out of the frame. One crucial way to read for silences is to read for context that has been removed. Reading for that context can help unmask power relations. In the essay "Reel Time/Real Justice," Crenshaw and Gary Peller use the legal framing and reframing of the 1991 Los Angeles police beating of motorist Rodney King as a point of departure to discuss more broadly "how racial power generally is produced, mediated and legitimated" (283). Through the police brutality trial, in which King was reframed as the dangerous agent, they explore the narratives constructed in legal discourses. "Law in general and the courtroom in particular are arenas where narratives are contested and the power of interpretation exercised. . . . The story lines developed in law *mediate* power in the sense that power is translated to appear as non-power" (286). In the courtroom, turning the video of King's beating into "frame-by-frame stills . . . mounted on clean white illustration boards" reframed the narrative and physically and symbolically permitted a "disaggregation" that removed the beating from any context. Crenshaw and Peller borrow the term *disaggregation* from Supreme Court Justice Thurgood Marshall's dissent in a 1989 affirmative action case, in which "disaggregating [the] local evidence" of racial exclusion permitted the Court to erase racial context and thereby mask unequal power relations.[12] Crenshaw and Peller write, "Through the typical process of 'disaggregation,' a narrative is created within which racial power has been *mediated* out, like the anesthetic effect of mounting stills on clinically-white illustration board" (290). Their focus in this article does not reach as far back as slave law, but I use their approach in my study to "examine critically how ideological narratives work as a form of social power, to show how a belief in formal legal equality—in the objectivity of 'the rule of law'—can help obscure the everyday character of racial power" (289). Such interactions of race, power, law, and objectivity can inform a study of nineteenth-century slave law.

Applying principles of critical race theory to discourses of slavery and resistance is important not only to understand a past moment in history but also to contribute to an understanding of racism and legal discourse in the present moment. The current political climate in the U.S. is marked by both retrenchments in civil rights law and claims of progress and "color blindness." From the Supreme Court's dilution of voting rights to California's statewide repeal of affirmative action, attacks on the gains of the last three decades are cloaked in the language of neutrality and fairness.[13] Judge and legal scholar A. Leon Higginbotham provides strategies for decoding such language through his examination of both slave law in U.S. history and racism in current law. Arguing that Americans must pay attention to the legal roots of slavery, he exposes various ways the seemingly neutral law sought to deny personhood to slaves and to African Americans more generally. "However tightly woven into the history of their country is the legalization of black suppression," he writes, "many Americans still find it too traumatic to study the true story of racism as it has existed under their 'rule of law'" (*In the Matter of Color* 11). That "true story" is difficult to grasp through a passive reading of law. Since "the language of the law shields one's consciousness from direct involvement with the stark plight of its victims," Higginbotham argues for a "skeptical reading" of legal discourse (11). Slave narratives and political oratory can provide some of the material for such a reading of antebellum law. While Higginbotham focuses on historical analysis, he also points to modern legacies: "The poisonous legacy of legalized oppression based upon the matter of color can never be adequately purged from our society if we act as if slave laws had never existed" (391). By examining the legal discourses of slavery and the challenges to those legal voices in the years leading up to the Civil War, we can confront the existence of slave law in a historical moment when debate over the legality of slavery was especially fierce. In the midst of modern-day claims of color blindness and race neutrality, it is particularly crucial to confront our history of *legalized* racial oppression and to provide alternative narratives.

Part of breaking down the appearance of univocality and neutrality is to locate oneself and one's perspective. I am engaging in this project as a contemporary critic wanting to examine legacies of slavery in modern legal discourses from a feminist and antiracist perspective. Constructions of race and gender emerging from slavery are important because they are not a brief historical moment secured in the past but remain with us in various forms. I also need to situate myself more specifically as a white, middle-class feminist activist and academic in the U.S.[14] Because of my political and geographical locations, I am particularly concerned with the history of racism in the U.S. women's movement and the legacies of U.S. slavery. I also sense the urgency of seeing activism and academia as intersecting and not mutually exclusive. Part of that urgency emerges from my experiences as a teacher, presenting issues of race, gender, and slavery to undergraduates who, for the most part, never have encountered slave testimony or slave law. It is important for my work to make visible the histories and stories that often are erased. I want to place at the center of the discussion issues of race and gender and, in particular, the voices of women of color who have been institutionally excluded from official histories in multiple ways.

In my pursuit of this project as a white feminist, there is a risk of repeating the colonization that I am analyzing. In considering the politics and ethics of my scholarship, I try to write with an awareness of positioning and not to presume to speak for any category of people. Many African American feminist scholars have written about always being called upon, as if it were their problem alone, to educate whites about racism and in particular to educate white women about racism in feminism. Audre Lorde writes: "Traditionally, in American society, it is the members of oppressed, objectified groups who are expected to stretch out and bridge the gap between the actualities of our lives and the consciousness of our oppressor. . . . In other words, it is the responsibility of the oppressed to teach the oppressors their mistakes" (114). While these voices, of course, should speak and echo loudly, relying on them alone functions as another excuse for inaction as "the oppressors maintain their position and evade responsibility for their own actions" (Lorde 115). In "Feminist Scholarship: Ethical Issues," bell hooks appreciates the interest of white students and scholars in the perspectives of black women, but she also warns that such gestures can "place black people once again in a service position, meeting the needs of whites" (47).[15] She cautions against the authority granted scholarship written by white women (or other people in the dominant group) about women of color (or other groups historically not allowed to write their own histories), but also cautions against avoiding such cross-cultural work to dodge responsibility. She expresses her "concern about the way in which recent feminist focus on differences, especially racial differences, has led to a sense that white women must abdicate responsibility for responding to works by 'different others'" (47). In a certain sense, I feel at once less authorized and more obligated to take on this project. As a white feminist, I see American racism as also my legacy and my problem. In this study I strive to listen to and register multiple voices while not avoiding my own accountability.

Overview

In each chapter, I create some form of multiple consciousness, articulating narratives that have been left out, highlighting a range of voices, and both generating and revealing juxtapositions. While this study centers on the mid-nineteenth century, I open with an earlier moment and close with a later one. As part of the introduction, chapter 2, "'Further Deponent Sayeth Not': Multiple Consciousness and Suppressed Narratives in Tellings of Slave Revolt," examines the inevitably incomplete texts surrounding the Middle Passage and slave resistance. This chapter helps to lay the groundwork for the rest of the book by addressing the silences in the record of slavery and raising concrete questions about how we can read, write about, and teach such compromised material. I place several texts alongside each other here, and this rapid juxtaposition of works from different periods and genres is intentional. Robert Hayden's twentieth-century poem "Middle Passage," Herman Melville's ambiguous retelling of slave mutiny cases, Wheatley's iambic pentameter verse, and later rewritings of Wheatley's rhetoric illustrate the need for a reading practice that enables us to read silences as well as what is there in plain sight. Wheatley survived the Middle Passage as a child and managed to leave behind a literary legacy as an eighteenth-century Boston poet. Reading her poetry alongside other tellings of slavery and resistance makes it easier to read the layers of resistance embedded in her tightly wrought lines of verse. Hayden reads multiple accounts of Middle Passage and slave mutinies in a way that both educates us and forces us to question the silences and gaps in such tellings; his poetic project helps us read with rhetorical and historical sensitivity Wheatley's multiple layers of meaning. I offer partial readings of inevitably partial texts to argue for simultaneously and critically examining multiple tellings of slavery and slave revolt.

Wheatley was not, in her daily life, what we would call a political activist, though her poetry and letters can be read as her activism. This study focuses especially on two later women, Truth and Jacobs, whose more explicit activism emerged from their experiences in slavery. Both are subversive voices challenging legal fictions of slavery, and they raise issues of race, gender, sexuality, and reproduction. Part two, "'I Want It Root and Branch Destroyed': The Radical Politics and Shifting Voices of Sojourner Truth," examines the legal and rhetorical lessons from Truth's activism. At a moment when African Americans and white women were disfranchised in various ways, Truth insisted on a public voice and both challenged and used the law. Chapter 3, "A Woman among the Pettifoggers: Truth as Legal Actor," focuses on Truth's role in the legal arena as she escaped slavery, won lawsuits, and lobbied the legislature. Anticipating the later project of critical race theory, Truth's legal agency reveals the law as both oppressive and potentially liberatory. Studying Truth's role as a legal actor is complicated by the deeply compromised textual record of her life and words. Chapter 4, "Framing Truth and Resisting Frames," analyzes the multiple sites from which Truth constructed her political arguments while examining the rhetoric of Harriet Beecher Stowe, Frances Gage, and other white women who transcribed, described, and packaged Truth to suit their own agendas. Truth was an orator and activist, not a writer, so others frame her words. They frequently construct her race and gender in order to distance and dehumanize her, even as they praise her, to establish their own authority, and to define notions of white womanhood in opposition to Truth's racial and sexual identity. Drawing attention to the layers of representation begins to make visible the erasures that continue to occur. This chapter deconstructs the literary tropes used to frame Truth and analyzes her rhetoric and politics. Truth's rhetorical and legal gestures revise nineteenth-century constructions of African American women and deploy a multiple consciousness of race, gender, class, and religion.

Part three, "'The Regulations of Robbers': Harriet Jacobs's Legal Critique," examines nineteenth-century legal writing alongside Jacobs's critique of slave law, in order to expose contradictions in discourses of slavery and to demystify legal fictions more broadly. Slave law rested on constructions of race and gender that attempted to erase black subjectivity and frame black sexuality as dangerous or illicit. Examining laws around various forms of voicing (such as bans on testimony and literacy) and laws around sex (including family, reproduction, and rape) reveals contradictions, gaps, and slippages in the discourses of slavery. The constructed objectivity of slave law in general and of antebellum legal scholar Thomas Cobb in particular is displaced through a reading of the legal aspects of Jacobs's slave narrative, *Incidents in the Life of a Slave Girl.* Chapter 5, "'We Could Have Told Them a Different Story': Slave Law and Slave Voices," contrasts Jacobs's methodology of multiple consciousness with Cobb's deployment of false neutrality. While Jacobs's narrative deconstructs fictions of slavery and womanhood, Jacobs does not merely replace fiction with truth. Her more complex goal is to demand that we pay attention to framing and to reinsert into the frame those perspectives that have been erased. In particular, I read Jacobs's deliberate deployment of testimony and literacy against the legal controls on slave voices. Chapter 6, "Reframing Legal Fictions of Womanhood," centers on Jacobs's critique of dominant standards of (white) womanhood. *Incidents in the Life of a Slave Girl* highlights personal, sexual, and familial issues, and Jacobs consistently connects those elements to legal questions. Her focus on the law (and on federal framings of the law) helps her to motivate Northerners to see slavery as an institutional problem and a national problem, and her focus on womanhood helps her appeal specifically to Northern women. Slave law and the politics of slavery construct the fiction of black female promiscuity to displace a discourse of the rape of African American women. Jacobs exposes the contradictory and hypocritical underpinnings of such fictions and offers alternate narratives of womanhood, family, and sexuality.

The epilogue, "Confronting the Legacies: Decoding Modern Rhetorics of Racism," examines the legacies of these nineteenth-century practices and discourses in modern legal and political rhetoric. I simultaneously interrogate these two periods in order to generate a politics of comparison. The moments I examine are not identical, but neither are they discrete, separate moments with surprising similarities—they are part of a continuum. The traces of nineteenth-century constructions of race and gender are evident in modern policy discussions, such as the attacks on African American motherhood and attempts to impose reproductive control on certain categories of women. The theory of black matriarchy, explicitly linked to slavery in the 1965 Moynihan Report, continues to have currency in policy discussions. Issues around birth control and sterilization often have been informed by racialized and racist notions, sometimes under the guise of neutrality. In the last decade, attempts to impose the long-term, surgically implanted contraceptive Norplant on certain groups of women reveal constructions of race and gender that recall nineteenth-century notions of erasing female agency and placing blame on black female sexuality.

Examining such cases in detail can offer us strategies for reading other reproductive cases and other policy issues that both highlight and obfuscate race.

A study of the history and rhetoric of slavery and resistance can inform how we represent, understand, and deconstruct gender and race in contemporary legal critiques. Racism works partly by erasure, omission, and the appearance of neutrality, particularly in its legal manifestations. It is important to place it in a context, make its history visible, and supply the erased connections. Examining simultaneously the period of slavery and the present moment helps to make these connections. I seek to expose the rhetoric of framing and representation, analyze intersections of race and gender, and trace historical legacies of racism and resistance.

chapter two

"Further Deponent
Sayeth Not"

*Multiple Consciousness and Suppressed Narratives
in Tellings of Slave Revolt*

Slavery necessarily produces an uneven record, marked by silences and
suppressed narratives. The official records emerging from the Middle
Passage and the American institution of slavery were produced by
beneficiaries of slavery who generally constructed Africans and African
Americans as nonhuman. Documents of this commercial enterprise, such
as shipping records or bills of sale, represented human beings as merchandise, cargo, and chattel. Records (official or unofficial) were unlikely to
emerge or endure from the Africans themselves. Upon arriving in the
"New World," survivors of the Middle Passage had their original languages suppressed, and, in the North American colonies and later the
United States, for the most part they were systemically denied education
and literacy in the new language imposed upon them. Voices from these
women and men emerged nonetheless, though constrained and compromised in many ways. A critical reading of historical and literary texts can
help recover and reread these voices.

This chapter juxtaposes several different tellings of slavery from different periods and genres to create and reveal multiple consciousness between
and within these works. Because of the instabilities and silences in the
record, it is necessary to read multiple tellings about the Middle Passage
and slave resistance and to read for multiple layers within those texts.

Voices that do emerge from the Middle Passage include that of
eighteenth-century poet Phillis Wheatley, who was kidnapped from Africa
at a young age and produced the first volume of poetry published by an
African in America. Her poetry can be read as expressing gratitude for her
removal from Africa, as ignoring her status as a slave, or as subversively

challenging slavery, racism, and hypocrisy. The rebellious undercurrents are more likely to appear if her testimony is read alongside other voices of slavery and resistance. Voices of resistance also emerge from slave mutinies that enter the public eye through legal records as well as political rhetoric. Nineteenth-century white American writer Herman Melville based his novella *Benito Cereno* on the court cases that resulted from several slave mutinies. A century later, African American historical poet Robert Hayden wove together multiple voices and incomplete documents to tell a compelling but frustrating story of the Middle Passage and slave rebellion. His poem "Middle Passage" is an instructive example of applying strategies of multiple consciousness to stories of slavery. Hayden deploys narrative silences to refigure issues of voicing and authority and to call for a more critical reading of historical records. Juxtaposing Hayden's poetry with other inevitably partial tellings of slavery can provoke a more nuanced understanding of those other works and can help uncover narratives of resistance.

This chapter begins with an analysis of Hayden's multivoiced poem and reads it alongside tellings of slave mutiny from slave trader Theodore Canot (Theophilus Conneau), novelist Herman Melville, and filmmaker Steven Spielberg. These readings provide a framework from which to consider the resistant voices in Wheatley's poetry and a range of poetic responses to Wheatley.

"We Find It Paradoxical Indeed": Compromised Documents and Multiple Ironies

European kidnapping and trading of Africans as slaves began in the 1400s. A triangular trade developed between the Americas, Europe, and Africa, exchanging across the ocean raw materials, manufactured goods, and human beings. "Middle Passage" is the term that emerged for the middle stage in the triangle, the deadly journey across the Atlantic from Africa to the so-called New World. Scholars disagree about the numbers of humans who survived the Middle Passage, perhaps nine million, perhaps fifteen million, perhaps more (Franklin 41). By any estimate, millions of Africans were subjected to this forced expatriation and millions died in the process. When Thomas Jefferson drafted the long list of King George's offenses that made up the bulk of the Declaration of Independence, the American revolutionary—and slaveholder—initially included a denunciation of George's participation in the international slave trade. The item read in part: "He has waged cruel war against human nature itself, violating its most sacred rights of life and liberty in the persons of a distant people who never offended him, captivating and carrying them into slavery in another hemisphere, or to incur miserable death in their transportation thither" (qtd. in Franklin 71). The Continental Congress deleted this clause from the final document. When delegates to the Constitutional Convention drew up the federal Constitution a decade later, not only did they not condemn the international slave trade, but they also guaranteed its legal protection for another two decades. After 1808, when the international slave trade finally was banned, the domestic slave trade within the United States remained legal. In addition, Africans still were kidnapped from Africa after the ban, in violation of the law. One famous case—that of the *Amistad,* a Spanish slave ship that became the name of a U.S. Supreme Court ruling—turned on the determination of whether the mutinous blacks on board were Africans who had been recently and illegally kidnapped or "New World" slaves whose African ancestors had been *legally* kidnapped. Writers Hayden and Melville, as well as filmmaker Spielberg and others who have interpreted this story, use the *Amistad* case and others like it to explore the contradictions of American slavery and resistance.

Hayden, whose body of work often reclaims key moments in African American history, includes his poem "Middle Passage" in the 1962 collection *A Ballad of Remembrance.* Much of Hayden's poetry emphasizes the importance and difficulties of remembering a history that has been silenced. Drawing upon actual documents gleaned from extensive research, Hayden's historical poem combines a number of "documentary" forms— legal deposition, entries in a ship's log, court testimony, reminiscence— written in various voices, telling different, fragmented, and incomplete parts of the story of the Middle Passage. In one case, the story of the *Bella J,* we learn of the stacking of bodies and the rape of women through the dispassionate, thrice-removed voice of a legal deposition. The words "Deponent further sayeth" begin the six-stanza segment, which is indented and quoted. Each subsequent stanza in this segment opens with the distancing word "that"—reminding us that this description is the poet quoting the court reporter, who in turn is paraphrasing the deponent, who is responding to the lawyer, who is questioning what "Deponent" witnessed:

"That there was hardly room 'tween-decks for half
the sweltering cattle stowed spoon-fashion there (52–53)

> "That Crew and Captain lusted with the comeliest
> of the savage girls kept naked in the cabins;
> that there was one they called The Guinea Rose
> and they cast lots and fought to lie with her (56–59)

The deposition exists because this particular ship caught fire, and the human "cargo" was burned alive. As with many of the examples in this section of the poem, the white slavers suffered along with the women and men they victimized: "that the Captain perished drunken with the wenches" (67).

These excruciating stanzas—their horrifying content juxtaposed with the detached tone—provoke more questions than they answer, and the segment ends with the lone quoted line, in archaic legal language, "Further Deponent sayeth not" (68), compelling us to look at the things not said in the official record. With the widespread outlawing of slave literacy and testimony (and often of free black testimony as well), evidence from black sources often was left unsaid or unrecorded. We will never hear this story from the perspective of the African woman "called [by the slave traders and rapists] The Guinea Rose" (58), and Hayden deliberately frustrates us with that silence. The aim of his poem is to teach us to read more carefully for that untold story.

Hayden presents the appearance of documentary objectivity (quoting voices that seem to speak for themselves) while undercutting the authority of those ostensibly objective voices. The poet weaves together depositions, logs, and other documents in this poem, rewriting them and juxtaposing them in ways to call attention to the gaps, silences, and lies of those primary texts that have endured. The first of Hayden's three numbered sections includes indented, quoted excerpts from the logs of two different slave ships in crisis.

> "10 April 1800—
> Blacks rebellious. Crew uneasy. Our linguist says
> their moaning is a prayer for death,
> ours and their own. Some try to starve themselves.
> Lost three this morning leaped with crazy laughter
> to the waiting sharks, sang as they went under." (8–13)

This fragmented tale of rebellious acts, from prayer to suicide to singing, is mediated by not only the captain's pen but also the translations of the linguist, who is needed to interpret what the captain reads only as moaning. We don't hear from the "rebellious" "Blacks" (9) themselves, though that opening description helps us read the subsequent details as human resistance and not just mindless acts of desperation. The quotation marks, sentence fragments, and reference to the linguist encourage us to pay attention to who is telling the story, in what language, and with what omissions.

Other quoted fragments in part 1 provide facts about the Middle Passage while emphasizing truths that are not articulated. "8 bells. I cannot sleep, for I am sick / with fear" (26–27), reports another white sailor, this time on a slave ship overtaken with illness. Nervously writing to stave off fear, he is mystified at the cause of his ship's adversity:

> . . . Misfortune
> follows in our wake like sharks (our grinning
> tutelary gods). Which one of us
> has killed an albatross? A plague among
> our blacks—Ophthalmia: blindness—& we
> have jettisoned the blind to no avail.
> It spreads, the terrifying sickness spreads.
> Its claws have scratched sight from the Capt.'s eyes . . . (31–38)

These deeply ironic lines about the physical blindness of "our blacks" no doubt point to the moral blindness of these merchants of human flesh who cannot imagine that they have sinned. "Which one of us / has killed an albatross?" wonders the sailor who, unlike Coleridge's ancient mariner,[1] cannot recall committing any wrong. Hayden's sailor writes largely to prove to himself that "still my eyes can see" (28), so instead of the public penance repeatedly executed by the mariner of Coleridge's poem (who knows he has sinned), this sailor tells his story to reassure himself that he has not yet been tainted.

Hayden here draws upon the actions of the slavers of the French ship *Le Rodeur*, who murdered thirty-six blinded Africans by throwing them overboard, "to save the expense of supporting slaves rendered unsalable, and to obtain grounds for a claim against the underwriters."[2] Again, Hayden tells the story of this crime through a document (indented, quoted, and written in first-person) produced by one of the culprits. The pronoun "It" (37) grammatically denotes the contagious medical condition, which spread from the maltreated Africans (who were provided with scant water or fresh air) to the crew and captain. "It spreads, the terrifying sickness spreads" (37) also suggests the whites' moral diseases of slavery, racism, and self-willed blindness to the sin of such inhumanity. The words are moving, but the context helps us read critically the pathetic story and look for the testimony left unuttered by this physically sighted yet spiritually blind sailor.

Throughout part 1 of the poem, interspersed with the ships' logs and the deposition, are other ironic voices—italicized or indented or oddly spaced, and suggesting prayers, hymns, a chorus of ironic ship names, and other interruptions. The poem opens with the names of Spanish slave vessels: "*Jesús, Estrella, Esperanza, Mercy:*" (1)—these hopeful and religious words, followed by a colon, fail to prepare us for the horrific details that follow. Other names appear in the section, and the third section also opens with reference to slave ships and their names:

> Shuttles in the rocking loom of history,
> the dark ships move, the dark ships move,
> their bright ironical names
> like jests of kindness on a murderer's mouth (94–97)

In Hayden's metaphor, history is a cloth woven not from objective records but from the commerce and lies of slavery. A shuttle is the device that weaves the thread back and forth in a loom. "Shuttle" also refers to a regular and well-traveled route. As Hayden weaves this poem, slave ships weave the fabric of history ("Shuttles in the rocking loom of history" [94]), leaving an ironic record of words that cannot be trusted.

In between each of the quoted testimonies of part 1 of the poem are woven other religious evocations. Lyrics from the nineteenth-century hymn "Jesus, Savior, Pilot Me" follow and precede the indented documentary excerpts, spaced so that they hauntingly slow down the pace of the poem: "Jesus Saviour Pilot Me" (20). A strange play on call and response, the refrains and interruptions add to the multiple voices of the poem and intensify the irony and the indictment of hypocritical Christianity. With the dizzying array of rapidly shifting voices and images of the first section, arranged in ironic counterpoint to each other, Hayden's poem questions historical records and official fact-making procedures. Its structure forces us to pay attention to voice—to the source of information.

Part 2 of the poem provides a rhetorical break from the quick shifts in perspective and speaks entirely in the voice of a retired and unrepentant slave trader, drawn from Hayden's reading of a 1928 reprint of a nineteenth-century journal by a slave trader. *Adventures of an African slaver; being a true account of the life of Captain Theodore Canot, trader in gold, ivory & slaves on the coast of Guinea* first appeared in 1854. Theophilus Conneau, whose name was Anglicized to Theodore Canot, was born in 1808 (shortly after the British and American bans on the slave trade took effect) and engaged in and profited immensely from the international trade long after it was illegal. From his very first words to the public, he is blunt about his interest in making money, be it from trading human souls or publishing this book. "My motive for publishing [these memoirs] is solely for the object of profit," he writes in his original preface (xiv).

Ironies, not surprisingly, fill his accounts. Reading his journals (written for publication) alongside his private letters also produces striking contrasts. In an 1854 letter to his American editor Brantz Mayer, Conneau complains of the "abominable" treatment he endured aboard the *Empire City,* an American ship taking white passengers from New York to Chile.[3] His indignation about difficult conditions and unfair hierarchies he experienced as a paying passenger are painfully ironic alongside his sanguine discussions of subjecting Africans to an involuntary and far more "abominable" passage for his own profit. He writes to Mayer:

> I will describe some of my troubles. First of all, the *E.C.* is a very slow boat and very neglectfully kept. Her dining saloon being in the lower deck, passengers are deprived of light, air, and ventilation during meal times. The berths are well enough, but full of insects and vermin.
>
> The table is certainly the worst served I have ever seen on board of any packets. The servants (Black Devils) are the greatest sauciest rascals in creation, and as their Chief is also a damned mustachio'd Negro, things are conducted with filthiness, impertinence, and neglect. Such is the imprudence of those demons that if a passenger calls for a drop of water during the day and does not place a shilling in their greasy hands, he is sure not to get it. I have known a second class passenger to ask for a glass of water, when a Mulatto rascal told her to go and get it. (364)

Such conditions clearly are unacceptable for white passengers of any class, in Conneau's estimation, and the outrage is compounded by the arrogance of the "Black," "Negro," or "Mulatto" servants. Such descriptions are a useful counterpoint to his tellings of the Middle Passage in his journal. His book, marketed to his nineteenth-century readers as "Adventures," focuses primarily on the immense profits from his trading. He defends the slave trade, which, he points out, just a few decades before "was not piracy, but a privileged monopoly powerfully practiced by the Christian potentates of Europe and the fathers of our present generation" (1). He repeatedly blames its cruelties (such as the tight packing of cargo holds with hundreds of humans) as "created" by "this arbitrary law" that banned the trade: he argues that profit-driven traders were compelled to take certain actions to evade capture and to insulate their huge profits from occasional losses (80–81).

In describing the Middle Passage, Conneau admits certain brutalities but maintains that they were necessary and were kept to the minimum. Such necessities included branding the Africans (a mark that usually fades in six months, he assures us, and that also helps to keep accurate logs of "every Negro thrown over the board during the voyage"), stripping them naked (hence "cleanliness is preserved with little trouble") and "stowing" them "spoon fashion" on planks of wood. He defends this last detail by asserting, "As it may appear barbarous that slaves should be made to lie down naked on a hard board, let me inform the reader that native Africans know not the use of mattresses" (84–85). His superior knowledge of ocean travel and of African custom reframes atrocities as necessities. He refers to this chapter as "the chapter of cruelties," but he opens it with discussion of a treaty enforcing the slave-trade ban (Spain and Britain's 1836 Treaty of Martinez de la Rosa) so that the cruelties are placed firmly in the context not of the slave trade but of the *ban* on the slave trade. "The danger becoming greater by this treaty," he writes, "it obliged slavers since that time to have recourse to greater economy in the stowage of slaves" (80). He simultaneously admits abuses, lessens their severity, and blames them on misguided and only ostensibly "philanthropic" lawmakers (81).

Conneau's tellings of the Middle Passage also reveal the resistance practiced by the Africans. In one chapter he describes an overt revolt during a voyage. Unlike the first captain in Hayden's poem, who traveled with a linguist, on this journey Conneau "had no interpreters as in other voyages, and the discipline of the slaves was carried on by the force of the lash." At first the acts of resistance were self-inflicted: "A slave in a fit of madness leaped overboard, while another choked himself during the night." Soon, however, collective revolt broke out as the African men and women "rose in a body" against the white sailors (208). With weapons superior to the Africans' pieces of wood, the sailors eventually suppressed the revolt. While Conneau says the revolt was unexpected ("The cause of this revolt I never could account for, as the slaves from Ayudah and its vicinity are generally humble, docile, and gentle to manage" [210]), his comments also reveal that resistance was a very common (if not always successful) occurrence. The cook, for example, "had orders on such occasions to distribute boiling water on the belligerents," suggesting that "such occasions" occurred with enough frequency to produce such a policy.

Conneau's unawareness of the impending attack moments before it took place also suggests his refusal to perceive resistance: "We had been at sea twenty-one days, and my apprehensions against a revolt had nearly worn away. Everything appeared as peaceable as could be expected. The slaves also *wore* a better countenance, and when *made to dance or sing,* it was done with better grace than before, when the whip had had to urge them to participate in the amusements" (208, emphasis added). Conneau wants to imagine the forced singing and dancing as evidence of contentment, and while his rhetoric reveals his awareness that the Africans' "countenance" is something they merely "wore," he still wants to believe that mask. His desire to see "mirth" in the Africans (who, he earlier complained, failed to appreciate his "kindness" on this journey) certainly blinded him to much of what took place (208). In this case, a confrontation ensued that resulted in several sailors and Africans being wounded or killed, so he was forced to see that something was amiss, even among these "humble, docile, and gentle" passengers.

Elsewhere, Conneau's descriptions of general conditions aboard slave ships reveal the everyday nature of African resistance. While he complains of the food service on the *Empire City,* he claims that the Africans in the Middle Passage are allowed to wash their hands and then partake of the food from the region of their origin. He also reports: "It is the sailor's duty to report when any one of the slaves refuses to eat, and if by the reconnoitering of the officer it is found that stubbornness is the cause of a voluntary abstinence (Negroes often starve themselves to death), the cat is applied till a cure is effected. (Here then is another instance of those unpleasant necessities resorted to, but it is only given as medicinal antidote)" (82–83). Here, physical violence (assisted by a cat-o'-nine-tails) is refigured as medicine. Such redefinitions occur throughout his journal and throughout the literature reporting and defending slavery. Conneau represents his occupation as being no more immoral than any other commercial venture; nevertheless, he sees the need to constantly defend and rationalize his practices. Part of the appeal of his story is that it tells the "adventures" of an outlaw, but the writer also seeks to justify his position outside the law to those same titillated readers. He defends his actions throughout, first by the unwavering attraction to profit, then by blaming abuses and cruelties on the "arbitrary law" itself.

When Hayden rewrites Conneau's tales in part 2 of "Middle Passage," he uses the most uniform poetic form in the poem, forgoing the choppiness and multiple voices of other sections. In this section—six uninterrupted stanzas of equal length sandwiched between the typographical and moral chaos of the other sections—the very lack of interruption seems to be Hayden's method of questioning the slave trader's unquestioning stance. Several lines describe African complicity in the slave trade. In dehumanizing language, the trader tells the unnamed male listener ("Aye, lad" [20]) that he has "seen the nigger kings whose vanity / and greed turned wild black hides of Fellatah, / Mandingo, Ibo, Kru to gold for us" (75–77). Hayden wants us to have the chilling information about Africans selling out their brethren, but the source of the information, a white trader grown rich from the sale of humans and looking back with no regrets, is also the point of the section.

> Twenty years a trader, twenty years,
> for there was wealth aplenty to be harvested
> from those black fields, and I'd be trading still
> but for the fevers melting down my bones. (90–93)

No counterpoint follows these lines, which close the section. Having been trained in the first section to read critically, we are left to form our own response to the slave trader's testimony and to wonder what this witness "sayeth not" (68). While the opening of the poem features slavers made uneasy by the misfortunes that befell them (even though they fail to see their own role in their hardship), this segment depicts the confidence that comes from success and the vast economic wealth produced by slavery.

The final section returns to multiple voices, though there are fewer shifts between documentary forms here. The poet's commentary seems to appear more directly, in stanzas that shift perspective and vary in length. Hayden continues using imagery of sight and blindness, including the following accusatory second-person stanzas:

> *But, oh, the living look at you*
> *with human eyes whose suffering accuses you,*
> *whose hatred reaches through the swill of dark*
> *to strike you like a leper's claw*

You cannot stare that hatred down

. . . .

cannot kill the deep immortal human wish,
the timeless will. (111–15, 118–19)

Hayden does not clearly identify the "you" in these stanzas: it is perhaps the confident trader of the previous section, or the various uneasy but still unaware sailors of the first section, or—given the second-person form— contemporary readers who perhaps also are denying awareness of their role in oppression. The indented, italicized lines stand out because of their appearance on the page and the sudden use of second person. These stanzas help emphasize how the white oppressors, whose voices control the testimony in this poem and in the historical record, in many ways are also defined by their relationship to the oppressed, whom the whites describe in dehumanizing ways but who also insist on looking back at them. The "human eyes" (112) reveal the humanity, subjectivity, and "will" (119) of the oppressed, but in their accusing stare they also define the subjectivity of the whites and reveal them as oppressors.

Immediately after placing the reader (as "you") in the position of white crew members, the poem shifts to the voice of one particular slaver who failed to "stare that hatred down" (115). This constructed and quoted testimony from the *Amistad* case,[4] the longest uninterrupted stanza, consists of explanations and disdain from one of the Spanish sailors, who demands that the court return his property. This stanza, which specifically names the *Amistad* and particular players in the case, is the only explicit description of this particular mutiny, but in a way all the other voices in the poem lead up to this case and the hero who emerges from it. Hayden's critique of American hypocrisy emerges ironically from the self-righteous perspective of the Spanish slaver:

We find it paradoxical indeed
that you whose wealth, whose tree of liberty
are rooted in the labor of your slaves
should suffer the august John Quincy Adams
to speak with so much passion of the right
of chattel slaves to kill their lawful masters
and with his Roman rhetoric weave a hero's
garland for Cinquez. (161–68)

An odd clarity comes through the obfuscations of the indignant slave trader, who exposes the hypocrisy of antislavery rhetoric from a nation founded on slavery. The slaver swears at the end of his testimony that "Cinquez shall die" (171). Cinquez and the other Africans are to be constructed as mere cargo or property, yet the mutineer is also considered agent enough to have to be extradited, tried, and executed for his violent acts. The sailor closes by calling for the death of Cinquez, but the poet closes, in unquoted lines, by celebrating the undying power of Cinquez:

> The deep immortal human wish,
> the timeless will:
>
>   Cinquez its deathless primaveral image,
>   life that transfigures many lives.
>
> Voyage through death
>   to life upon these shores. (172–77)

The larger-than-life hero of Hayden's poem is Cinquez, the leader of the *Amistad* rebellion, yet like "The Guinea Rose" he has no directly quoted voice in this long, multivoiced poem. This is not a careless omission by Hayden but a crucial part of his argument. While Hayden presents multiple glimpses into the horror of the Middle Passage, noticeably absent are black voices of this horror. This absence compels the reader to look actively for subtext, for the underlying narratives of resistance and humanity.

"That Hive of Subtlety": Masks of Silence and Resistance

Hayden explicitly invokes multiple voices, marked by different rhetorical and typographical details, each revealing different blind spots, biases, and agendas. Through these devices—which cite but also interrogate multiple voices and their markers of facticity—he directs us to read closely, critically, and skeptically. A century earlier, Melville, in the initially bewildering 1855 novella *Benito Cereno* (based on the *Amistad* and other slave mutinies),[5] also forces us to scrutinize narrative voice and question sources of information. The serialized narrative appeared five years after passage of the Fugitive Slave Act, which mandated the return of fugitives who had made their way to the "free" North. Melville's father-in-law, Massachusetts Supreme Court Chief Justice Lemuel Shaw, handed down key rulings enforcing that law (including the 1851 *Sims* case, which Harriet Jacobs responds to in her narrative), and those decisions form part of the context of Melville's publication.

Melville uses a third-person narrator who is linked to the perspective of Amassa Delano, an ostensibly benevolent Massachusetts captain. The story opens when Delano boards a Spanish slave ship that appears (like the ships in Hayden's poem) to be in distress. Like Hayden, Melville breaks away from the narrative and devotes a large section of his work to a quoted— and even notarized—legal deposition, which offers sworn testimony from the Spanish captain Cereno (the title character). But these seemingly authorized viewpoints are undercut and questioned. As in Hayden's constructed deposition, the story told in Melville's deposition only generates more questions.

Prior to the supposed clarity that comes from reading Cereno's testimony, Melville repeatedly calls attention to Delano's inability to read signs as he tries to comprehend what is happening on the Spanish ship he has boarded. Despite the relentlessly ambiguous and gray setting (the sea is full of swells but seems fixed; gray birds mix with gray vapors in the gray sky [46]), the American captain insists on seeing everything in black and white. His attachment to his racist constructions of "negroes," whites, and Spaniards makes him unable to perceive two crucial facts: the Africans aboard the ship are humans (and neither Newfoundland dogs nor wolves, the only two extremes he can imagine),[6] and these same Africans have mutinied and are in control of Cereno's ship. On the deck of the ship, the oakum pickers and hatchet polishers—armed Africans who in fact are threatening violence and enforcing order during the disguised mutiny— are perceived by Delano as mindless laborers. Like the captain writing his log in Hayden's poem, Delano hears communication between these Africans only as moaning or noise: the oakum pickers "accompanied the task with a continuous, low, monotonous chant, droning and druling away." The hatchet polishers "sat intent upon their task, except at intervals, when, with the peculiar love in Negroes of uniting industry with pastime, two and two they sideways clashed their hatchets together, like cymbals, with a barbarous din" (50). Delano not only misinterprets individual actions but also generalizes from his incorrect conclusions to the race as a whole.

In another episode of misinterpretation, when rebel leader Babo is shaving Cereno while the two captains talk, Delano again fails to see evidence of the mutiny because he can see only his own expectations. In the shaving episode, as in the image of the hatchet polishers and oakum pickers,

Melville demonstrates how the fictions of slavery allow an armed African to be perceived as a happy servant. In this scene, Babo shaves his master/captive so that he can control how Cereno answers Delano's questions. He compounds the physical threat of the razor with the deliberate political violence of using Cereno's Spanish flag as an apron. Delano processes the imagery of the flag to make Babo's subversive gesture fit his racist assumptions: "'The castle and the lion,' exclaimed Captain Delano—'why, Don Benito, this is the flag of Spain you use here. It's well it's only I, and not the King, that sees this,' he added, with a smile, 'but,'—turning towards the black—'it's all one, I suppose, so the colors be gay'; which playful remark did not fail somewhat to tickle the Negro" (85). Melville's story is about mutiny, but it is also about interpretation and the failure to read carefully.

Like Hayden, Melville does not offer a direct African voice of resistance, and he calls attention to the silence of that perspective. "The black," he tells us in the closing paragraph, "met his voiceless end" (116). While Babo, the rebel leader, doesn't speak before his execution, his silent and accusatory gaze closes the story: "The head, that hive of subtlety, fixed on a pole in the Plaza, met, unabashed, the gaze of the whites" (116). Like the easily fooled Delano, the reader—at the mercy of an unreliable narrator and the unreliability of racial fictions—does not at first understand what is taking place. Only after the story concludes do we reread everything that came before and see the physical and political resistance in everything from the din of the hatchet polishers to Babo's use of the Spanish flag as an apron when he shaves, with sharp razor, his supposed beloved master.

Hayden's poem explicitly celebrates resistance through the figure of Cinquez, but by denying us his voice, Hayden additionally exposes fictions about narrative authority and voicing. He forces us to question the authority granted certain documentary forms. Melville does not directly celebrate Babo, but he does call into question sources usually granted authority. He too denies us the voice of the slave rebellion leader (who is based partly on Cinquez/Sengbeh Pieh), perhaps less to silence him than to call attention to his silencing. Spielberg's Hollywood film *Amistad*,[7] which brought this story to a wide audience in 1997, celebrates Cinqué's rebellion, but by telling the story primarily through white eyes without any critical examination of issues of narrative, it duplicates precisely the erasures that Hayden and Melville critiqued decades ago.[8]

Spielberg's production opens with the rebellion and offers compelling scenes with the African characters, filmed in the Mendi language. The film's central drama, however, is the ensuing court battle, and at its center is former president John Quincy Adams, played by Anthony Hopkins, who successfully argues the case. In the film, the amiable Adams must explain to a fictional former slave (Joadson, played quietly in the shadows by Morgan Freeman) that it is important to tell a compelling story, as if this abolitionist—presumably familiar with the workings of political persuasion—would not already know that. "What is their story?" asks Adams, and the white lawyer proceeds to enlighten the African American activist about the value of telling a story in the right way. (To illustrate his point, Adams retells Joadson's own story, concluding: "*That's* your story, isn't it?") Spielberg makes Adams the character with the answers: he knows what is important (telling "the best story"), and his ability to act on that premise in the courtroom allows the successful denouement of the film. Hayden and Melville, on the other hand, make it clear that the answers are not to be found in one place and that the "story" is a contested and slippery object. A courtroom is an especially compromised place for the telling of stories, and the film might have accentuated the ironies of the *Amistad* court case. Instead, it keeps Adams and his courtroom speech as an unproblematized center. "Who we are is who we were," intones Adams when he invokes the proud heritage of the American founders— a list that includes slaveholders who made compromised choices about protecting slavery in a democracy, an irony lost in the film's courtroom climax.

"Remember, *Christians*":
Antiracist Imperatives in Iambic Pentameter

Whereas Hayden's "Middle Passage" emphasizes the unlikelihood of black voices documenting the slave trade, his later poem "A Letter from Phillis Wheatley" more subtly addresses issues of documentation and voice through a black writer who did document her own experiences. Hayden appropriates and empowers Wheatley's voice, still pressing us to read carefully for suppressed stories of slave resistance. Wheatley was no slave mutineer. Many have read her as a co-opted voice of early African American assimilation. But in fact she also can be read as a powerful and multilayered agent and symbol of resistance to slavery. Melville's depiction of Babo's masking combined with Hayden's exposure of silences in the record of slavery might provide an interesting way to read Wheatley's seemingly nonthreatening and refined poetry. We might read her rhetoric like

Melville encourages us to reread Babo's gestures during the hidden mutiny. Babo's signs of apparent fidelity are intended to keep Delano credulous and distracted, secure within his racist schemas, while revolt seethes under the surface and under his nose. Babo, and perhaps Wheatley, are capable of displays that perfectly fit a Massachusetts liberal's expectations for a loyal slave. Reading all these works together might lead us to ask, where is Wheatley (like Babo) shaving her readers with their own flag as apron?

Wheatley's volume of poetry, the first by an African American, was titled *Poems on Various Subjects, Religious and Moral.* Her most famous poem, "On being brought from AFRICA to AMERICA," tells a version of her passage to this country in what seems an intense understatement: "'Twas mercy brought me from my *Pagan* land" (1). Defying the odds that some-one subjected to kidnapping, forced expatriation, and legalized enslave-ment would seize the pen, Wheatley does claim a literate—and I would argue a legal and political—voice in the eighteenth century. To do so, her words must be prefaced, literally, by white authentications of her African voice. Hayden, with his interest in the multiple documents produced by slavery, certainly found the half dozen pages of authenticating documents that precede Wheatley's words a revealing record of the power relations under slavery. Both the "LETTER sent by the Author's Master to the Pub-lisher" and the official "Attestation" offered "To the PUBLICK" inform the reader that Wheatley came to this country from Africa. Both documents make use of Wheatley's language, which refers to kidnapping and forced transport as "being brought." Her owner, John Wheatley, opens by stating that "PHILLIS was brought from Africa to America, in the Year 1761, between Seven and Eight Years of Age" (vi). His words come before hers in the text, but her poem was written before his letter; hence, his phrasing echoes hers, even as her phrasing echoes white constructions of African kidnapping.

To be allowed to publish at all, Wheatley had to prove to an assembly of powerful white men that her poems were indeed written by herself. In 1772 she met with a gathering of eighteen titled public figures that con-sisted of (using the italicized honorifics of the document): the *Governor, Lieutenant-Governor,* five *Honorables,* three *Esquires* (including John Han-cock, soon to grace the Declaration of Independence with his famous sig-nature), seven *Reverends,* and *her Master.* Implicitly, she also had to prove that publication of these poems would not be threatening to the interests represented by these "most respectable Characters in *Boston.*" In a short document marked by legalistic language and format, the eighteen men signed a statement that: "We whose Names are under-written, do assure the World, that the POEMS were (as we verily believe) written by PHILLIS, a young Negro Girl, who was but a few Years since, brought an uncultivated Barbarian from *Africa,* and has ever since been, and now is, under the Disadvantage of serving as a Slave in a Family in this Town. She has been examined by some of the best Judges, and is thought qualified to write them" (Wheatley vii). Again, the language of being "brought . . . from *Africa*" reappears, this time heightening the racist implications of African origins to a white audience: she lived, prior to her American status, "an uncultivated Barbarian." The sense of this meeting as more legal than literary—the sense of Wheatley on trial for her authorship—is emphasized by the assembly calling themselves "Judges" and describing the exchange as an "examin[ation]." The sense of documentary authenticity also emerges in the closing note: "*N. B.* The original Attestation, signed by the above Gentlemen, may be seen by applying to *Archibald Bell,* Bookseller, No. 8, *Aldgate-Street*" (vii). It is the seemingly official nature of such documentation that authorizes Wheatley as author.

While the attestation supposedly ensures "that none might have the least Ground for disputing" (vii) the origin of the poems, the evident racism of the language and the admission that slavery is a "Disadvantage" also serve to feed doubts about a slave's authorship. Such doubts are expressed, for example, in a handwritten note inserted in a leather-bound first edition of Wheatley's poems now held in the Library of Congress. The note, from Philadelphian Edward Ingraham to Cambridge's George Livermore, Esquire, is dated 1850, when the abolitionist movement was well underway and many former slaves were publishing their writings. Ingraham cautions: "I have always had misgivings about these Poems, and have thought that there must have been an elaboration of them by someone other than Phillis herself. The inclination in old times to derive a little celebrity from the performance of a pet negro, which she seems to have been, or a pet race horse, was very strong, and to that I attribute the preparation and publication of the Work in question. Doubts, as you will discover from the strangely worded attestation of Gov. Hutchinson and others, were not a little prevalent before the poems appeared in print." Four days later, Livermore inscribes the volume to another "Esquire," Peter Force, and apparently inserts the note. The attestation supposedly intended to authenticate the volume apparently assisted these readers in dismissing its authenticity and reasserting dehumanizing constructions of slave as pet and as horse.

The documents cited and rewritten in Hayden's "Middle Passage" orig-inally were produced in support of slavery. The documents appended to Wheatley's poetry were produced ostensibly in support of this particular slave, but evidently supported the ideology of slavery as well. Again, what might be most compelling is what these documents, these deponents in the literary trial of Phillis Wheatley, "sayeth not." While these poetry-exchanging esquires may have believed Wheatley's poems to be "the performance of a pet negro," Wheatley probably was quite aware of the performance required in the documents and rhetoric that framed her poems.

Subsequent volumes of slave-authored literature are similarly marked by multiple layers of verification, including carefully worded title pages, affidavits, and portraits. Wheatley's volume is dedicated to an English countess and opens with a portrait of herself, an unsigned preface about the author's intentions, the signed letter from her master, and the signed attestation. These authenticating strategies might feed the prejudices of esquires Livermore and Force, and they also might do work similar to Babo's seemingly submissive gestures, intended for Delano's benefit. True, Wheatley is not masking a violent mutiny. Her framing documents and heroic couplets, however, do cloak mutinous subtexts—perhaps only rhe-torical but mutinous nonetheless.

Wheatley's autobiographical and polemical "On Being Brought from Africa to America" might be offering thanks or might be an ironic and piercing indictment of those who decided they knew better than she what she needed. The poem reads:

> 'Twas mercy brought me from my *Pagan* land,
> Taught my benighted soul to understand
> That there's a God, that there's a *Saviour* too:
> Once I redemption neither sought nor knew.
> Some view our sable race with scornful eye,
> "Their colour is a diabolic die."
> Remember, *Christians, Negros,* black as *Cain,*
> May be refin'd, and join th' angelic train. (1–8)

While Wheatley once was read as a passive and co-opted voice, I would argue along with more recent readings of her poetry (see for example Foster's *Written by Herself*) that the way to understand her experience of the Middle Passage and slavery is to listen for what is not explicitly there—

to read for irony and to probe between the lines for the more subversive messages veiled by the language of Christianity and gratitude. Each of those italicized words, for example, can be read ironically, as can other key terms such as "mercy" and "benighted." The apparently thankful lines of the opening seem intended to tell a white readership that she is grateful for the introduction to Christianity made possible by her kidnapping (described here only as "being brought," words anticipated by the prefatory material). The second half of the poem, however, turns the terms of Christianity against the racists (the "Some" of line 5) who would use religion to condemn her and others of "our sable race" to hell—and thereby forces us to rethink the first half of the poem. If we are to believe the terms of this religion that she never requested, then she and her sable kinfolk may in fact be saved, as certainly as any other "*Christians*" might be. The imperative of that closing couplet might command "*Christians*" to recall that, by their own doctrine, "*Negros*" may be saved, or it might remind everyone that Christians *and* blacks are both metaphorically "black as *Cain*"—are equally sinful—and equally may be saved.

Wheatley posits a horizontal and egalitarian image of an "angelic train" over the exclusive and hierarchical terms of those "Some" who view her people with scorn. What sounds like gratitude may in fact be anger. What sounds like assimilation into white Christianity becomes instead a strategic deployment of the enemy's paradigm against the enemy. The shocking understatement of kidnapping as "being brought" tells us to look for other acts of understatement and indirection. "Cain" and "die," for example, also evoke sugar cane and indigo dye (Levernier 26), key items in the "triangle trade," which would imply that the real motivations of the Middle Passage were mercantile, not spiritual, contradicting the apparent claim of the opening line. In a precise frame of iambic pentameter rhymes, a form she learned from her education in white literature, Wheatley is calling satiric attention to precisely those things which are not allowed in that frame.

In some ways Wheatley rewrites this poem in the middle of another poem, one dedicated to an English nobleman. Her 1772 poem "To the Right Honourable WILLIAM, Earl of DARTMOUTH, His Majesty's Principal Secretary of State for North America, &c." is framed with exalted words of praise for this newly appointed British official. "Hail, happy day, when, smiling like the morn, / Fair *Freedom* rose *New-England* to adorn" is the optimistic opening (1–2). The two middle stanzas, however, draw pointed parallels between literal slavery and the metaphoric "iron chain" (17) that

white colonists feel enslaves them to England. Writing in Boston during
the historic moment bracketed by the Boston Massacre and the American
Revolution, Wheatley identifies herself as a Patriot and takes the part of
New England colonial subjects clamoring for political rights. With empathy perhaps not due her enslavers, who are chafing against British rule and
hoping the earl of Dartmouth will prove more sympathetic, Wheatley
assures white America: "No longer shalt thou dread the iron chain, /
Which wanton *Tyranny* with lawless hand / Had made, and with it meant
t' enslave the land" (17–19). She makes concrete that metaphoric language
of slavery by refiguring her own "being brought" from Africa:

> I, young in life, by seeming cruel fate
> Was snatch'd from *Afric's* fancy'd happy seat:
>
> .   .   .   .
>
> Such, such my case. And can I then but pray
> Others may never feel tyrannic sway? (24–25, 30–31)

Although John Wheatley and the Attestation both paraphrased the poet's
telling of the Middle Passage as "being brought," suggesting no irony in
the wording, here Wheatley significantly rewords her telling and their
retelling of that forced journey. The object "me" in the first line of "On
Being Brought" ("'Twas mercy brought me from my *Pagan* land") here
becomes the subject "I," modified and humanized by the age reference
(no "Barbarian," but rather a child). "Mercy" becomes "cruel fate." Her
unnamed *"Pagan"* land" becomes *Afric,* still italicized, but now specified
as a "happy seat." And the passive and even gentle "brought" becomes the
more violent (in meaning and even sound) "snatch'd." This powerful revision is tempered, however, by words that interrupt the shocking and vivid
description. The cruel fate is modified as "seeming" and Afric's seat is
only "fancy'd" happy. These words—which call attention to mistaken, surface interpretations—might prove her assimilated, co-opted position. Or,
these may be the outlines of her mask, her performance, like that enacted
by Melville's Babo.

The closing couplet of this stanza (30–31) explains her patriotic position, should readers "wonder from whence [her] love of Freedom sprung"
(21). Having herself experienced tyranny, she asks, how can she not support the colonists' bid for freedom? Of course, by the same token, the
reverse is true: how can the American colonists, writhing in their metaphoric chains, not pray that "others"—that is, American slaves—may no

longer feel tyrannic sway? The celebration of King George's earl is actually a political call for American colonial rights, and the call for American rights is actually a revolutionary claim for African American justice. But a Delano reading this poem can dwell in the framing stanzas (which mention *"Freedom"* [2] but not slavery) and cling to words like "seeming" and "fancy'd" to allow *him* to fancy that this loyal servant is only thinking of him and is as content in her position as he assumed Babo to be.

"When Thou Hunger Hast": Reading Wheatley

The double-edged effect of Wheatley's masking can be seen in the response to her poetry of one of her contemporaries, New York–born slave-poet Jupiter Hammon. Unlike Wheatley and another early African American poet, Lucy Terry (who composed oral poetry and presented oral arguments in the Supreme Court), Hammon was born on American soil and did not experience the Middle Passage. His poetry seems to argue for freedom only in the hereafter, a sentiment also expressed in his most famous prose piece, "An Address to the Negroes in the State of New York," in which he states (in 1787, the year of the U.S. Constitution), "Getting our liberty in this world is nothing to our having the liberty of the children of God" (Kaplan and Kaplan 199). His other most noted work is a 1778 poem he dedicated to his more famous contemporary: "An Address to Miss Phillis Wheatly [*sic*], Ethiopian Princess." Published as a broadside with biblical citations printed in the margins, the poem praises Wheatley for her piety more than her literary role and is filled with appeals for her to "seek for heaven's joys." Hammon seems to rewrite Wheatley's "'Twas mercy brought me from my *Pagan* land" yet again, seemingly without any suggested irony. He repeatedly echoes some of her language, using the words "mercy" and "brought" for example:

> God's tender mercy brought thee here;
>   Tossed o'er the raging main;
> In Christian faith thou hast a share,
>   Worth all the gold of Spain. (13–16)

He praises "The wisdom of thy God, / In bringing thee from distant shore" (2–3) and emphasizes "God's tender mercy set thee free" (19), and yet again "Thou hast left the heathen shore, / Thro' mercy of the Lord" (41–42). It *seems* he reads her work with no sense of her revolutionary subtext. At the same time, his repeated articulation of the same sentiment suggests he is trying to convince her (along with his other readers and perhaps himself) to read her arrival here as only an act of mercy. Perhaps perceiving the more resistant sentiment under the surface of her poetry, he seeks to set her on a more straight and narrow path. Hammon seems concerned that Wheatley keep her energies focused on God and Jesus, lest she seek other forms of salvation. The thirteenth stanza reads:

Thou, Phillis, when thou hunger hast,
   Or pantest for thy God,
Jesus Christ is thy relief,
   Thou hast the Holy Word. (49–52)

Hammon seems uneasy that Wheatley might hunger for salvation in *this* world or pant for *her* god (who might be someone other than America's Christian god). She may be deploying her own Word too freely, prompting him to offer "the Holy Word" as a more appropriate alternative. "Come, dear Phillis, be advis'd" (61), he repeats a few stanzas later, ". . . There nothing is that shall suffice, / But Christ's redeming [*sic*] blood" (63–64).

Hammon's own deeply compromised writing occasionally betrays less than perfect comfort with things as they are. Lines such as "liberty is a great thing" make his 1787 speech simultaneously antislavery and pro–status quo (qtd. in Kaplan and Kaplan 199). Hammon's reading and possible rewriting of Wheatley's poetry is mostly a conservative and co-opted one. At the same time, his uncomfortable response might reveal just how two-toned her poem is: he could read it as obedient appreciation to white mercy and God's will, but he also senses something more. In his position, he could not celebrate that additional something, but his nervousness about what lies under the surface might show the impact of Wheatley's Babo performance on a fellow slave.

Other contemporaries had mixed responses to her work. Thomas Jefferson, the antislavery slaveholder who wrote the Declaration of Independence and declared that blacks had no intellect, did not quite know how to respond to black intellectuals. His theory was that although African Americans could imitate well, they were limited in creativity and greatly inferior in mathematics. African American scientist and mathematician Benjamin Banneker wrote Jefferson a respectful yet highly critical letter, to which Jefferson sent a polite reply, saving his more scornful language about Banneker for a letter to a white friend. After seeing Wheatley's volume of poems, Jefferson dismissed the work "published under her name" as "below the dignity of criticism" (qtd. in Kaplan and Kaplan 189). His comment implies he found the poems quite terrible, yet he also reveals that he found them good enough that he was forced to wonder if she really wrote them. She and Banneker both had to be pushed from his mind for him to hold onto his theories about black intelligence. Despite Jefferson's great intellect and creativity—and like Melville's Delano—he processed the information he encountered until it fit his existing frames. But also like Delano, his acts of interpretation show traces of the struggle.

We might think that Wheatley wrote her poems for readers such as Jefferson, Hancock, the countess, the earl, her owner Susanna Wheatley, and other supposedly open-minded white readers. But the evidence of her literary exchanges with not only Hammon but also Obour Tanner (a fellow African and a slave in Rhode Island), Scipio Moorhead (a fellow slave and, as she addressed him in a poem, "*African* painter"), and Samson Occom (a Native American missionary and writer, to whom she dedicated some of her earliest writing) shows that she was part of a community of literate people of color.[9] If her work seems written to whites and for their benefit, she also clearly has an audience of color as well. She certainly wrote on more than one level, and no doubt the same poems spoke very differently to different readers.

"Forgive th'Intrusion"

Wheatley's own rewriting of her words challenges us to reread her words far more carefully than most critics have attempted in the past. Hayden rewrites Wheatley's constrained voice in his 1978 epistolary "psychogram" (as he termed it) entitled "A Letter from Phillis Wheatley" (Hatcher 329). The poem is unrhymed, formatted in paragraphs, dated ("London, 1773," locating it during Wheatley's trip to England to publish her book), addressed to Obour Tanner (who was the recipient of much of Wheatley's actual correspondence), and composed with syntax and punctuation similar to Wheatley's actual letters; in a crowded anthology the poem could be mistaken for an actual "letter from Phillis Wheatley." Hayden's poem, written entirely in Wheatley's voice, opens:

Dear Obour
     Our crossing was without
event. I could not help, at times,

reflecting on that first—my Destined—
voyage long ago (I yet
have some remembrance of its Horrors)
and marvelling at God's ways. (1–7)

This voyage took Wheatley from Boston to England and evokes her earlier
crossing of the Atlantic. Perhaps again rewriting the opening of "On Being
Brought from Africa," Hayden's Wheatley makes oblique and parenthetical references to the horrors of the Middle Passage. While mentioning
such things, she also mentions certain things she holds back. Of the "illus-
trious" Londoners she meets she says, "I scarce could tell them anything /
of Africa, though much of Boston / and my hope of Heaven" (10–12). At
the countess's praise, she says, "I held back tears, as is my wont" (16). As,
with "Sombreness," amusement, and understatement, this Wheatley tells
her friend and fellow African about the ironies of her visit, we are left to
wonder what else she chooses to hold back. Her hosts praise her, but will
not eat with her: "At supper—I dined apart / like captive Royalty—"
(19–20). The speaker reveals the information between dashes, setting the
description itself "apart." England is "idyllic," but observers still call her a
"Cannibal Mockingbird." Like Jefferson, the English here can see black
literary production only as an imitation of white intellect. Offered a presentation at court, Hayden's Wheatley declines "as Patriot" (38), but she
also recalls an earlier racially inflected irony: "(I thought of Pocahontas)"
(26). This brief parenthetical statement links African American and
Native American encounters with patronizing white racism.

A final irony in Hayden's poem, often read by critics as merely humor-
ous, links racial oppression in America with class oppression in England:

Today, a little Chimney Sweep,
his face and hands with soot quite Black,
staring hard at me, politely asked:
"Does you, M'lady, sweep chimneys too?" (46–49)

Hayden's figure here evokes the young exploited workers in William Blake's
"The Chimney Sweeper." His image of blackness caused by soot recalls
Wheatley's ironic quoting of racists who attribute her sable race's blackness to "a diabolic die." Wheatley frames the incident by calling it "Droll"
(45) and amusing, but again Hayden lets us wonder what she (and he)
might be holding back. The exploited child's innocent question, addressed

to the American slave with an English honorific of nobility, like the quoted testimony in Hayden's earlier poem, points to issues and connections that are left largely unsaid. The paragraph opens with Wheatley reminding Obour (and Hayden reminding his readers) that there are some things that cannot be shared with an audience of outsiders:

> Sister, forgive th'intrusion of
> my Sombreness—Nocturnal Mood
> I would not share with any save
> your trusted Self. (39–42)

Hayden writes in Wheatley's voice, both respecting and resisting its silences, to make it say perhaps what she might have meant, all the while not letting us forget that she could not say exactly what she meant. The very form of Hayden's poem—it looks like a letter but it is not—calls attention to how texts are marked as authentic voices of experience. Its form and tone are very different from "Middle Passage," but it grapples with some of the same textual issues raised by slavery and resistance (both physical and rhetorical), that is, who can speak and with what constraints? What texts endure and why? How can we read, and perhaps rewrite, the highly compromised texts that emerge from slavery?

"How Should There Be Black Poets in America?"

Contemporary African American poet and essayist June Jordan even more radically rewrites Wheatley's voice in her poetic essay entitled "The Difficult Miracle of Black Poetry in America, or, Something Like a Sonnet for Phillis Wheatley." Kidnapped from Africa, sold to the Wheatleys as a child, fed exclusively white literature, allowed to publish only after an examination by eighteen of the most powerful white men of Massachusetts, young Wheatley produced poetry that, not surprisingly, is quite compromised. "Come to this country a slave and how should you sing?" asks Jordan, marveling that Wheatley sings at all (252). In nonetheless struggling to find the revolutionary notes in Wheatley's poetry, Jordan quotes, responds to, and pushes at bits and pieces of Wheatley's poetry. Jordan reads and rereads Wheatley's "On Being Brought from Africa to America," contextualizing why it would be so compromised but also finally rewriting one line—one that seems most compromised—to release the power and resistance implicit there:

But here, in this surprising poem, this first Black poet presents us with something wholly her own, something entirely new: It is her matter-of-fact assertion that "once I redemption neither sought nor knew," as in: Once I existed beyond and without these terms under consideration. *Once I existed on other than your terms.* And, she says, *but* since we are talking with your talk about good and evil/redemption and damnation, let me tell you something you had better understand. I am Black as Cain *and* I may very well be an angel of the Lord: Take care not to offend the Lord! (255–56)

Jordan first quotes the entire poem as it appeared in 1773, so we can see what in her analysis is direct quotation, what is paraphrase, and what is Jordan's own exasperated, astonished, and admiring release of Wheatley's enslaved song. The quotation marks drop off, but Jordan retains Wheatley's first-person voice and, seemingly, her spirit. "And, she says, *but*" frames the objective statement of quotation ("she says") with two contrasting conjunctions: "and" suggests Jordan is merely adding something, while the italicized "*but*" suggest a change, a turn, and marks Jordan's stronger shift in tone.

Christianity supposedly taught Wheatley's soul to "understand" certain things—in this rewrite, Wheatley's poem insists on telling her readers "something you had better understand." There is a not very veiled threat in "you had better," setting up the command that the reader should "Take care" not to offend the poet, perhaps rewriting Wheatley's subtler but now even more strikingly assertive "Remember, *Christians*." These are not Wheatley's "original" words, and yet perhaps they are closer to the origin than the words Wheatley managed to print. Like Hayden, Jordan both respects and resists Wheatley's silences. She understands what constrained Wheatley's voice, and she also refuses the consequences of those constraints. This contradictory approach might be the most responsible one.

Jordan's work to contextualize Wheatley's silences begins with the opening paragraph of her essay. The two opening sentences, ironic and contradictory, are repeated throughout the essay, forming a refrain of sorts. The next sentence is a long, fragmented, breathless, and unrelentingly concrete description of the Middle Passage and slavery, images that contextualize why "Black Poetry in America" is such a "Difficult Miracle" (a seeming redundancy—when is there an easy miracle?). The paragraph closes with a series of second-person questions that ask Wheatley herself—still unnamed and unspecified except in the title of the essay, so perhaps the "you" is any slave writer, or metaphorically any black poet—to explain how such conditions could possibly produce a poet.

It was not natural. And she was the first. Come from a country of many
tongues tortured by rupture, by theft, by travel like mismatched clothing
packed down into the cargo hold of evil ships sailing, irreversibly, into slavery; come to a country where, to be docile and dumb, to be big and breeding, easily, to be turkey/horse/cow to be cook/carpenter/plow to be 5′6″ 140
lbs. in good condition and answering to the name of Tom or Mary; to be
bed bait; to be legally spread legs for rape by the master/the master's son/the
master's overseer/the master's visiting nephew; to be nothing human nothing family nothing from nowhere nothing that screams nothing that weeps
nothing that dreams nothing that keeps anything/anyone deep in your
heart; to live forcibly illiterate forcibly itinerant; to live eyes lowered head
bowed; to be worked without rest to be worked without pay to be worked
without thanks to be worked day up to nightfall; to be ⅗ths of a human
being at best: to be this valuable, this hated thing among strangers who purchased your life and then cursed it unceasingly: to be a slave: to be a slave:
come to this country a slave and how should you sing? After the flogging
the lynch rope the general terror and weariness what should you know of a
lyrical life? How could you, belonging to no one, but property to those
despising the smiles of your soul, how could you dare to create yourself:
A poet? (252)

This opening to Jordan's essay perhaps again rewrites the opening to
Wheatley's famous Middle Passage poem that seems to refuse to talk
about the Middle Passage. Jordan invokes slave law implicitly throughout
the description and more explicitly through her references to the three-
fifths clause of the Constitution and the failure to outlaw the rape of
slaves. The slashes, internal rhymes, alliterations, and repetitions make
poetry out of prose, make song out of sheer horror, and prove the possibility of that difficult miracle of black poetry in racist America. Having
defined slavery, Jordan next sets up the contradictions in the notion of a
slave poet: "A poet can read. A poet can write. . . . A poet is somebody
free. A poet is someone at home." And so, "How should there be Black
poets in America?" Clearly, it was not natural. And yet, she was the first.
"First" implies that Wheatley managed to be that miracle, and "first" also
implies there were and are others to follow.

The expansiveness and constraints of Jordan's writing help us rethink
what could be underneath Wheatley's constrained lines. Jordan clearly
establishes the reasons that the Middle Passage and slavery in America
seem to make the production of black poetry impossible. She also reminds

us why the poetry that does miraculously appear might be constrained: "Consider what might meet her laborings, as a poet, should she, instead, invent a vernacular precise to Senegal, precise to slavery, and therefore, accurate to the secret wishings of her lost and secret heart?" Jordan queries (257). If Wheatley wrote to "speak her pain" or to "stir her people into insurrection," would anyone have published such verse? The literature that does endure needs to appear nonthreatening enough to appear in the first place. While Wheatley's testimony may come from a source more trustworthy than the official voices complicit in slavery that produced the official testimony quoted by Hayden and Melville, it is still filled with silences and omissions. But reading Wheatley's seemingly nonthreatening lines alongside writers who teach us how to read between and underneath the lines may help us see Wheatley as Babo, Wheatley as potential angel of the lord. Such juxtapositions help to shift the frames set up by the laws and practices of slavery and racism.

The writers and activists who came after Wheatley face both more and less stringent constraints on their expression. The challenges raised by her poetry and by other textual engagements with the Middle Passage help explain the context of the literature of slavery and resistance and help force us to devise strategies for reading such material. We should read and teach Hayden's poetry of Middle Passage alongside Melville's story of slave mutiny, and both of them next to Wheatley, Olaudah Equiano, Douglass, Jacobs, and other slaves who did tell their own stories, though not without constraints. We can watch Spielberg's Hollywood blockbuster, but we have to seek out other voices at the same time—those eighteenth- and nineteenth-century African and African American voices, as well as contemporary voices from alternate perspectives. The multiple voices articulated here teach us not to rely upon the official or the blockbuster voices alone.

PART TWO

"I Want It Root
and Branch Destroyed"

The Radical Politics and Shifting Voices of
Sojourner Truth

A Woman among the Pettifoggers

Truth as Legal Actor

Two years after the Union victory and Confederate surrender, instead of yielding to pressure to keep the painful issues of the war in the past, Sojourner Truth insisted on keeping slavery in the public eye. "I come from another field—," she tells a mostly white New York audience in one of her recorded speeches, "the country of the slave. They have got their liberty—so much good luck to have slavery partly destroyed; not entirely. I want it root and branch destroyed. Then we will all be free indeed." She also assures this gathering of suffragists: "I want women to have their rights. In the courts women have no right, no voice; nobody speaks for them. I wish woman to have her voice there among the pettifoggers. If it is not a fit place for women, it is unfit for men to be there."[1] Truth advocates and claims legal agency in a United States that from its beginnings restricted slaves, free African Americans, and white women from a legal voice.

Although the law asserted otherwise, Truth's life demonstrates the capacity of disfranchised Americans to seize such agency. Through her escape from slavery (on the eve of legal emancipation), her multiple lawsuits, and other examples of private and public activism, Truth functioned as a legal actor, revealing the law as both an agent of oppression and a potential tool for resistance. Truth's relationship to the law anticipated the relationship described by critical race theorists more than a century later: law as both subordination and liberation.[2] We will never have a complete picture of Sojourner Truth, especially given the compromised textual record of her words, but examining her persistent legal agency helps to provide another dimension to this iconic figure and helps to deconstruct the myth of all-powerful slave laws and silenced slaves.

Like many African American activists in the nineteenth century, Truth had escaped from slavery. The terms of her escape reveal the contradictions and pettiness in the rhetoric and behavior of lawmakers and slaveholders, even as they worked toward emancipation. Though often identified with Southern slavery, Truth (called Isabella as a slave) was born in the slave-holding state of New York in the closing years of the eighteenth century. She was to be officially freed July 4, 1827, under New York's emancipation legislation (which was passed March 31, 1817), and her freedom often is framed as a legislative achievement. The subtitle of her 1850 book gives the state credit for her freedom: *Narrative of Sojourner Truth, a Northern Slave, Emancipated from Bodily Servitude by the State of New York, in 1828.*[3] The title page of the 1878 edition, published after the end of legal slavery, locates agency specifically in the state legislature and seems to place Truth's servitude and freedom further in the past: *Narrative of Sojourner Truth: A Bondswoman of Olden Time, Emancipated by the New York Legislature in the Early Part of the Present Century.* In this description, Truth's bondage was "olden" and her freedom came "early," thanks to the lawmakers of New York. In fact, Truth did not wait for the New York lawmakers. She escaped prior to the official date of emancipation, after her owner, John Dumont, went back on his word to free her early.

Combined with earlier legislation, New York's emancipation statute provided gradual and staggered freedom for enslaved African Americans in the state, revealing anxiety about creating a free black population too quickly. Slaves who were born before July 4, 1799, including Truth, would be free on July 4, 1827. Slaves born after July 4, 1799, including Truth's children, would be technically free but remain in mandatory servitude ("shall remain the servant of the owner of his or her mother") until age twenty-five for women and twenty-eight for men (Laws of New York 137: Sec. 32 and 4). Further, those born after passage of the act would remain in servitude until age twenty-one. These staggered dates, based on age and gender, meant there was no single day of collective emancipation. Slaveholders would be eased into this postslavery era, but wives and husbands, parents and children, sisters and brothers, inevitably would remain bound until different moments. The oldest slaves became free in 1827, others became free in 1824 (e.g., a woman born July 5, 1799), still others not until 1845 (e.g., a man born March 30, 1817). Another cruelty of such laws is the reliance upon birthdays—information often kept from slaves.

Maryland slave Frederick Douglass commits the first paragraph of his 1845 *Narrative* to analyzing the motivation and impact of denying slaves such knowledge. While he offers great detail about where he was born, he cannot offer similar detail about when: "I have no accurate knowledge of my age, never having seen any authentic record containing it. By far the larger part of the slaves know as little of their age as horses know of theirs, and it is the wish of most masters within my knowledge to keep their slaves thus ignorant. I do not remember to have ever met a slave who could tell of his birthday. They seldom come nearer to it than planting-time, harvest-time, cherry-time, spring-time, or fall-time" (39). Following a 1799 statute, New York owners were required to register the birth of new slaves (Higginbotham, *In the Matter of Color* 143). This requirement helped guard against the enforced ignorance that Douglass condemns, but it still places authority for knowledge with slaveowners. A mother's memory that her child was born at "cherry-time" would be unlikely to carry legal weight, if her owner recorded it differently. Making a slave a bit older or younger could produce a few more years of state-sanctioned servitude before state-sanctioned emancipation began.

Ironically, the key dividing points and the gradual dates of emancipation fell on the fourth of July, Independence Day. "Independence" was parceled out over several days and decades, and if one were born on the wrong side of that patriotic holiday, it meant more years of slavery. As Douglass declares years later in his "What to the Slave Is the Fourth of July?" speech (delivered July 5, 1852), "I am not included within the pale of this glorious anniversary! Your high independence only reveals the immeasurable distance between us" (284). His speech explicitly calls for "scorching irony" as he exposes the many ironies of American slavery (287). Another key irony in New York's emancipation debates is the odd contradiction that emerged when the legislature faced the dilemma posed by its own democratic history: the state constitution, written in 1777 and full of revolutionary fervor, granted voting rights to *all* free propertied men, without reference to color or prior condition of servitude. Hence, simply freeing slaves could have the side effect of giving some of them the civil rights of white men. Legislators tentatively resolved this problem in 1785 by placing some limits on slavery while also limiting the political rights of free blacks and continuing to debate emancipation for three more decades.[4] So although New York was somewhat early to debate the emancipation of slaves, the state also was early to articulate limits on the rights of former slaves.

Truth did not know the details of these legislative ironies, but she knew that she was entitled to be free by both state decree and her owner's word, so when Dumont revoked his promise of freedom, she decided to dissolve the terms of their contract. Of course, they never had a freely entered mutual contract, but even under the unilateral terms of slavery, Truth believed that Dumont had failed in his obligations. Dumont gave a reason for going back on his word: she had sustained a serious injury to her hand, and so he had sustained an economic loss and she therefore (by the logic of slavery) owed him another year of her labor. Her injury, needless to say, was sustained while she was providing him free labor in the first place, but slaveholders often invoked the rhetorics of fairness and entitlement when breaking their word. Harriet Jacobs, for example, details the legalistic excuses allowed to her grandmother's owner, her owner, and her children's owner. She describes the twisted legal reasoning as if readers already understood: "The reader probably knows that no promise or writing given to a slave is legally binding; for, according to Southern laws, a slave *being* property, can *hold* no property. When my grandmother lent her hard earnings to her mistress, she trusted solely to her honor. The honor of a slaveholder to a slave!" (Jacobs 6). Truth is quoted in her *Narrative* as offering the following analysis of the honor of slaveholders in keeping to their own contracts: "Slaveholders are TERRIBLE for promising to give you this or that . . . if you will do thus and so; and when the time of fulfilment [*sic*] comes, and one claims the promise, they, forsooth, recollect nothing of the kind; and you are, like as not, taunted with being a LIAR; or, at best, the slave is accused of not having performed *his* part or condition of the contract" (Truth and Gilbert 39–40). Slaveholders imposed their own contracts and devised their own loopholes, as did Dumont. So Truth determined to throw off such government, as resolutely as Jefferson decided to throw off King George's government a half century earlier,[5] and in late 1826 she walked away with her youngest child. She decided, however, to finish her current project first—spinning Dumont's wool—perhaps to demonstrate to him her superior sense of fulfilling one's obligations. If Dumont could not live by even his own laws, she would take justice "into her own hands."[6]

Like that of Douglass and Jacobs, Truth's freedom came from a combination of escaping her bondage and being purchased by white antislavery friends. After her escape, she stayed with the Van Wagenen family, who eventually paid Dumont for the last months of her service to which he imagined himself entitled. Unlike Douglass and Jacobs, Truth did not spend years living as a fugitive slave, and she had the additional legal protection of being officially emancipated by the state within months of her escape. Unlike those who fled from Southern slavery, Truth was able to remain in her home state as a free woman. While denied full citizenship rights there, Truth nonetheless claimed herself a citizen of New York and exercised legal prerogatives in a variety of contexts.

Truth's activism was multifaceted, involving political as well as religious appeals, in personal and public battles. Although she was best known as an orator, Truth's multiple approaches to personal and political ends, to social change, can be represented in her courtroom battles. Those efforts suggest a broader image of the struggles of African American women in the nineteenth century as well. Truth successfully initiated court action in three different cases: to free her son; to sue a respected white couple for libel; and to charge a conductor with assault and battery. Time and again, she was willing to use the law even as she challenged its legitimacy. Although Truth was not legally the defendant in the cases she initiated, she did have to defend herself in various ways, proving her right to claim precisely those things denied under slavery.[7] Securing the freedom of her son was contingent upon proving her motherhood. Suing for libel required her to prove her good name. And prosecuting a white man for assault meant proving that "a colored woman" (as newspapers identified her) had a right to bodily integrity. All of these efforts—asserting her motherhood and hence "womanhood," protecting her right to be secure in her person, and fighting for her name and control over representations of herself—play out in her other forms of activism as well, including her use of rhetoric.

Truth sued for her young son's freedom shortly after she secured her own. Her suit challenged the not uncommon practice of circumventing the emancipation laws by selling or transporting New York slaves into permanent slavery in other states. In the years leading up to full emancipation, New York laws barred such removal of soon-to-be-free slaves, but New York slaveholders and out-of-state slave traders (wanting to take advantage of the drop in slave prices that resulted from the emancipation laws) regularly engaged in such illegal behavior.[8] When Truth learned that her son (five-year-old Peter) had been illegally sent South, she refused this circumvention of the law—just as she earlier refused her owner's circumvention of his own agreement with her—and used the law to regain her child.

The story Truth tells reveals the sadism of slavery (particularly through the violent acts of her son's southern owner) as well as the indifference and hypocrisy of those complicit in slavery (particularly through the reactions of the white mothers to whom she appeals for help). At the same time, the story depicts a series of white people, from Quakers to lawyers, who offer assistance. Most importantly, the victory presents Truth as a woman who, despite few resources and many obstacles, was able "to have her voice there" in court (Stanton, Anthony, and Gage 2:193).

Truth's court battle for her son demonstrates both how slavery divides families and how family bonds remain important nonetheless. While defenders of slavery asserted that slave families generally remained intact,[9] slave narratives and other testimonies reveal otherwise. While Truth was busy spinning John Dumont's wool and planning her escape, Dumont sold her five-year-old son, Peter, to a New York doctor who was heading to England. Young Peter then changed hands twice more, moving from brother to brother to brother-in-law over a short period of time. The doctor's brother, Solomon Gedney, sold Peter to an Alabama planter, Fowler, who was married to Gedney's sister.

Peter was already in Alabama when Truth learned of her son's illegal sale. In the narrative, Truth appeals first to Dumont's wife, Sally, herself a mother, for justice. While Harriet Beecher Stowe's *Uncle Tom's Cabin* and other antislavery works argue that the common instincts of motherhood could create a sympathetic bond between white and black women, Truth's experience suggests the opposite. Sally Dumont expresses no sympathy and dismisses Truth's concern by invoking an image of excessive black motherhood. The *Narrative* quotes her vicious response: "*Ugh!* a *fine* fuss to make about a little *nigger*! Why, have n't you as many of 'em left as you can see to and take care of?" The overreproductivity of slaves proves their *lack* of true motherhood, in the eyes of Sally Dumont and other slaveholders. Faced with this excess of African Americans (scheduled to be emancipated within a few years), Sally Dumont echoes the racist sentiments behind arguments for removing blacks to Africa instead of freeing them and allowing them to remain in the U.S. as free people:[10] "A pity 'tis, the niggers are not all in Guinea!!" (41). Truth's response asserts her motherhood and her power: "*I'll have my child again.*" Her description of her feeling of empowerment uses the language of nationhood, countering Dumont's effort to render her powerless and nationless: "Why, I felt so *all within*—I felt as if the *power of a nation* was with me!" (45). Truth refuses the racist and gendered stereotype and replaces it with an image of determination and power, foreshadowing the power she will claim in her successful lawsuit.

Truth's appeal to another white mother meets equal indifference and hostility. In this confrontation, Truth refigures another common political comparison. White women's rights advocates often invoked analogies between marriage and slavery, between white wife and black slave. Truth challenges the simplicity of such parallels. After Sally Dumont's rejection, Truth visits Mrs. Gedney, whose three children each had been in possession of Truth's child. Gedney also rejects Truth's plea for sympathy and justice, using their common motherhood to establish division, not solidarity,[11] and making a derisive comparison between slavery and marriage to support her dismissal of Truth's concerns:

"Dear me! What a disturbance to make about your child! What, is *your* child better than *my* child? My child is gone out there, and yours is gone to live with her, to have enough of everything, and to be treated like a gentleman!" And here she laughed at Isabel's [a variant of Truth's slave name] absurd fears, as she would represent them to be. "Yes," said Isabel, "*your* child has gone there, but she is *married* and my boy has gone as a *slave,* and he is too little to go so far from his mother." (45)

Truth's response reasserts her motherhood (and the right of a five-year-old child—even a slave—to remain close to his mother) and insists on the significant difference between marriage and slavery. To the extent that the white mother thinks her daughter's marriage and move to Alabama increases her security, the parallel does not hold for the boy who joins her as property.

As the tragic end of this story reveals, had Gedney been wiser in her use of comparison, she might have seen that, indeed, a man given absolute authority over the body of another human might not hesitate to be equally violent with the other humans in his domain. After Truth recovers her son from Gedney's daughter and son-in-law (the Fowlers) and discovers how Mr. Fowler had brutalized Peter, she later learns—in graphic detail—that Mr. Fowler had beaten his wife to death: "He knocked her down with his fist, jumped on her with his knees, broke her collar bone, and tore out her wind-pipe!" (56). Instead of assuming slavery to be as benign as marriage, Mrs. Gedney might have interrogated more thoughtfully the nature of slavery and rethought her daughter's marriage to a Southern planter. Similarly, after painting an unfavorable portrait of Southern homes to her readers, Jacobs indicts Northerners whose daughters marry slaveholders: "They are not only willing, but proud, to give their daughters in marriage to slaveholders" (36). Jacobs and Truth would advise that the ownership of many acres and many slaves predicts not comfort but habits of tyranny.

Further details about Peter's experience in Southern slavery vividly depict the violence and sadism made legal by slavery and help to refigure sympathy further. Whereas Mrs. Gedney is incapable of sympathy for a fellow mother, her daughter, Eliza Fowler, appears in a different light. Once reunited with her son, Truth discovers, through his reports and his scarred body, that Mr. Fowler "whipped, kicked and beat" the five-year-old child and treated other slaves similarly. His other tale of torture also reveals the slaveholder's violence toward motherhood: one of the slave women, Phillis, "had a little baby, and Fowler cut her till the milk as well as blood ran down her body. You would *scare* to see Phillis, mammy." Truth also learns that Eliza Fowler tried to soothe Peter's injuries and told him "she wished I was with Bell [Isabella]" (54). Eliza's gentleness is contrasted with Mr. Fowler's cruelty, and her desire that Peter be with his mother contrasts with her own mother's indifference about Peter's motherless position.

Motherhood turns out to be at the core of Truth's suit for her son's freedom. Though not the defendant, she still has to prove herself. She is compelled to prove not whether Solomon Gedney really sold Peter to Fowler or whether Fowler really transported him out of the state; these points are not contested. The disposition of the case finally turns on whether or not Truth was really the child's mother. Slavery ironically both emphasizes motherhood (laws passed as early as 1662 declared that "the child follows the condition of the mother") and tries to obliterate it (except for guaranteeing a child's slave status, the mother has no legal influence over her child). Lawsuits for freedom often turned on questions of maternity. When Polly Berry (who was born free but kidnapped in Illinois) sued in a Missouri court for the freedom of her daughter, Lucy Delaney, she had to prove her motherhood:

> At the time my mother entered suit for her freedom, she was not instructed to mention her two children . . . so the white people took advantage of this flaw, and showed a determination to use every means in their power to prove that I was not her child.
>
> This gave my mother an immense amount of trouble, but she had girded up her loins for the fight, and, knowing that she was right, was resolved, by the help of God and a good lawyer, to win my case against all opposition. (Delaney 35)

Berry's "good lawyer" presented sympathetic testimony from slaveholders to prove Delaney's status as daughter and Berry's original free status, and he invoked in their favor the law dooming the children of slave women to bondage, arguing: "No free woman can give birth to a slave child, as it is in direct violation of the laws of God and man!" (42). Berry won her case, ironically by using the laws of slavery to her advantage and using her own former master to testify to her motherhood.

In Truth's case, she too had to persuade a court of her status as a mother in order to protect her child. As depicted in her *Narrative,* the chief testimony against Truth's motherhood is instigated by Fowler but comes in the voice of her own child. Coached by his Southern owner, Peter repeatedly denies that Truth is his mother (and also provides false explanations for the source of his many scars). The judge finally "allowed the mother to identify her son" and further declared that he be not only removed from Fowler but also returned directly to Truth (and not to slavery in New York, where he still owed fifteen years of servitude, under the emancipation act). Truth's *Narrative* quotes the court as ruling that the "boy be delivered into the hands of the mother—having no other master, no other controller, no other conductor, but his mother" (53). Through her successful use of the law, "the mother" here manages to displace the "master," in a Northern state moving toward emancipation but still entangled in slavery.

Through her own agency and through supportive white figures, Truth achieved a victory in court. She rescued her son from permanent servitude in Alabama and from shorter-term servitude in New York. Her white helpers included Quakers, who directed her to the grand jury and who provided her with needed funds, and two lawyers: "Esquire Chip" and "lawyer Demain." They are depicted as crucial to her success but not necessarily as fully sympathetic or understanding figures. Chip, when he first hears her story, leads her away and compels her repeatedly to swear to its truth. This performance is for the amusement of the law clerks, who cannot suppress their laughter, though he justifies it by saying it is for the law: "'Stop, stop!' said the lawyer, 'you must swear by this book'—giving her a book, which she thinks must have been the Bible. She took it, and putting it to her lips, began again to swear it was her child. The clerks, unable to preserve their gravity any longer, burst into an uproarious laugh; and one of them inquired of lawyer Chip of what use it could be to make *her* swear. 'It will answer the law,' replied the officer." He unnecessarily tortures the desperate mother, and offers the law as the excuse. He also invokes the law to quiet her impatience: "The law must take its course" (49). When Truth objects to the long wait, fearful her son might be endangered, Chip offers, like King Solomon without the wisdom, half the defendant's bond if he were to abscond with Peter: "'Well,' said the lawyer, very coolly, 'if he puts the boy out of the way, he must pay the $600—one half of which will be yours.' . . . She assured him, that she had not been seeking money, neither would money satisfy her; it was her son, and her son alone she wanted, and her son she must have" (49–50). Truth's legal efforts and her complex depiction of the various players show that whites and the law can act as both obstacles and helpers to freedom.

While white lawyers helped her bring her secular case to court, Truth also sought and received a form of justice directly from a higher court. After learning of Eliza's death and her family's grief, Truth was uneasy: "She thought she saw clearly, that their unnatural bereavement was a blow dealt in retributive justice: but she found it not in her heart to exult or rejoice over them. She felt as if God had more than answered her petition, when she ejaculated, in her anguish of mind, 'Oh, Lord, render unto them double!'" (58). The legal language (her "petition" was answered with "justice") suggests a parallel to her success in the courtroom struggle. She did not rejoice in this divine delivery of justice, but the example furthers an image of her as powerful and successful in her petitions. There is also an implied threat to those complicit in slavery: the laws of god and the state can turn a blind eye for only so long, particularly when agitated by a woman who carried within her "the power of a nation."

Truth's second lawsuit raises issues of representation and identity that continue to be important in her public life. Her 1835 libel suit allowed her to reclaim her good name from the white couple who wrongly accused her. Truth's involvement with a religious community (the Kingdom of Matthias) led to her being accused of attempted murder when the community fell apart after one of its members, Elijah Pierson, died. The Pierson family accused Matthias, the prophet of the community, of murdering him. The respectable Ann and Benjamin Folger wanted to deflect blame from themselves for the scandal, and they accused Truth of attempting to poison them. Truth simultaneously prepared to testify in defense of Matthias (because of the presumption against black testimony, she had to secure white attestations to her character), and she sued the Folgers for slander and libel.

Truth was facing verbal and written accusations, not criminal charges, but her lawsuit indicates the power of discourse and her refusal even to be named as a criminal. She sued for her good name, something that the daily slanders and stereotypes of slavery and racism try to refuse to African

Americans. The Folgers probably assumed the only African American woman (and ex-slave) in the group might be the easiest target and least likely to defend herself. Truth proved them wrong. Matthias was acquitted, and Truth won her lawsuit. The Folgers had to pay her $125 in damages— quite a settlement in the 1830s (Vale 2:3). In the course of defending herself, Truth gave her most detailed testimony not in a courtroom but in a book. British immigrant and radical journalist Gilbert Vale interviewed Truth and published an 1835 account of the story largely from Truth's perspective.[12]

Truth's successful lawsuit enabled her to keep her name clean. A few years later, Truth rid herself of that name altogether. She renamed herself in 1843, perhaps not only as a response to the ever-changing names of slaves but also as an even more radical way to reclaim her good name from the Folgers and others who would malign her. Many former slaves described the process of renaming themselves after they attained freedom. That rite of naming often was a combination of keeping and shedding identity, and the new names often came from white sources. William Wells Brown as a child was whipped for keeping his first name after his mother was ordered to change it because of the arrival of a white child named William. As an adult and a fugitive, he added to his name that of the Ohio Quaker who aided him shortly after his escape. The grateful fugitive asked the white man to rename him:

> "If I name thee," said he, "I shall call thee Wells Brown, like myself."
>
> "But," said he, "I am not willing to lose my name of William. It was taken from me once against my will, and I am not willing to part with it on any terms."
>
> "Then," said the benevolent man, "I will call thee William Wells Brown." (34–35)

Frederick Douglass renamed himself several times after his escape, changing his last name for safety but holding onto his first name "to preserve a sense of my identity" (*Narrative* 101). He finally settled on a name his abolitionist host drew from Sir Walter Scott's *The Lady of the Lake* (the poem's Lord James of Douglas, "the great Scottish chief" [*My Bondage* 209]). Booker T. Washington (who created his last name so that he could properly respond to his teacher's roll-call) observes that changing names was one of the first things that former slaves did upon emancipation. He describes how they would drop the master's last name (if they had been allowed to use it at all) and invent a new one (and often a middle initial), frequently drawing upon the names of Civil War heroes: "If 'John' or 'Susan' belonged to a white man by the name of 'Hatcher,' sometimes he was called 'John Hatcher,' or as often 'Hatcher's John.' But there was a feeling that 'John Hatcher' or 'Hatcher's John' was not the proper title by which to denote a freeman; and so in many cases 'John Hatcher' was changed to 'John S. Lincoln' or 'John S. Sherman,' the initial 'S' standing for no name, it being simply a part of what the coloured man proudly called his 'entitles'" (14). ("Susan" disappears from his example, and he does not specify whether women used Civil War names as well.) Since slaves' names are not their own, renaming can be a powerful act of self-definition.

When Isabella Dumont escaped in 1826 and was benevolently purchased by the Van Wagenens, she became Isabella Van Wagenen. In 1843, Isabella Van Wagenen became Sojourner Truth. She asked no white protector or "benevolent man" to rename her, and she drew upon no white inspiration for her new identity. Her new name is wholly her own. She reclaimed her name from Dumont, who owned her, from the Folgers, who slandered her, and even from the Van Wagenens, who protected (and purchased) her. Her new name reflects not the past but the future she carves out for herself: she would be an itinerant preacher, sojourning in various places and telling the truth to various audiences. Truth's escape (after Dumont went back on his word) and her court cases (for her son and her name) were battles over the truth. In the context of the lies of slavery and racism, she made explicit her commitment to truth in her choice of a new (and permanent) last name. Her new first name asserts a consciously chosen mobility, perhaps a response to the forced instability of slavery. She chose to sojourn and move on, for her own purposes and on her own terms.[13]

Truth traveled to preach and to agitate on political issues in the years leading up to and following the Civil War. She attained significant fame, but she was not always greeted with hospitality. Her speaking tour in proslavery Indiana was marked by legal struggles, but she prevailed in court even here, in cases that she did not initiate. Her 1861 speaking tour in the state came shortly after the outbreak of the Civil War and after Indiana passed legislation barring African Americans from entering the state. Many states, North and South, took measures to keep free blacks from their borders. Truth was arrested more than once, as were whites who hosted her. The descriptions of her tour quoted in the "Book of Life," appended to later editions of her *Narrative,* emphasize her triumph and her right to invoke American icons and liberties: "The band struck up the 'Star Spangled Banner,' in which I joined and sang with all my might, while amid flashing bayonets and waving banners our party made its way to the platform upon which I went and advocated free speech with more zeal than ever before, and without interruption" (141).

In this state run by Copperheads (Confederate sympathizers in the North), she had ongoing struggles with the law but also consistent support from a range of community members. She describes the legal incompetence of her opposition when she appeared at the courthouse to be tried for the crime of being black in Indiana: "My enemies, thinking I would probably run away, had made no preparation for the trial; but when they saw us come, hunted around and procured a shabby room into which I went with a few friends and waited for some one to appear against me. After a while, two half-drunken lawyers, who looked like the scrapings of the Democratic party, made their appearance, eyed us for a few moments, then left. Presently we saw them enter a tavern across the way, and this ended the trial" (143). Her victory serves as an affirmation of free speech— if not to the court, at least to the wider public to whom she told her tale— and it also provides her an opportunity to criticize her political opponents. Her success seemed to come partly because her accusers made the mistake of believing their own racist constructions. They assumed she would not even appear for the trial—the threat of legal action presumed to be enough to frighten off an ignorant black woman. Instead, they appeared the ignorant ones and Truth prevailed again.

The third court case initiated by Truth is linked to the post–Civil War desegregation of streetcars in Washington, D.C., and prefigures twentieth-century battles led by Rosa Parks and other African Americans willing to confront laws of segregation. Truth made a point of riding the segregated streetcars and insisting upon equal treatment. When confronted by antagonistic drivers, she did not back down. Her perseverance led to personal injury but also to the desegregation of public transportation and another successful court case. Stories about her struggles appeared in letters (both private and published), in newspaper articles, and in her "Book of Life." Her efforts again reveal her willingness to both challenge and use the law.

"Jim Crow" segregation generally is associated with post–*Plessy v. Ferguson* America[14] and the South in the 1950s and 1960s (when the Montgomery bus boycott, Greensboro lunch counter sit-ins, Freedom Rides, and other civil rights efforts brought national attention to the legal practices of segregation). Slave narrators, however, make it clear that Jim Crow was thriving in the "free" North of the mid-nineteenth century. Individual and organized opposition to this segregation also thrived. Jacobs describes learning that her money could not purchase first-class seats for the train ride from Philadelphia to New York: "This was the first chill to my enthusiasm about the Free States. Colored people were allowed to ride in a filthy box, behind white people, at the south, but there they were not required to pay for the privilege. It made me sad to find how the north aped the customs of slavery" (162–63). In her chapter entitled "Prejudice against Color," she relates that she was spared some of the indignities of Jim Crow in New York only because she was nursemaid to a white woman: "Being in servitude to the Anglo-Saxon race, I was not put into a 'Jim Crow car,' on our way to Rockaway, neither was I invited to ride through the streets on the top of trunks in a truck" (176). The chapter closes with her refusal to stand for discriminatory treatment and her call to fellow African Americans to resist: "Finding I was resolved to stand up for my rights, they concluded to treat me well. Let every colored man and woman do this, and eventually we shall cease to be trampled under foot by our oppressors" (177).

In 1855, Douglass writes of challenging Jim Crow practices: "The custom of providing separate cars for the accommodation of colored travelers, was established on nearly all the railroads of New England, a dozen years ago. Regarding this custom as fostering the spirit of caste, I made it a rule to seat myself in the cars for the accommodation of passengers generally. Thus seated, I was sure to be called upon to betake myself to the '*Jim Crow car.*' Refusing to obey, I was often dragged out of my seat, beaten, and severely bruised, by conductors and brakemen" (*My Bondage* 244). Douglass uses the arbitrariness of segregation practices to deconstruct color and color prejudice: "Some people will have it that there is a natural, an inherent, and an invincible repugnance in the breast of the white race toward dark-colored people; and some very intelligent colored men think that their proscription is owing solely to the color which nature has given them. They hold that they are rated according to their color, and that it is impossible for white people ever to look upon dark races of men, or men belonging to the African race, with other than feelings of aversion. My experience, both serious and mirthful, combats this conclusion" (246). Douglass then describes riding to Albany on an integrated train and finding that the white passengers all chose to segregate themselves from him, leaving the seat next to him empty, even though it was the only seat available. The Governor of Massachusetts chanced to enter the train and, knowing of Douglass's fame, sat next to him and engaged in conversation. "The despised seat now became honored. His excellency had removed all the prejudice against sitting by the side of a negro; and upon his leaving it, as he did, on reaching Pittsfield, there were at least one dozen applicants for the place. The governor had, without changing my skin a single shade, made the place respectable which before was despicable" (246). Douglass and others who refused the laws and practices of segregation exposed the fictions upon which those behaviors rested. While various legal and political efforts were underway, many nineteenth-century Rosa Parkses also placed their bodies on the line to challenge the practices and assumptions of segregation.

By the time of the Civil War, legal segregation of transportation had ended in many Northern cities. The nation's capital continued to segregate its streetcars legally until 1865, when President Lincoln signed a law banning such racial exclusions (Mabee and Newhouse 130). During legal segregation, Truth challenged the law by refusing to use the Jim Crow car and complaining to the company. The description offered in the "Book of Life" links her resistance to the passage of the law: "Unwilling to submit to this state of things, she complained to the president of the street railroad, who ordered the Jim Crow car to be taken off. A law was now passed giving the colored people equal car privileges with the white" (184).

However, even after the law changed, segregation and discrimination continued from both conductors and passengers. Truth now used the law to challenge these violations. She physically persevered and strategized to ride the cars, and she verbally confronted conductors who objected. "The Book of Life" describes several confrontations. In one incident, after the conductor ignores her, she yells "I want to ride! *I want to ride!!* I WANT TO RIDE!!!" and in the confusion of the crowd that gathered, Truth climbs aboard. "The angry conductor told her to go forward where the horses were, or he would put her out. Quietly seating herself, she informed him that she was a passenger. 'Go forward where the horses are, or I will throw you out,' said he in a menacing voice. She told him that she was neither a Marylander nor a Virginian to fear his threats; but was from the Empire State of New York, and knew the laws as well as he did" (184–85). She invokes her status as a Northerner and her knowledge of the laws to hold her ground. In another incident, she confronts racist passengers who are offended by the presence of Truth and an African American companion. One white woman asks the conductor "in a weak, faint voice" if "niggers" were allowed to ride. "He hesitatingly answered, 'Ye yea-yes,' to which she responded, "Tis a shame and a disgrace. They ought to have a nigger car on the track.' Sojourner remarked, 'Of course colored people ride in the cars. Street cars are designed for poor white, and colored, folks. Carriages are for ladies and gentlemen. There are carriages [pointing out of the window], standing ready to take you . . .' Promptly acting upon this hint, they arose to leave" (186). Objecting to the conductor's half-hearted support of the law, Truth assertively declares the right of African Americans to ride, and she further manages to compel the women to leave, successfully segregating the white racists away from the desegregated car.

Truth's confrontations led to the firing of more than one conductor. A particularly brutal encounter resulted in her third successful court case, a charge of assault and battery. She describes the incident in a letter to Amy Post:

> As I assended [sic] the platform of the car, the conductor pushed me, saying "go back—get off here." I told him I was not going off, then "I'll put you off" said he furiously, clenching my right arm with both hands, using such violence that he seemed about to succeed. . . . The number of the car was noted, and conductor dismissed at once upon the report to the president who advised his arrest for assault and battery as my shoulder was sprained by his effort to put me off. Accordingly I had him arrested and the case tried before Justice Thompson. My shoulder was very lame and swolen [sic], but is better. It is hard for the old slaveholding spirit to die. But *die* it *must*. (letter, 1 October 1865, dictated to Laura Haviland, qtd. in Sterling 254.)

Here she names segregation and brutality as legacies of slavery. The "Book of Life" describes the outcome this way: "The [Freedmen's] Bureau furnished me a lawyer, and the fellow lost his situation. It created a great sensation, and before the trial was ended, the inside of the cars looked like pepper and salt" (187). In several of these descriptions, it is the white conductors who are described as "hesitating," "furious," or "angry." Truth on the other hand seems consistently calm, even as she is the one being abused, suggesting her security in being in the right. Her efforts with the streetcars appear in the "Book of Life" as well as in several newspaper accounts in 1865, including the *National Anti-Slavery Standard, Weekly National Republican,* New York *Commercial Advertiser,* and Detroit *Post*

(Mabee and Newhouse 262), so the story of her successful resistance spread beyond Washington, D.C. Her actions and the publicity surrounding them help demonstrate that more than laws are needed to change discriminatory practices. Even good laws require activism—and often a willingness to put one's body at risk—to make them effective.

Desegregation is but one issue in postemancipation America, and court cases are but one strategy used by Truth. The Civil War amendments (the Thirteenth, Fourteenth, and Fifteenth Amendments, ratified between 1865 and 1870) officially freed the slaves, articulated principles of due process and equal protection, and allowed African American men the right to vote, but there was tremendous work still to be done. In her travels and in her relief work in the nation's capital, Truth saw intimately the economic and social strife facing former slaves. The minimal government support provided to these freed women and men clearly did not pay off the debt the country owed them for generations of slavery. In this postemancipation moment, Truth embarked on a new initiative: she lobbied the government to secure land in the American West where the former slaves could live and work. Her target was the U.S. Congress, but she took her appeal directly to the people, circulating a congressional petition among her various audiences over a period of about three years. She began this effort in 1870, the year the Fifteenth Amendment technically gave (male) African Americans the right to vote. In reality, racist laws and practices kept African American men from voting in many states.[15] Women did not gain the vote nationally until 1920. In the 1870s, no women and only a handful of African American men served in Congress (throughout Reconstruction, two African Americans served in the Senate and a total of twenty in the House). Despite these disfranchisements, Truth circulated her petition among women and men, African American and white. The petition offered separate columns for men and women, but it did not segregate the signatures by race. It did not ask signers if they were registered to vote (or eligible to register). It claims a political voice for all Americans, regardless of voting status.

In her public oratory and in letters to the newspapers, Truth urges people to support and sign the petition. The text reads:

To the Senate and House of Representatives, in Congress assembled: —

Whereas, through the faithful and earnest representations of Sojourner Truth (who has personally investigated the matter), we believe that the

Freed Colored People in and about Washington, dependent upon Government for support, would be greatly benefitted and might become useful citizens by being placed in a position to support themselves.

We, the undersigned, therefore earnestly request your Honorable Body to set apart for them a portion of the Public Land in the West, and erect Buildings thereon for the aged and infirm, and otherwise so legislate as to secure the desired results. (Sojourner Truth File, Library of Congress)

Truth conceived of the petition, paid for its printing, is named in its first line, and oversaw its circulation. Unlike her lawsuits, which sought personal redress, the petition calls for larger commitment from the state to a class of people. And unlike her lawsuits, the petition did not meet with success. This effort was a very different project, even though the goal was still justice. Here the appeal was for collective justice and collective relief, not just making whole an exceptional individual. The cost would be a commitment of resources not from an individual (whether Gedney's loss of a slave, the Folgers' $125 settlement, or the D.C. conductor's job) but from the federal government. The proposal might not have been the most pragmatic or effective solution, but it was certainly more ambitious than anything the U.S. government did try. As with many petition efforts, however, part of the goal was to raise consciousness among the signers, and in this Truth may have been successful. The petition motivated and focused her speaking tours in the 1870s, when there was no longer a clear project (that is, the abolition of slavery) around which activists could organize. It allowed her to speak about racial justice and legacies of slavery at a time when many citizens and even many activists wanted to believe that the Civil War had settled the issue of race in this country.

Nineteenth-century legal fictions tell us that slaves, free blacks, and women had no legal voice. Under various laws and practices, these groups officially had limited or nonexistent access to the courts, ballot box, legislature, or other arenas where laws are made and enforced. Nevertheless, Sojourner Truth—an African American woman and former slave—won three lawsuits, attempted to vote before it was legal, petitioned Congress, and in many ways insisted upon a legal and political voice. Studying the traces we have of her legal activism against slavery and racism complicates our picture of Truth (often seen only as orator or as larger-than-life icon of early feminism) and challenges some of the silences in the intentionally incomplete American record of slavery and resistance.

chapter four

Framing Truth
and Resisting Frames

xamining representations of Sojourner Truth is highly problematic.
No historical figure can be reconstituted fully or accurately, even
with an abundance of written texts. These problems are especially
pronounced with Sojourner Truth, however, who was an orator and activist, not a writer, and who belonged to multiple disfranchised groups.
Others wrote down the words attributed to her that we read today, choos-
ing what to put in the frame and how to represent it. These representations are deeply compromised: Orality does not transfer easily to paper,
and those who wrote down her words were never neutral transcribers.
Still, though Truth was not a writer, she was not simply an activist uncon-
cerned with the power of language. She was deeply involved in rhetoric,
communication, and the production of texts: she was active in American
discourse. Fields such as American literature, feminist criticism, ethnic
studies, and critical race theory need to continue to find ways to contend
with Truth and her texts, because of her contribution to these fields and
because of the methodological problems she brings to light.

Literary analysis of Truth includes not only a deconstruction of the
tropes used to represent her (in her time and into the present) but also an
exploration of her rhetoric in its own terms. Analysis of Truth's rhetoric
and politics reveals her radical revisions of nineteenth-century constructions of identity and multiple consciousness of race, gender, class, and religion. This chapter first examines the recent critical work that addresses the
complexity of the textual record around Truth and proposes new methodologies for examining her work. That discussion is followed by analysis of
how Truth's voice was framed by others, particularly white women who

"transcribed" Truth and her words. This analysis of framing is divided into sections on descriptions of Truth, representations of dialect, and packaging of Truth's texts. Finally, having discussed the complicated textual record, I analyze the multiple aspects of the public voice that Truth created through her activism.

Historical and Textual Contexts

Part of the context of Truth's activism is the racialized history of political movements in the U.S. Many African American women were active in abolition, women's suffrage, temperance, the antilynching campaign, and other nineteenth-century reform movements. Truth, Maria Stewart, Frances Ellen Watkins Harper, Mary Ann Shadd Cary, several women from the Charlotte Forten family, Mary Church Terrell, Anna Julia Cooper, Ida B. Wells, and many others spoke, wrote, and organized on behalf of these issues. Racism and exclusion were prevalent, however, and the white leadership of these movements systematically marginalized African American women. The debate over the exclusion of (white) women from the 1840 World's Anti-Slavery Convention is a well-known story in the genesis of the women's movement. Elizabeth Cady Stanton and Lucretia Mott met at the London convention, where women were barred from participation in the proceedings. The women in attendance were not to speak or vote, and they were "fenced off behind a bar and a curtain similar to those used in church to screen the choir from public gaze" (Stanton, Anthony, and Gage 1:60–62). Abolitionist sentiment did not imply feminist sentiment, these women learned. That experience resulted in the alliance between Stanton and Mott, which led to the 1848 Women's Rights Convention in Seneca Falls, a meeting that included at least one African American man, Frederick Douglass, but no African American women.

As it turned out, abolitionist sentiment did not imply antiracist convictions either. Local women's antislavery societies often were segregated, and the attendance of African American women could result in controversy. The Massachusetts Female Anti-Slavery Society at Fall River, for example, almost dissolved in the uproar resulting from the attendance of African American women in 1835 (Terborg-Penn, "Discrimination" 19). African American women often were excluded from the women's clubs that formed during the last part of the nineteenth century, encouraging the growth of the black women's club movement. In the suffrage movement, expediency often won out over justice; for example, in order to appease

Southern whites, Susan B. Anthony asked Douglass not to attend an Atlanta convention. Activist and journalist Ida B. Wells quotes Anthony as saying: "I did not want anything to get in the way of bringing the southern white women into our suffrage association. . . . Not only that, but when a group of colored women came and asked that I come to them and aid them in forming a branch of the suffrage association among the colored women I declined to do so, on the ground of that same expediency" (Wells Barnett, *Crusade for Justice* 230). Wells commented that Anthony "had endeavored to make me see that for the sake of expediency one had often to stoop to conquer on this color question" (229). Wells herself was dedicated to "women's" issues such as suffrage but also worked tirelessly for "black" issues such as the antilynching law. Unlike Anthony, she was not willing to betray one group for the other. As the battle for the vote wore on, many white suffragists invoked increasingly racist arguments, and African American activists were increasingly alienated from the movement.[1]

Rereading the history of the women's movement and the cultural documents produced by activists can help expose the racist subtexts (and texts) of the nineteenth century and their legacies into the present. My own education into feminism included reading and celebrating various (white) foremothers: Anthony, Stanton, Alice Paul, and others. In the history I encountered, in both academic and activist settings, women of color tended to be nonexistent, in the margins (sometimes literally—in the footnotes, appendix, or epigraph only), or, often, present only as grateful beneficiaries of their white sisters' efforts on their behalf. In applauding the victory of women's suffrage, (white) students of the women's movement often fail to identify racial tensions among early (and later) feminists and the racist compromises made by suffrage leaders.

Historian Rosalyn Terborg-Penn goes further to argue that Northern white suffragists did not merely compromise with Southern racists, they "made their southern counterparts the scapegoats for the racism they shared" (*African American Women* 6). An example of the slippery rhetoric used by white feminists as they sold out their sisters comes again from Anthony, in her patronizing reply to an African American suffrage leader who was not permitted to speak at a meeting: "I would not on any account bring on our platform a woman who had a ten-thousandth part of a drop of African blood in her veins, who should prove an inferior speaker . . . because it would militate so against the colored race" (qtd. in Carby, *Reconstructing Womanhood* 119). Anthony deploys the proslavery imagery of single drops of African blood as she justifies her racial double standard, disguising her motivation as concern for the "colored race" and blaming it on the black woman's own supposed "inferior[ity]."

Despite the suffrage leaders' attempts to silence the voices of African American women, activists such as Truth insisted on being heard. The unstable textual record of Truth's activism, depending as it does upon the reportage of others, offers a particularly rich opportunity to trace the racial problematics of the relationship between white activists and African American women in the nineteenth century. Even as white feminists critiqued aspects of the dominant ideologies of womanhood, often they invoked the slave woman's body—and her evident distance from standards of womanhood—to authorize their own speaking position. In the hands of white representors, Truth often is used to reinscribe existing definitions of womanhood, which she resists with her own redefinitions.[2]

In her life, Sojourner Truth walked away from slavery, initiated lawsuits, agitated for social and political change, and preached to an ever-changing congregation of both supporters and opponents. Because she was an activist and not a writer, her words seem particularly compromised. Reading any texts emerging from slavery challenges traditional approaches to history and literature. Attempting to read the texts or the life of Truth in particular forces a reevaluation of categories. Truth's politics and her identity crossed many boundaries. Part of the radicalism of her politics was her location in multiple sites. But because those sites were not in traditionally powerful arenas—as an African American, a woman, and an orator who did not write, she was outside the standard history-making spaces—it is very hard to trace her words and actions. Historian Nell Irvin Painter, in more than a decade of work on her biography of Truth, concluded that Truth's life compels us to rethink history-making procedures and to redefine biography. Early in her research, she wrote: "The Sojourner Truth biographical problem becomes a larger question of how to deal with people who are in History but who have not left the kinds of sources to which historians and biographers ordinarily turn. In order not to cede biography to subjects who had resources enough to secure the educations that would allow them to leave the usual sources for the usual kind of biographies, we need to construct new biographical approaches" ("Sojourner Truth in Life and Memory" 14). Painter calls on us to find ways to confront the complexity of the textual record of someone whose texts were primarily oral, to examine the history of someone who did not enter institutional facticity.[3]

The challenge in Truth scholarship and teaching is to contend with the problematic textual record while not letting those problems take over the study. The recent critical work on Truth tries to acknowledge the ways in which she has been mythologized while keeping her—and not her mythologizers—at the center of the analysis. As a historian, Painter strives in her biography to separate the historical woman from the myth. In its very structure, Painter's *Sojourner Truth: A Life, a Symbol* separates chapters on Truth's life, with detailed information culled from multiple historical sources, from chapters on what Truth becomes as a symbol. For example, Truth's famous Akron speech is contextualized and described in the chapter entitled "Akron, 1851," but its multiple versions and constructions are explored in a later chapter on the same event called "Ar'n't I a Woman?" (the query, probably never uttered by Truth, by which the speech has become known). The organization of Painter's book sometimes is frustrating, but she does not want to indulge our desire to see all the imagery before we take in the historical details.

Another biography is historian Carleton Mabee's *Sojourner Truth: Slave, Prophet, Legend* (written with Susan Mabee Newhouse). It provides valuable research, especially for locating multiple versions of speeches, but is very literal in its analysis. Painter's surprising closing chapter, "Coda: The Triumph of a Symbol," sums up how her book—along with Mabee's and Erlene Stetson and Linda David's—critiques the centrality of white abolitionist Frances Dana Gage's "Ain't I a Woman" version of Truth's 1851 Akron speech, yet students and even scholars still insist on holding on to that heroic framing of Truth and her oratory. Painter concludes that the "symbol of Sojourner Truth is stronger and more essential in our culture than the complicated historic person" (287).[4] Her scholarship offers powerful alternatives to how Truth has been constructed, but it also offers a warning that such scholarship will be resisted.

Stetson and David's groundbreaking *Glorying in Tribulation: The Lifework of Sojourner Truth* provides some of the most cogent literary and political analysis of Truth's discourse. They recover her history but also insist on uncovering her words. They simultaneously analyze multiple versions of Truth's speeches and assert her role in discourse, refusing to "see Truth's orality as a pathology" (11). To permit a multiple reading of the 1851 Akron speech, for example, "parallel passages from the three accounts are grouped, so that the reader can compare the substance and style of the transcripts" (114). They interweave their careful analysis with five sets of grouped passages, lining up similar moments in the *Anti-Slavery Bugle*, *National Anti-Slavery Standard*, and *New York Tribune* (114–18).[5] The technique is effective and persuasive, yielding a historically contextualized and textually specific reading of the speech and the multiple agendas shaping it. At times they offer innovative and sometimes bold alternatives to being bound to painfully problematized and compromised versions of Truth. For example, they quote from one powerful speech in which Truth parallels sick wheat and the sick Constitution, both of which look big and healthy until she takes hold of them:

> Children, I talk to God and God talks to me. . . . This morning I was walking out, and I got over the fence. I saw the wheat holding up its head, looking very big. I go up and take hold of it. You believe it, there was *no* wheat there? I say, God, what *is* the matter with *this* wheat? and he says to me, "Sojourner, there is a little weevil in it." Now I hear talking about the Constitution and the rights of man. I come up and I take hold of this Constitution. It looks *mighty big*, and I feel for *my* rights, but there aint any there. Then I say, God, what *ails* this Constitution? He says to me, "Sojourner, there is a little weevil in it." (132)

They analyze her rhetoric here in the context of political debates over the role of the Constitution, associating her view with the Garrisonian refusal to rely upon a document legitimating slavery. This discussion works to contextualize a famous confrontation between Truth and Douglass (who came to reject William Lloyd Garrison's dismissal of political action).[6] Their analysis keeps us focused on the politics of her speech. Their endnote, however, reveals that the indented quotation from Truth was in fact "our translation of the following dialect rendering of Truth's vision" from the *National Anti-Slavery Standard,* which they quote only in the note, complete with hard-to-read misspellings and bracketed insertions. This move might be read as yet another colonizing transcription of Truth to serve an agenda. Yet somehow it instead reads as a bold refusal to be limited by the limiting textual record. We might disagree with details of their rewriting, and obviously they marginalize the "original" version by tucking it into the notes (which are at the end of the chapter, not at the bottom of the page), but this framing is one of the various ways they try to displace the centrality of those nonoriginal "originals."[7]

As previously discussed, the body of work making up the public record of Truth is inherently unstable. She frequently was described, transcribed, and edited by friends and critics alike, all with a variety of agendas. Such framing and reframing make multiple layers of representation inevitable.

There are no original words to which to return. The initial "text" was a speech (or meeting, song, dictation, or other oral event), which does not exist outside of representation. What we receive is the writing down or reporting of that f-act (simultaneously the "original" event, the act of reporting, and the received "fact"), as transcription, interpretation, or reminiscence. Power relations are encoded in these transcriptions, where we encounter the attempt to "capture" aural elements (e.g., inserting dialect) and the attempt to "standardize" her language (e.g., removing dialect), as well as the colonization that transcription entails. Often what become "facts" about Truth are simply those items that are printed and reprinted, cited and re-cited. Like the children's game of "telephone," in which a statement is whispered from person to person until it emerges again completely altered, each reprint is likely to contain at least small changes.

Beyond the setting down of her words, there are also the characterizations and other framing descriptions of Truth. Whoever the describer, many similar tropes persist. Further, we have to consider the editing and packaging of those texts, which necessarily involve categorizing Truth in one way or another. These three gestures—transcription, description, and packaging—have different functions but often have similar results. They frequently work together to construct a particular version of Truth, emphasizing or creating characteristics that serve the creator well. Truth is the object of these representations, but she is also an agent in making use of and resisting these moves.

Representing Truth

The transcribers of Truth's voice make many choices about how to frame quotations and how to describe Truth and her speech. Often that framing forces a reader to receive her words in a particular way, and the image that comes with that frame frequently becomes more memorable and lasting than the words themselves. I am particularly interested in constructions of race and gender that set "black" against "woman" and against "American" and place Truth in an alien and foreign camp. Truth is often exalted and praised in these pieces, but she is also discredited and distanced in many ways. Underlying the praise are rhetorical moves that render Truth foreign, inanimate, nonhuman, nonwoman, and otherwise "Other." In this section, I will juxtapose representations of Truth published by three white women: Olive Gilbert, Frances Gage, and Harriet Beecher Stowe. These texts prove particularly enduring and appear in multiple versions.

Instabilities and contradictions within these representations reveal the contradictory projects of these writers and Truth's resisting rhetorics.

In 1850, Truth collaborated with Gilbert, a white abolitionist, to produce *The Narrative of Sojourner Truth*, copies of which she carried with her and sold to support herself. The book is sometimes referred to as dictated autobiography, although Gilbert puts the story in the third person and at times comments on the events as an outside (though unnamed) narrator. Gilbert was not a particularly public figure, and her name appears nowhere in the original text. Throughout the narrative, there are tensions between Truth's voice and Gilbert's. Sometimes the struggle is quite visible, as when Truth insists on including certain stories that Gilbert wants to suppress. Sometimes the tensions are subtler and appear through gaps, slippages, or misunderstandings. The presence of multiple voices was intensified when subsequent editions of the *Narrative* were published (in 1875, 1878, 1881, and 1884) by white abolitionist Frances Titus, who included additional framing material and appended Truth's "Book of Life," a collection of news stories and other tellings of Truth's public events and private correspondence, mostly collected by Truth but arranged, supplemented, and, at times, altered by Titus. The original narrative focuses on events prior to Truth's political activism, while the "Book of Life" depicts Truth more in her public life as orator, activist, and itinerant preacher. These depictions are often through Truth's "own" words, but the vastly different rhetorics in the speeches and letters remind the reader to pay attention to who is writing down the words. The *Narrative of Sojourner Truth* is a dynamic text that takes on different forms and authorships in multiple incarnations.

The texts that originally produced Truth's fame as an advocate were oral, but their translation into written documents helped to expand her reputation. Truth's most famous speech, delivered on May 28, 1851, at the Akron Women's Rights Convention, was not printed in the official proceedings. The *Liberator* published a four-sentence article about her speech, which mainly stated that it was impossible to report what she said. As noted above, the *New York Tribune* published a longer description of the speech and its effect on the crowd, while the *Anti-Slavery Bugle* attempted to reprint her words.[8] The next detailed version appeared twelve years later, in a *National Anti-Slavery Standard* article written by Frances Gage, composed in response to an essay in the *Atlantic* by Harriet Beecher Stowe. In 1881 the editors of the *History of Woman Suffrage* revised Frances Gage's article and included it in their book. The *Bugle* version of Truth's speech, while perhaps the most reliable, did not circulate until the 1990s, but Gage's account became the most quoted—as well as most trans-formed—version of a Truth speech. Revisions based on her version still are reprinted in anthologies (as well as on posters, cards, T-shirts, and other feminist paraphernalia).

In her *Atlantic* essay, Stowe—by 1863 one of the most famous American writers of race issues—recalls and embellishes her meeting with Truth from a decade earlier, leading to another "text" influential in framing Truth: Stowe had described Truth to her sculptor friend William Wetmore Story, prompting his 1860 statue *The Libyan Sibyl.* Story was a Massachusetts artist and son of Supreme Court Justice Joseph Story (who had anti-slavery sentiments but who also wrote the opinion in a critical proslavery case).[9] Story never met Truth, and Stowe never saw his statue, yet Stowe named her article "Sojourner Truth, the Libyan Sibyl" and closes with a lengthy description of the statue. Before describing the work, Stowe explains its inspiration: "The history of Sojourner Truth worked in [Story's] mind and led him into the deeper recesses of the African nature,—those unexplored depths of being and feeling, mighty and dark as the gigantic depths of tropical forests, mysterious as the hidden rivers and mines of that burning continent whose life-history is yet to be. A few days after, he told me that he had conceived the idea of a statue which he should call the Libyan Sibyl" (480–81). Stowe's story becomes Truth's "history," which becomes the thrice-deep nature of Africa. These images of Truth and Africa, both rendered unfathomable, merge to become a statue. The statue's name becomes Truth's, and Truth becomes similar to the statue that she supposedly inspired.

Story himself emphasized the African specificity of his intentions: "I have taken the pure Coptic head and figure, the great massive sphinx-face, full-lipped, long-eyed, low-browed and lowering, and the largely-developed limbs of the African. . . . I made her head as melancholy and severe as possible, not at all shirking the real African type . . . —Libyan African of course, not Congo" (James 1:70–72). Stowe's description of an individual African American thus becomes "*the* African." Story is after essences: the Coptic head is "pure," the African type is "real." While Story may not have intended to represent Sojourner Truth, such an equation is the result, thanks to Stowe's descriptions and her use of the title "Sojourner Truth, Libyan Sibyl." The appositive endures, appearing in subsequent articles, frontispiece captions, and even essays published more than a century later.

While the word "Libyan" places Truth in Africa, "sibyl" might be read as putting Truth in the ranks of the gods. More specifically, however, a sibyl is a mythological mortal woman who transmitted messages from the ancient gods—in some depictions, a male priest transcribes her incoherent utterances. In one of the most widely known accounts, the Cumaean sibyl in the *Aeneid* speaks in a mad frenzy, caused and tamed by the god who bestrides her like a horse, "pull[ing] her up" and "whip[ping] her on" (Virgil 6.142). Virgil's hysterical and sexualized images suggest power from another source and loss of control:

> And as she spoke neither her face
> Nor hue went untransformed, nor did her hair
> Stay neatly bound: her breast heaved, her wild heart
> Grew large with passion. Taller to their eyes
> And sounding now no longer like a mortal
> Since she had felt the god's power breathing near. (6.77–82)

Unlike Truth, the sibyl does not preach from her own inspiration. Rather, upon orders from god or mortal, she enters a trance or frenzy and reveals the god's words in this possessed state. This image contrasts sharply with Truth's public oratory, which did not emanate from any sponsor.

Sibyl imagery often was invoked in nineteenth-century depictions of fictional women who spoke in public, for instance in Henry James's *The Bostonians* and Nathaniel Hawthorne's *The Blithedale Romance*, perhaps as a way to depict the power (and potential subversiveness) of a woman seizing public space while still displacing the source of the power from the woman herself. Woman as sibyl is simultaneously a radical and reactionary image. Story's white marble statue depicts a woman, bare-breasted, reclining, leaning on a closed scroll. The image seems powerful but in fact helps to exoticize Truth and disempower her voice. The final sentence of Stowe's essay refers to the importance not of Truth or her impact but of her statue (in which she played no active role): "We hope to see the day when copies both of the Cleopatra [Story's other "African" sculpture] and the Libyan Sibyl shall adorn the Capitol at Washington" (481). Truth—who in real life petitioned the U.S. Congress—is contained and removed, turned into white marble, merely adorning instead of lobbying the Capitol. Stowe constructs her as an ornament, not a political actor.

Framers such as Frances Gage and Stowe simultaneously praise and discredit Truth. She is constructed as foreign, exotic, primitive, ancient, "barbaric," or "Amazon." Stowe describes Truth singing a hymn, "carried away with her own feeling." The description places Truth safely far away, savage and singular: "She sang with the strong barbaric accent of the native African, and with those indescribable upward turns and those deep gutturals which give such a wild, peculiar power to the negro singing" (477). Like the priest translating the frenzied sibyl's rantings, Stowe transcribes Truth's lyrics in "standard" English. Frances Gage refers to the many anecdotes about "the weird, wonderful creature, who was at once a marvel and a mystery." She praises Truth but also makes her strange and nonhuman. Once Truth appears at the convention, Gage describes the reaction: "The tumult subsided at once, and every eye was fixed on this almost Amazon form, which stood nearly six feet high, head erect, and eye piercing the upper air like one in a dream." "Which" and "high" denote a thing, not a person. The eyes of both Truth and her audience are mentioned, but the crowd's eye is the subject, and Truth's eye is another objectified, viewed piece of her body. As in Stowe's piece, Truth is described with abstract and dehumanizing words like "form." The Amazon image mythifies her and her race, size, and gender. Like Stowe, Frances Gage seems hesitant to credit Truth with too much conscious ability. The dream language suggests the sibylline trance. Truth's power is rendered supernatural instead of human. For Gage, it was a "magical" power that subdued the crowd, not the human Truth and her human qualities. "I have never in my life seen anything like the magical influence that subdued the mobbish spirit of the day" (4). Magic, rather than Truth herself, is credited, just as Apollo, not the sibyl, is considered the real source of power.

Truth is made into an object, often literally. She is described variously as a "palm-tree," "ornament," and "statue."[10] Truth is repeatedly "singular," "strange," "original." In her opening line, Stowe declares that Truth's "singular name" is known by the "few" readers of "radical" papers (473). Truth lacks the mainstream fame and acceptability that Stowe enjoys. After observing her guest, Stowe states: "By this time I thought her manner so original that it might be worth while to call down my friends" (474). Stowe beckons her friends from above (their relative location in the house and in the social structure) to observe what has been constructed as an intriguing but quirky spectacle. Sibyls were not gods, but they were not treated as mortals either. Aeneas and other ancients sought them out to observe and decipher their frenzied trance. Mortals would watch and listen, not interact. An observed performance, not a conversation, is what occurs in classical myth and in Stowe's account. Stowe's friends descend, and "Sojourner" (already known by her first name alone) is joined by "Dr."

Beecher and "Professor" Allen. If she stands above the titled men, it is as inanimate object: "She stood among them, calm and erect, as one of her own native palm-trees waving alone in the desert" (474). She becomes a tree: natural, passive (if "waving," it is by the wind), isolated (she waves "alone") and African ("native"). Truth often is rendered African rather than American. Stowe even describes Truth's journey from Africa, placing her in the Middle Passage even though she was born in New York.

For Stowe, Truth's gendered identity as a woman does not come into play until she is rooted firmly in the African desert. Truth's maternal role is evoked in anecdotes she relates to the gathered audience. The stories cited by Stowe are examples of aberrations of motherhood. The first reference is to Truth's discovery that her son had been sent South. Truth may have recounted these stories to Stowe, but the text here seems largely lifted—and not carefully—from the *Narrative* (see 44–58). Stowe retells the anecdotes with additions, inaccuracies, and altered dialect. Stowe quotes Truth quoting herself: "'Missis,' says I, '*I'll have my son back again!*'" (477). Truth's declaration reveals her as a committed mother, a key attribute of a true woman. But the fact that she has lost her child (and regains him) in an economic and legal transaction unique to slaves reminds Stowe's audience that Truth is a different kind of mother. The description of the mother-child reunion is decidedly unsentimental and sounds more like a restoration of goods: "Well, finally they got the boy brought back. . . . They gave him to me, an' I took him an' carried him home." That story of motherhood temporarily denied is immediately followed by a symbolic mothering. When the mistress responsible for sending Truth's son to the South finds that her only daughter has been murdered, Truth takes on the nurturing role in Stowe's telling: "I held her poor ole head on my arm, an' watched for her as if she'd been my baby. An' I watched by her, an' took care on her all through her sickness after that, an' she died in my arms" (478). This scene is not described in the *Narrative* and may be Stowe's creation.

While these nurturing, maternal characteristics befit a nineteenth-century "true" woman, again the circumstances reveal a perversion of real motherhood emerging from the circumstances of being a slave first and a woman second. Truth's audience—Stowe and company—distance themselves from her and from her story, and the readers are expected to join those observers in that distancing. After listening to Truth's story of finding her son, climaxing in the wrenching scene of Truth holding her former mistress like her own baby until she died in her arms, the audience responds with: "Well, Sojourner, did you always go by this name?" (478). "Well," begins this nonsequitur, as if the question had anything to do with the testimony just delivered. These passages are brief vignettes to show off different elements of Truth's dialect and presentation. Readers are not really meant to engage in the content of her comments. Like the sibyl who is asked a series of questions without generating any actual interaction, Truth is not to expect genuine reactions from her seekers either.

Truth's physicality as a woman emerges in Stowe's article in response to a question about women's rights. In this passage, Stowe reduces Truth's views on feminism to a comment about Truth's own body. Stowe manages here to trivialize both Truth and women's rights activists. She quotes Truth on speaking at suffrage meetings and being asked if she wore bloomers: "'I told 'em I had bloomers enough when I was in bondage. You see,' she said, 'dey used to weave what dey called niggercloth, an' each one of us got jes' sech a strip, an' had to wear it width-wise. Them that was short got along pretty well, but as for me'—She gave an indescribably droll glance at her long limbs and then at us, and added, 'Tell *you*, I had enough of bloomers in them days'" (479). The passage is the only one about Truth as a political orator, but it shifts quickly to a focus on her physicality. The focus is on the femaleness of her body but in a racially specific way. And the details of her body—she is too tall—serve to defeminize her.[11] Truth is described as making fun of her own body, even turning her own glance at it in an objectifying way. Our attention to her gendered body is in the context of her slave's body being treated as ungendered. Rather than using the detail to criticize slavery or gendered expectations in clothing, Stowe employs the example to mock feminists.[12] Truth may have offered this description, but as the only discussion of women's rights and public speaking in the frame that Stowe constructs, it offers a reductive picture of Truth's role as feminist thinker and orator.

Frances Gage's focus on Truth's physicality also serves to mediate Truth's agency. When Gage does grant agency to Truth, she simultaneously fragments her so that it is her parts that have agency. In one of Gage's hyperboles, "Rolling thunder could not have stilled that crowd as did those deep wonderful tones, as she stood there with outstretched arms and eye of fire" (4). The image is impressive, but Truth is not a complete subject and instead is made up of tones, arms, and eyes. Gage already emphasized Truth's powerful arms, interrupting her words to state that "she bared her right arm to the shoulder, showing its tremendous muscular power." She recalls those arms again in one of the concluding images: "She had taken us up in her strong arms and carried us safely over the slough of difficulty" (4). While Gage praises Truth, she also reduces her to her physicality. No longer a mere statue, Truth is now a heroic—but still not quite human—figure. Or, if human, she might be a version of the Mammy figure—large and strong, adored and relied upon, but not an agent in her own right. That image also recasts Truth's success as an act of physical strength rather than oratory. As Yellin argues, rather than rejecting patriarchal definitions of womanhood, Gage "cast the black woman as a powerful rescuer and herself and the other white women at the convention as the powerless rescued female victims" (81). While honoring Truth's magical and physical power, Gage and her fellow "tender-skinned" (coding race and class—these are white ladies who can stay out of the sun, unlike Truth with her "hard palms") white women "with streaming eyes and hearts beating" can retain their femininity (4).

Frances Gage's final description of Truth at the Akron convention is as "the glorious old mother" (4). The label is somewhat ironic, as Gage's descriptions throughout have not been particularly maternal. The only reference to Truth's literal role as a mother is her quoted line: "I have borne thirteen chillen, and seen 'em mos' all sold off into slavery and, . . . I cried out with a mother's grief" (4). The rules of true motherhood are reinscribed as we see Truth at her moment of being denied any but the biological maternal role. As in Stowe's description, here Truth is physically a mother, but as a slave and black woman she has none of the social prerogatives of a white mother. The number here is an exaggeration—she had five children, not thirteen. Truth herself might have engaged in this hyperbole, but it is also possible that Gage, not remembering the details, filled in with her own picture of the highly reproductive slave woman.[13]

Frances Gage's famous telling of Truth's Akron speech is most often drawn not from the original abolitionist newspaper article but from the 1881 excerpt in the *History of Woman Suffrage*. The original piece appeared a month after Stowe's essay and uses it as a point of departure. Truth is first named in quotes, as if Stowe's fictional creation: "The story of 'Sojourner Truth,' by Mrs. H. B. Stowe, in the April number of *The Atlantic,* will be read by thousands" (4). Gage invokes the authority of the more famous Stowe but also authorizes herself as one of "those who knew this remarkable woman" and personally "witnessed" her speech in Akron. In the *History* reprinting, the editors remove the first three paragraphs of Frances Gage's piece but make their own references to Stowe. This 1881 introduction, written two decades after Stowe's piece, opens by referring to Truth as "Mrs. Stowe's 'Lybian [*sic*] Sibyl'" (115). The Libyan sibyl association persists (though misspelled). Whereas Stowe opens by invoking white sculptors Story and Cumberworth, the suffragist editors invoke white author Stowe. The white suffragists do not construct Truth as the product of a white male artist but rather as the possession of a white woman writer. The white woman is named with the married honorific—Mrs. Stowe—while the African American woman has no title (and sometimes no last name).

Frances Gage's narration, in the original and in 1881, repeats the comparison to the *Sibyl*, emphasizing its existence as a stationary and silent statue. In the midst of tumult and excitement, "old Sojourner [only in her fifties at the time], quiet and reticent as the 'Libyan Statue,' sat crouched against the wall on a corner of the pulpit stairs, her sun-bonnet shading her eyes, her elbow on her knee, her chin resting on her broad, hard palm" (4). Truth is an orator, yet she is introduced as silent ("quiet" and "reticent") and compared to a permanently silent statue. The description of her body is identical to the positioning of Story's statue. Truth again is more an imitation than the real thing.

While Stowe and Frances Gage each play a prominent role in their first-person pieces about Truth, Gilbert is an anonymous presence in Truth's 1850 *Narrative*. The original edition appeared without Gilbert's name and with an unsigned preface by William Lloyd Garrison. The title page provides many details—*Narrative of Sojourner Truth, a Northern Slave, Emancipated from Bodily Servitude by the State of New York, in 1828. With a Portrait*—but no author. Without the phrase "written by herself," Truth is not announced as the author, and no white author or editor appears either. Modern reprintings tend to echo the 1850 silences, listing neither Truth nor Gilbert as authors and naming only the modern editor.[14] Gilbert's unnamed presence might be read as an act of modesty or self-effacement, but in some ways the lack of a clear authorial identity makes the narrative declarations seem more sweeping. The descriptions seem commonly agreed upon and without an identifiable source.

Similarly, Titus's name also does not appear as editor on the 1878 title page, though she is listed on the following page as having entered this text in the Library of Congress. Her preface is signed simply "THE AUTHOR," which might mislead the reader to think she is the author of the text to follow. This preface is respectful toward Truth (who is referred to by her first name again) but also objectifies her. Her height and movements "remind the observer of her lofty cousins, the Palms, which keep guard over the sacred streams where her forefathers idled away their childhood days. Doubtless, her blood is fed by those tropical fires which had slumberingly crept through many generations, but now awaken in her veins" (vi). Truth is part of a foreign, tropical nature here, and she is again compared to palm trees and other passive images that "idle" and "slumber." She is an important object for our observation but is not developed into a fully sentient subject. The 1878 frontispiece illustration is captioned SOJOURNER TRUTH, "THE LIBYAN SIBYL." Titus's language about Truth's awakening tropical blood also evokes the sibyl. The very nature of this genre—a third-person "autobiography" written down and edited by someone other than the autobiographical subject—might suggest the sibyl metaphor as well. Truth's name and face open the book, but the words are not necessarily hers.

Many nineteenth-century African American figures create a public persona through their first-person autobiographical slave narratives, "written by herself" or "himself." Significantly, two of the most iconic figures in nineteenth-century African American culture come to us through texts they did not write. Both Truth and Virginia slave rebel Nat Turner produced texts about their lives in collaboration with a white scribe. Though created under very different circumstances, the texts they produced might be considered dictated narrative or collaborative autobiography. The narrative Truth produced was written in the third person by a white abolitionist and was first published before her most famous public activities. Turner's first-person account of his life and the 1831 slave insurrection he initiated was solicited and written down by a white lawyer who wanted to make money off the tale. Both Turner and Truth utilized their transcribers to tell their stories while they also struggled against the representations of themselves in the works.

These works do not fit easily into any one category. Not strictly autobiography, they have similarities with the autobiographical genres of slave narrative and spiritual narrative even as they do not conform to the expectations of those forms. They are acts of testifying in a culture that banned slave testimony (and often free black testimony) in a court of law. The fictions of self-representation present in any autobiography are compounded here by representations of race and gender relied upon by the dominant culture and by the white "coauthors" of these works. Although both books purport to tell an individual life, both contain multiple voices and competing agendas.

Whereas Truth spoke as a traveling orator and former slave, Turner spoke as an imprisoned slave condemned to death for instigating an insurrection. Lawyer Thomas Gray interviewed Turner in his jail cell and published *Confessions of Nat Turner* days after Turner's execution. This is a very different type of collaboration than Truth's voluntary one with Gilbert. Gray's framing controls what we read: he asks the questions, and he can include, exclude, and phrase Turner's words as he pleases. At the same time, Turner can be using Gray to advance his own agenda. Some readings see Turner as trickster, controlling the message through what he includes and what he omits.[15] This document is the primary source of information about Turner, but many other texts contribute to the legend around him.[16] As with Truth's narrative, reading Turner's life involves attempting to analyze his self-representation while dissecting his transcriber's framing and contending with the popular constructions of Turner, who in 1831 had already become a powerful icon of both fear and inspiration. Partly as a result of the ambiguities around their lives, Truth and Turner both became larger-than-life American icons. Tensions and gaps fill their collaborative autobiographical texts.

These contested works reveal not only the complexities around the lives and words of these figures but also the tensions and anxieties around slavery and race in nineteenth-century U.S. culture. Both works, created under very different circumstances, are examples of white appropriations of African American voices, pointing to literary and political considerations still with us. These works also reveal how, even under unequal or involuntary collaboration, the subject of the autobiography still exerts control over her or his text.

As mentioned above, tensions appear in a variety of ways in Truth's narrative collaboration. Like many of Truth's transcribers, Gilbert acknowledges the difficulties of transcription. She writes of Truth's religious expression: "Her prayers, or, more appropriately, 'talks with God,' were perfectly original and unique, and would be well worth preserving, were it possible to give the tones and manner with the words; but no adequate idea of them can be written while the tones and manner remain inexpressible" (60). The "words" are inadequate because they cannot convey tone and manner. Using Truth's slave name (even though she no longer went by the name Isabella at this time), Gilbert writes of the inexpressibility of Truth's communication to others: "The impressions made by Isabella on her auditors, when moved by lofty or deep feeling, can never be transmitted to paper, (to use the words of another,) till by some Daguerrian art, we are enabled to transfer the look, the gesture, the tones of voice, in connection with the quaint, yet fit expressions used, and the spirit-stirring animation that, at such a time, pervades all she says" (45). Adequate transcription requires the precision of a camera, not a pen. Gilbert's discussion of the impossibility of transmitting Truth's voice and performance on paper calls out the multiple problems of transcription and simultaneously reveals the problems of constructing Truth as this odd, untranscribeable creature.

Stetson and David describe the struggle between Truth's dictation and Gilbert's transcription:

> Truth's "I" becomes Gilbert's "she," although this is by no means a simple metamorphosis. Their contending dialogue reveals itself throughout, in interruptions of chronology and through corrections, amplifications, clarifications, second thoughts and deliberate suppressions. As an interactive document, *Narrative* highlights a dynamic of corrective unrest and retrospective remembering of remembering in its self-conscious attempts to establish an authentic and enduring identity for its speaker through the medium of its anonymous scribal voice. Their efforts are both collaborative and resisting, as Truth's recollection, reconstruction, and reconstitution strive against Gilbert's censoring authorial control. (15)

Coauthors Truth and Gilbert work together and are at odds. Gilbert has an abolitionist agenda that may be shared by Truth, though Truth does not necessarily want the details of her life to be simply pressed into the service of the movement. Five years later, Douglass would write in his second autobiography that his comrades in the abolitionist movement would take him as their text in a variety of colonizing ways, constructing him as they imagined a former slave *ought* to appear, constraining his own expressions in the process.[17]

As part of her condemnation of slavery, abolitionist Gilbert depicts Truth failing to fulfill standards of womanhood. On some levels, the *Narrative,* especially with the appended "Book of Life," narrates Truth trying to establish her womanhood. From tales of the slave Isabella's motherhood to retellings of arm- and breast-baring episodes in the "Book of Life," Truth is depicted as physical and gendered. That gendering, however, is filtered through Truth's race and class positions. Gilbert uses the narrative to make her own statements about abolition and to displace certain physical or sexual issues that she cannot talk about as a white woman. Through suggestive omissions, Gilbert points to how removed Truth is from true (white) womanhood, especially in her susceptibility to sexual abuse and her inability to be a traditional mother. For example, after relaying stories of Truth's childhood in great detail, Gilbert introduces her new owners, the Dumonts: "From this source arose a long series of trials in the life of our heroine, which we must pass over in silence; some from motives of delicacy. . . . Therefore, the reader will not be surprised if our narrative appear somewhat tame at this point, and may rest assured that it is not for want of facts" (30). Gilbert does not say she is omitting stories of sexual abuse, but the ambiguity and suggestiveness of the passage permits the reader to imagine just such indelicate trials. The gap serves as a reminder of the gap between Truth's experiences and those of a white woman whose life does not need such censorship. Gilbert's "we" and "the reader" do not include African American women. White readers are to join the white author in distancing themselves from this "heroine."

Margaret Washington states in her 1993 introduction to the *Narrative* that Gilbert's omissions are surprising: "Gender-specific devaluation is an implicit, underlying theme in Isabella's story. It is peculiar that Olive Gilbert's censoring of Isabella's story is strongest in the female 'sphere' and in sexuality" (xxix). Such censoring is less peculiar given constructions of (white) womanhood as sexually pure. Gilbert is simultaneously safeguarding her own propriety as a writer, "protecting" Truth from problematic disclosures, and highlighting the shock value of what those disclosures might be.

In addition to sexual standards of womanhood, familial roles of women are reinscribed when Gilbert describes Truth inevitably failing to fulfill properly the roles of wife and mother. Isabella's slave marriage is performed by a fellow slave, "as no true minister of Christ *can* perform . . . a mere *farce*, a *mock* marriage, unrecognized by any civil law" (36–37). Her marriage—a key element of her candidacy for womanhood—is defined by its lack of validity. Denial of marriage rights means that slave relations are licentious, according to Gilbert, but she also links that failing to Southern law and implies that *white* Southern sexuality is no less licentious under these laws. She writes that slaveholders "are well aware that we know how calmly and quietly they contemplate the present state of licentiousness their own wicked laws have created, not only as it regards the slave, but as it regards the more privileged portion of the population of the South" (37). She cites here the South's awareness of the North's knowledge of their sin while she provides the context for Truth's inability to marry legally.

Gilbert further dissects Truth's compromised womanhood in a chapter ironically titled "Isabella as a Mother." Truth eventually "found herself" the mother of five and, according to Gilbert, "rejoiced" in increasing her master's property.

> Think, dear reader, without a blush, if you can, for one moment, of a *mother* thus willingly, and with *pride,* laying her own children, the "flesh of her flesh," on the altar of slavery—a sacrifice to the bloody Moloch! But we must remember that beings capable of such sacrifices are not mothers; they are only "things," "chattels," "property."
>
> But since that time, the subject of this narrative has made some advances from a state of chattelism towards that of a woman and a mother; and she now looks back upon her thoughts and feelings there . . . as one does on the dark imagery of a fitful dream. (37–38)

Gilbert here separates definitions of black and white motherhood and implicitly defines true motherhood as white. To make this point, she turns directly to the constructed reader, who is "dear" and is likely to "blush," suggesting a white woman of tender sensibilities. The "we" who "must remember" are set in opposition to the "beings" and "things" produced under slavery. Gilbert's dehumanizing language certainly is intended to condemn the dehumanizing effects of slavery, but her descriptions reveal the assumptions from which she launches her attack. The categories of "woman" and "mother" cannot include a slave or even a free black woman, for Truth's emancipation has only pointed her "towards" womanhood: she has not arrived and perhaps cannot arrive at that endpoint. Gilbert's word choice describing the bad dream of slavery—"dark imagery"—reminds us that it is blackness which keeps Truth from true womanhood.

The narrative is filled with tensions between Gilbert and Truth, sometimes explicit and sometimes veiled. Occasionally Truth insists on telling a story that Gilbert finds trivial (e.g., "one comparatively trifling incident she wishes related" [30]). At times Truth's anecdotes seem to give us instructions about how to read compromised texts. In a chapter entitled "Some of Her Views and Reasonings," Gilbert writes:

> I had forgotten to mention, in its proper place, a very important fact, that when she was examining the Scriptures, she wished to hear them without comment; but if she employed adult persons to read them to her, and she asked them to read a passage over again, they invariably commenced to explain, by giving her their version of it; and in this way, they tried her feelings exceedingly. In consequence of this, she ceased to ask adult persons to

read the Bible to her, and substituted children in their stead. Children . . .
would re-read the same sentence to her, as often as she wished, and without
comment; and in that way she was enabled to see what her own mind could
make out of the record, and that, she said, was what she wanted, and not
what others thought it to mean. She wished to compare the teachings of
the Bible with the witness within her; and she came to the conclusion, that
the spirit of truth spoke in those records, but that the recorders of those
truths had intermingled with them ideas and suppositions of their own.
(108–9)

Truth warns us through her transcriber to be skeptical about the texts
produced by transcribers, readers, and interpreters who invariably inter-
mingle truth with their own suppositions. Earlier in the chapter, Gilbert
discusses Isabella's interpretation of God by narrating and then providing
"direct" quotations from Truth that slip from first-person to third-person
narration (while still within the quotes), reminding us through her own
inconsistency to beware the transcriber (107–8).[18]

"Tickety-Ump-Ump-Nicky-Nacky": The Politics of Dialect

Once Truth's appearance, character, and language are described by her
reporters, her words then appear. Her language in these versions usually is
filled with an exuberant rendering of dialect. Truth was born in upstate
New York and her first language was Dutch; nevertheless, her written
words often appear with what could be labeled as a heavy Southern
"negro" dialect. The transcribers are registering something other than her
voice; assumptions about race are being coded here. Dialect helps to mark
Truth as black, and perhaps Southern, and in some ways not-American.
The Northern white transcribers of Truth's words often use dialect to foreground her race and validate their own dialect-free voices. Multiple accounts
of the same speech sometimes help to reveal the choices being made. The
textual history of Truth's most famous speech provides a striking example.
The *Anti-Slavery Bugle*'s account of her 1851 Akron speech is written without the heavy dialect, without audience interruption, and without the
famous "ain't I a woman" refrain by which it is now known. It was written immediately after the event, unlike Frances Gage's essay, making it
perhaps likely that Gage would remember Truth's blackness more than her
words and that she would use that blackness to extrapolate a dialect.
    The dialect imposed on Truth usually suggests not her geographical

origins (New York) or linguistic background (Dutch) but her racial status. Critic Michele Birnbaum analyzes the racial implications of the nineteenth-century move toward perceiving written dialect as an unmediated representation of the spoken word: "By conflating literary and linguistic discourse through the scientific institutionalization of literary transcriptions of speech, realists and philologists alike legitimized racialist (and inevitably racist) evaluations of language based on sociopolitical hierarchies" (37). The notion of dialect implies the existence of "standard" speech. Dialect often was viewed as revealing race more effectively than color, class, or geography might. Birnbaum quotes nineteenth-century linguist William Whitney asserting the reliability of dialect to convey what other factors conceal: "Language shows ethnic descent, not as men have chosen to preserve such evidence of their kindred with other communities and races, but as it cannot be effaced" (38). While Whitney seems to fear efforts to efface ethnic descent, Truth's transcribers' fixation on ethnic descent at the exclusion of other factors effaces other truths, such as the presence of slavery in the Northeast (and not just the Deep South).

Truth seems to have noted the inaccuracy of dialect impositions on more than one occasion. An 1879 article in the *Kalamazoo Daily Telegraph* reported: "Sojourner also prides herself on a fairly correct English, which is in all senses a foreign tongue to her, she having spent her early years among people speaking 'low Dutch.' People who report her often exaggerate her expressions, putting into her mouth the most marked southern dialect, which Sojourner feels is rather taking an unfair advantage of her" (qtd. in Fitch and Mandziuk 37–38). The use of dialect is described here as not only inaccurate but also "unfair."

Truth is aware that such "exaggerat[ions]" are not simply colorful but in fact do harm and construct hierarchies. A *New York Tribune* report on Truth's appearance at an 1870 women's rights meeting quotes her without thick dialect and then states, "Sojourner wanted to be reported in a grammatical and smooth way, 'not as if I was saying tickety-ump-ump-nicky-nacky'" ("American Woman Suffrage Association" 2). Shortly after the appearance of Stowe's article, Truth told the abolitionist editor James Redpath: "I related a story to her and she has put it on me, for I never make use of the word honey" (*Commonwealth*, 3 July 1863, qtd. in Stetson and David 27). The use of "honey" might imply a speaker's intimacy with her audience, but its invention here suggests Stowe's construction of an uninvited intimacy with Truth. These and other comments reveal Truth's awareness of the power of transcriptions and the dismissive impact of constructed illiterate dialect. These quotations might be as problematic as any other quoted words from Truth, but they do suggest that the accounts offered by Stowe, Frances Gage, and others did not go unanswered.

As one of the most widely referenced accounts of Truth, and as one of the first "literary" renditions, the Stowe article and its construction of dialect set the stage for later references to Truth. Stowe reproduces a dialogue format that alternates between what is constructed as Stowe's brief but fully articulate statements and Truth's thick colloquial dialect:

> "Well, honey, de Lord bless ye! I jes' thought I'd like to come an' have a look at ye. You's heerd o' me, I reckon?" she added.
>
> "Yes, I think I have. You go about lecturing, do you not?"
>
> "Yes, honey, that's what I do. The Lord has made me a sign unto this nation, an' I go round a-testifyin', an' showin' on 'em their sins agin my people." (473)

The content is compelling: This lecturer testifies against a nation, exposing evidence of its crimes against her people. The framing, however, serves to disempower and distance this voice of testimony. The dialect categorizes Truth as black, Southern, illiterate. The dialogue emphasizes how deviant from the constructed norm Truth's language is. By contrast, we know how literate Stowe is. In this linguistic strategy, Stowe sets the standard from which Truth's dialect deviates. In addition, the dialogue form intensifies the sense of distancing. While Truth's statements are always clearly assigned to her, her audience's lines appear anonymously and without personal identification. That voice sets the agenda: It decides what Truth discusses and when she should stop (not entirely unlike lawyer Thomas Gray shaping Nat Turner's testimony). That voice appears simply neutral, while Truth's voice is always marked.

In Frances Gage's article, Truth's words are interspersed with Gage's commentary. The dialect is thicker than in Stowe's piece. Whereas Stowe occasionally writes a full sentence in Truth's voice without indicating "non-standard" pronunciation, in Frances Gage's account, sometimes every other word attributed to Truth is in dialect, beginning with her first sentences: "Well, chillern, whar dar's so much racket dar must be som'thing out o' kilter. I tink dat, 'twixt de niggers of de South and de women at de Norf, all a-talking 'bout rights, de white men will be in a fix pretty soon." The *History of Woman Suffrage* version rendered even more deviant the dialect in Truth's quotations, changing many words into more vernacular

spellings: wall (for well), neggers, Souf, womin, talkin', hab, gibs. Frances
Gage's contraction "ar'n't" becomes the more informal "a'n't." While it is
not clear who made these changes (Stanton is the first of three editors
listed for the volume), it is clear that these changes are conscious efforts
to render the already vernacular speech in an even thicker dialect. As
with the sibyl, Truth's words or information may be powerful, but they
are hardly decipherable. Every sentence constructs how Truth varies from
the standard—a standard set up by the transcriber's seemingly literate
commentary.

It is precisely Frances Gage's use of dialect and colloquialisms that
makes her version sound so accurate to many readers. One of Truth's early
biographers, Arthur Huff Fauset, incorporates Frances Gage's account into
his narrative, interspersing his own commentary and not crediting Gage
by name. He praises the accuracy and authenticity of the text: "It is one
of the few times that a speech of Sojourner's has come down to us in its
pristine form, so that we know exactly the kind of language and dialect she
employed, and what it was in her speeches that brought people of the
highest grade of intelligence and training under her spell" (131). Frances
Gage disappears, but the "pristine" words of Truth—the Southern negro
dialect imposed on the Northern Dutch-speaking orator—remain. Today,
discomfort with that dialect creates new problems of retranscription.
Modern citations often silently rewrite the Gage version. Reprinted in a
1996 *Norton Anthology of Literature by Women* (which uses Miriam Schneir's
1970s revision of the 1881 Stanton version of Gage's 1863 rendering of the
1851 speech), Gage's commentary is omitted and the language is standardized—that is, dialect is removed and the term "nigger" changed to "negro."
Editors Sandra Gilbert and Susan Gubar call the changes "modernization"
("We are indebted to Miriam Schneir for her modernization of Truth's
speeches" [253]). Such changes, often invisible, and perhaps well-meaning,
help erase the history of how white women talked about and used Truth.
Modern editors "clean up" the references, so we do not have to face the
colonization or the potential racism in these relationships. Contending
with the many frames around Truth is challenging because there are multiple and contradictory layers of representation.

Some elements from Truth's rhetoric appear in multiple places, and
the comparisons might suggest different agendas. A pint/quart metaphor
appears in the Gage and *Bugle* articles as well as in the Stowe piece. The
passage reads very differently in each version and suggests slightly different
arguments. The Gage version seems in some ways the most demeaning in

how it depicts Truth. In any case, the repetitions also suggest that Truth probably really used that metaphor, while the variations reveal that choices are being made in these representations:

As for intellect, all I can say is, if woman have a pint and man a quart—why can't she have her little pint full? You need not be afraid to give us our rights for fear we will take too much, for we can't take more than our pint'll hold. [*Anti-Slavery Bugle*]

"Den dey talks 'bout dis ting in de head. What dis dey call it?" "Intellect," whispered some one near. "Dat's it, honey. What's dat got to do with woman's rights or niggers' rights? If my cup won't hold but a pint, and yourn holds a quart, wouldn't ye be mean not to let me have my little half-measure full?" [Gage]

S'pose a man's mind holds a quart, an' a woman's don't hold but a pint; ef her pint is *full*, it's as good as his quart. [Stowe 479]

The interruption in Gage's version emphasizes Truth's ignorance and need for aid. Gage depicts Truth's literate companions supplying her with a key word: "intellect." Another interpretation could be that Truth is calling on her audience to supply a word in order to engage them, not because she doesn't know the word. The *Anti-Slavery Bugle*, however, does not interrupt her speech and shows Truth knowing the word "intellect" without assistance. In this version, Truth uses generalized third-person and then first-person plural. Her concluding "we" statements strengthen the breadth of her argument and suggest solidarity and group identification. Stowe's version is shorter and, like Gage's, written in dialect. Gage puts the passage in first and second person, personalizing the argument and obscuring whether the constructed differences are attributed to gender, race, or simply personal differences. Truth is constructed as the half-full half-wit, and the audience (at the convention or reading the essay) is the "you" with a full quart. The *Bugle* version seems more political, in that it makes an argument about collective groups, power, and rights ("You need not be afraid to give us our rights"). It also employs a strategy that appears in other passages attributed to Truth—accepting a reactionary premise (racist, sexist, or otherwise hierarchical) only to transform it into support for political change. Accepting a hierarchical notion of intellect becomes support for an egalitarian notion of rights. The Gage version also mentions rights—specified as "woman's or niggers' rights"—but the assertion stops at suggesting that denying full expression of limited intellect would be "mean." The statement does not go on to conclude that rights should thus be given. The *Bugle* account also never uses the racial epithet that Gage has Truth use repeatedly. Stowe's version omits any reference to rights and suggests nothing about power relations. That passage seems to denote mental comparisons between men and women with no explicitly political conclusion. This juxtaposition does not tell us which version is most accurate, but it helps demonstrate what might be missing if we examine only one version of Truth's words.

Stowe and Gage are both strong presences in their first-person essays on Truth. Gilbert writes supposedly from Truth's perspective but in the third person and with present perspective. The book is mostly narration of events, some political pontification, and occasional dialogue. When dialogue appears in Truth's voice, there is no suggestion of dialect. Truth and the other people in this book speak like characters in a sentimental novel. For example, the narrative retells an exchange between Truth and her father: "'Oh, my child,' replied he, 'I cannot *live* that long.' 'Oh *do*, daddy, do live, and I will take such *good* care of you,' was her rejoinder" (Truth and Gilbert 23). Such rhetoric suggests that Gilbert is shaping Truth's story into a particular acceptable form. Truth is framed as the sentimental protagonist in the novel about her life. She is very different from us, the narrator stresses, but she speaks in a recognizably feminine way, familiar at least in terms of other popular women's texts. Instead of a masculine Apollo speaking through a sibyl's body, here a feminine and sentimental Gilbert speaks through Truth's novelistic persona.

When the *Narrative* includes the "Book of Life," several different accounts of Truth sit side-by-side: Gilbert's sentimental language, Gage's use of heavy dialect, an abolitionist paper's journalistic telling, letters from friends recounting a story, and so on. Editor Titus chooses what to include and in what order, and she engages in some editing. For the most part, however, the different versions appear without changes and without justifications for the resulting contrasts. This odd multiple perspective reminds us that representations of Truth form a montage.

Transcription is just one element of the montage making up Truth. To some extent, it is one of the most insidious ways Truth is framed. Physical descriptions and other kinds of labeling are more easily identified as written by someone else. Quoted words, on the other hand, are assumed to be the actual uttered syllables. Readers are accustomed to taking quotation marks as reliable markers of speech. And once a transcriber puts words in quotes, other writers quote those quoted words as if they were fact. In addition, dialect often appears a realistic element, bringing readers closer to the genuine oral experience. Stowe, Gage, and Gilbert each strive to authorize their own voices and make their renditions appear authentic. Consequently, it is crucial to analyze these texts, question the facticity of these transcriptions, and take apart the various ways these quotations are representations.

Packaging Truth

Another layer of framing is the packaging of these representations. Once described and transcribed, Truth and her words still face a variety of editorial choices. Categorization and editing decisions affect nineteenth-century depictions as well as modern representations of Truth. Part of Truth's "singularity" is her membership in various groups. Then and today, she might be packaged as an abolitionist, suffragist, feminist, woman, African American, orator, or some combination.[19] She might be canonized (in the *Norton Anthology*, for example), marginalized (left in a footnote, for example), or have her specificities erased (such as in an anthology of men of America). In any package, editors make a variety of choices about how to use the "original" texts: which version to choose, how to edit, whether to add or remove dialect, whether and how to repeat legends, even how to name and alphabetize her. All these choices affect readings of Truth. The Stowe, Frances Gage, and Gilbert texts all are packaged and presented in certain ways in the modern editions in which they appear. These packaging decisions, more often than not, tone down or try to erase some of the most problematic elements of these texts.

Stowe's essay about Truth is not easy to locate in its original form. The library at the University of California–San Diego, for example, carries bound volumes of the *Atlantic Monthly*, but the early volumes are stored in the Annex facilities, so the interested researcher must put in a request and wait. Alternatively, the essay is reproduced in the *Heath Anthology of American Literature*. This more easily accessible text makes editorial decisions that affect the possible readings of Stowe's piece. The Heath editors omit the last eight paragraphs, which form more than one-fifth of the original essay. The excerpt ends strategically with the story of Truth listening to Douglass's speech about the hopelessness of seeking justice from whites without taking up arms. Truth replies to the hushed audience:

"Frederick, *is God dead?*"

The effect was perfectly electrical, and thrilled through the whole house, changing as by a flash the whole feeling of the audience. Not another word she said or needed to say; it was enough. . . . (in Lauter et al. 2393, italics and ellipsis in original)

Stowe's comment praises if not Truth at least her "effect" without also demeaning or marginalizing her in some way. The reader might be left with a sense of Truth's power and her voice, quoted here without dialect. The ellipsis is the only clue that something is omitted. This ending is not, however, the ending Stowe chose. In the original, Stowe shifts immediately to a general discussion of noble ex-slaves who "come to us cramped, scarred, maimed," and from that transition she ponders for three columns of text the mysteries of Africa and the wonders of Story's *Libyan Sibyl* (480). This version has a very different impact from the *Heath* excerpt. In Stowe's original, Truth's story is completely framed and bounded by statue images. Stowe opens with Cumberworth's "statuette of the Negro Woman," closes with Story's sculpture, and titles the piece and Truth after the *Libyan Sibyl*. As previously noted, Stowe's last words praise neither Truth nor her words but rather Story's statue. Since Stowe herself provided the description that produced the sculpture, her lavish praise reflects back on herself.

The quotations in the last eight paragraphs of Stowe's piece come not from Truth's testimony but from authorized white male sources. Stowe cites a London review describing Story's statue and precedes that reference with a passage from Milton describing the blackness of, in Stowe's words, "an African type of woman" (480). Truth is rendered inanimate, silenced, and absent. One of the lines omitted by Heath reveals that Stowe mistakenly thinks Truth is dead and therefore must be replaced: "But though Sojourner Truth has passed away from among us as a wave of the sea, her memory still lives in one of the loftiest and most original works of modern art, the Libyan Sibyl, by Mr. Story" (480). In fact, Truth was still alive and active and lived another twenty years. *Heath's* editors offer no commentary warning that they are selectively editing the piece. Other excerpts are labeled clearly as excerpts: the next piece, for instance, is headed "*from* Oldtown Folks" (2393). The alteration is subtle and almost invisible, but it drastically changes the impact of the essay. It omits an ending that further dehumanizes and distances Truth, and the near invisibility of this repackaging makes it difficult to track the changes.

Frances Gage's essay about Sojourner Truth is reprinted in many more sources than is Stowe's piece, so there are even more opportunities for repackaging. The original version from the *National Anti-Slavery Standard* (which can be found as a clipping in the Sojourner Truth file in the Manuscript Division at the Library of Congress or in the rare places where 1863 issues of the *Standard* are held) is rarely reproduced, quoted, or even cited. Most often cited is the rewrite in the *History of Woman Suffrage* (or later revisions based on that 1881 version). Beyond adding their own introduction and intensifying some of the dialect, the suffragist editors also shorten and reedit Frances Gage's narration. They omit one of her anecdotes and much of her opening comments, leaving out her admission that she had produced "but a faint sketch" of the speech and the information that she was writing twelve years after the fact. These edits grant more authority and facticity to Gage's telling. When reprinted, in the *Heath Anthology* or *The Concise History of Woman Suffrage* (a modern abbreviated version), for example, the *History* version usually appears without the *History* introduction, so we do not see the brief Truth biography that precedes Gage's essay. Omitting the introduction also removes the original editors' labeling of Truth as "Mrs. Stowe's 'Lybian Sibyl.'" Such framings and reframings make it difficult to trace the agendas of the original versions.

In the *Norton Anthology of Literature by Women,* the editors use the 1970s "modernized" version, omitting Frances Gage's commentary and her imposition of dialect. One goal of such changes might be a desire not to repeat racism. Without calling out that desire and those changes, however, the reframers consequently cover up—whitewash—evidence of racialized framing. Such repackaging helps to elide race and racism. In addition, modern editors often insert their own descriptions that echo some of the problems that they try to obscure with their editing. After omitting the *History* introduction, *Norton* precedes what they title the "Ain't I a Woman" speech with their own biographical notes in which they use the sibyl image ("the subtle power of this 'sibyl'"), emphasize Truth's illiteracy (saying she was "illiterate all her life"), and disempower her act of naming herself ("mystical visions and voices gave her the new name") (369). Editors Gilbert and Gubar echo Stowe's tendency to downplay Truth's agency. Although the introduction is brief, numerous names of Truth's white contemporaries are invoked. Included in the name-dropping are Garrison, Stowe, and Stanton. In this version of Truth's life, what the editors call "her white friends" are credited with encouraging her every achievement—lessening her agency and erasing some of the problematic elements of these relationships (370).

Reading the nineteenth-century texts about Truth only through modern anthologies can cover up a range of problematic references. Even looking up the nineteenth-century appearances can be revealing. The original edition of the *History of Woman Suffrage* includes Truth in the index but alphabetizes her by her first name, so she is in the S's, a couple of entries above "*South, what the, can do.*" Such a choice sets Truth apart, puts her in a separate category. The name of a book or a ship would be alphabetized like this, but not that of a person. The practical effect is that it makes references to her harder to find. Modern sources do not alphabetize Truth by the name Sojourner, but until very recently they have almost invariably referred to her by her first name, not with an honorific and almost never by her last name alone. It is admittedly problematic to make a decision about how to refer to Sojourner Truth. She renamed herself, replacing what is traditionally a patriarchal and hierarchical naming system and what in her case had become a series of names of white men. White women had the names of fathers and then husbands, while slave women often had the last name of male owners, if they had surnames at all.[20]

Rejecting both systems, Truth renamed herself. The systems—genealogy under patriarchy and under slavery—are certainly not equivalent or parallel. White fathers passed their name to "legitimate" white offspring, whereas black mothers passed their condition to their children, as pointed out by Hortense Spillers, who traces the symbolic order of naming under slavery and other elements of what she calls an "American grammar," uncovering power relations and their consequences. Truth's act was more radical than, say, white feminist Lucy Stone's decision not to give up her (father's) name when she married Henry Blackwell in 1855 (Stone 104–5). Truth challenges and steps outside dominant systems of naming—and all that is associated with such systems, including parental lineage, marital law, and economics—when she names herself. She did not inherit her name from anyone, nor did she pass it on to anyone. She chose her first name first, according to the story Stowe tells and others repeat, and wanted a last name only because other people had two names. Perhaps that story endures in order to justify using her first name only. It might be rhetorically powerful for modern writers to reject traditional naming patterns and use her first name instead of an invented "family" name. On the other hand, given the particular historical and current context—in which African Americans and white women are often labeled by their first names as a way to demean them[21]—and given the near unanimity until recently of writers *not* calling her by her last name, I choose to call her Truth. Using

Truth's first name alone is particularly problematic when other figures—usually white—appear by their last names. Such asymmetry suggests hierarchy or at least separation. In any case, using the first name assumes a familiarity and creates a nonparallelism that has to be justified. The ease of using Truth's first name suggests criteria that are gendered, raced, and classed, when men and white women are referred to by their last names.

Truth appears primarily as "Isabella" in her 1850 narrative. Various kinds of labeling shape how the narrative will be read, including whether it is listed as biography or autobiography. A recent printing is a 1991 edition for the Schomburg Library of Nineteenth-Century Black Women Writers. This edition precedes the text with forty-seven pages of editorial material, placing Truth in the category of black women writers, though she did not herself write. The editors do not consider the Gilbert text autobiography, but little reference is made to Gilbert, and her name appears on neither the original nor the new title page. Jeffrey Stewart's fine introduction highlights issues of voicing and transcription; nevertheless, he refers to Truth as Sojourner or Isabella, while he refers to all the white figures by their last names (including Gage, Gilbert, and Stowe). In the 1993 Vintage edition, Margaret Washington precedes the text with a thirty-three page introduction that provides cogent historical context and analysis. She consistently refers to her subject as "Sojourner," and as with Stewart, this naming is particularly jarring next to other figures who are referred to by their full names or last names alone. For example, Washington writes, "The article enhanced Sojourner's reputation, since *Uncle Tom's Cabin* had made Stowe one of America's most popular writers" (xi). Beyond the content of the sentence, Stowe is made to sound more important, influential, respectable, and professional than Truth. The asymmetry of language makes it hard to read the two women as peers or equals.

Like Stewart, Washington also omits Gilbert's name in the cover or title page. In the framing material Washington refers to Gilbert as the person who wrote down Truth's story, Truth's "amanuensis."[22] Downplaying Gilbert's role obscures that she was more than a scribe. While Truth may indeed have "dictated" her story, Gilbert clearly makes choices in her presentation of the narrative—from referring to Truth in the third person to deciding what details to omit (xxiii). The final section of Washington's introduction does address Gilbert's role in "censoring" details of Truth's story and how Gilbert's own notion of "true womanhood" could have influenced her telling of Truth's life. Washington places the 1850 preface by William Lloyd Garrison in an appendix at the end of the text, displacing its original prominence as an introductory piece. Washington does not include the "Book of Life" that was appended to the Titus editions of the narrative. These editorial choices highlight the narrative of Truth's life as the central text. That highlighting is powerful, but there is the risk of forgetting the framing choices that shaped that narrative in the first place.

A key element of how Truth is packaged is which versions of Truth and truth are used. Much of what is "known" about Truth consists of legends that have no clear referent. Truth's framers will use particular stories or legends differently and will find support in different "original" texts, depending on the purpose. For example, different versions of Truth's meeting with Abraham Lincoln will be cited, depending on the editor's agenda regarding Lincoln and Truth.[23] The story of Truth baring her breasts to prove her womanhood also occurs in many different versions (and even in different states). Even though there are many variations, the story endures perhaps because it somehow fits what many people want to remember about Truth. A letter to the *Liberator* included in the "Book of Life" tells the story, placing it in Indiana in 1858 and emphasizing Truth's physical femaleness and race while removing her from traditional womanhood or motherhood: "Sojourner told them that her breasts had suckled many a white babe, to the exclusion of her own offspring . . . that, although [those white babies] had sucked her colored breasts, they were, in her estimation, far more manly than they (her persecutors) appeared to be; and she quietly asked them, as she disrobed her bosom, if they, too, wished to suck!" (139).

In addition, this story is told in different versions to convey specific arguments about Truth's detractors. To condemn antisuffrage males, the story is placed at a women's rights convention, sometimes at the site of the 1851 Akron speech (adding a different level of physicality than just baring her arm [e.g., Love 24]). To condemn proslavery men, it is placed at an antislavery meeting disrupted by a man (Stewart xliii). To criticize white abolitionist women, the trigger is the women at the antislavery meeting who do not support Truth (Terborg-Penn, "Discrimination" 20). To critique a patriarch without implicating his politics, the event is placed at a generic "meeting" with a generic "clergyman" doing the denouncing (Lebedun 360, placing it in Michigan). If "true," the story could be seen as Truth powerfully and audaciously asserting her self in the face of racist and sexist oppression. But the varied uses of this myth also turn Truth into a sibyl again, if not in terminology then metaphorically. These authors speak through her, use her body as a hollow reed, sibyllize her, to get their own message across.

"I Am a Woman's Rights":
The Multiple Voices of the Personal and the Political

Analyzing the layers of framing around Truth's status as symbol and icon is intended to lay the groundwork to discuss her actions and her words (unrecoverable as they may be in any "pristine" form). Truth's rhetoric at times both relies upon stereotypes and subverts them. She makes use of multiple representations of race and gender in order to make her arguments. She frequently invokes religion as well as personal experiences or identity to establish her authority. She uses her own multiple identities—former slave, African American, American, woman, mother, worker—to persuade her audience and in particular to argue for a conception of feminism that includes African American women and others who were often left out of the middle-class white-dominated suffragist movement. Some of the specific patterns emerging in a range of her speeches and other statements include accepting a stereotypical premise and turning it around to support her argument, expressing pity for the oppressors and asserting they eventually will feel better if they stop oppressing, refusing simplistic generics and making black women visible, invoking her personal experiences and identity as a source for her authority, and using biblical references to invoke a higher authority even while she transforms that authority. These conclusions might be compromised because of the instability of the textual record, but it is possible to trace the patterns across several texts and identify multiple sources in order to attribute these characteristics to Truth's rhetoric and politics.

These patterns, taken together and not resting on any one representation alone, produce a political rhetoric of multiple voices and shifting perspectives. Truth uses her location in multiple sites to draw upon a range of perspectives and discourses and to displace the false univocality of dominant discourses. As abolitionist, feminist, and preacher, Truth's rhetoric and political arguments seek to replace narrow definitions of womanhood with multiple consciousness of race, class, gender, and religion.

A repeated pattern in Truth's speeches is irony, which is a form of multiple perspectives: saying one thing and meaning another. A variation of irony is when Truth seems to take one position and then uses that seeming concession to support the opposite position. For example, she often appears to accept a reactionary premise or to sympathize with the oppressor and then turns the premise around to support her own position. Opponents of women's rights often invoke the Bible in their defense, particularly the story of the Fall, caused by Eve. Truth counters that biblical argument by accepting it. "If" Eve caused the downfall, she conditionally suggests—but she shifts the conclusion—then, we should use women's power to reposition the world. In the *Bugle* version of the Akron speech, she says: "I have heard the bible and have learned that Eve caused man to sin. Well, if woman upset the world, do give her a chance to set it right side up again." In the Frances Gage version, Truth says: "If de fust woman God ever made was strong enough to turn de world upside down all her one lone, all dese togeder . . . ought to be able to turn it back and git it right side up again" (4).

Truth similarly repositions reactionary arguments about the intellect. "If" women have less capacity, then the call for equal rights becomes even more, not less, valid: why not permit full expression of that allegedly limited intellect? Again quoting from the *Bugle:* "As for intellect, all I can say is, if woman have a pint, and man a quart—why can't she have her little pint full? You need not be afraid to give us our rights for fear we will take too much,—for we can't take more than our pint'll hold." She turns the criticism against the critics. Either they are right and would be cowards to fear the liberation of such a population, or they are wrong. Even in the more self-deprecating language of the Gage version, the example is still an imaginary proposal: "*If* my cup won't hold but a pint. . . ." Truth's irony in taking on the opponents' arguments can lead to misreadings of her own argument, if her words are taken too partially or too literally.

Another form her irony takes is to acknowledge the suffering of the oppressor class, to admit that change is painful, and then to deploy that seeming sympathy to call for change. In Akron she refers to "the poor men"; in New York she says giving up power "cuts like a knife." In both cases, Truth moves from acknowledgment to the assertion that acquiescing to the painful change eventually will make the oppressor "feel better." In Akron, according to the *Anti-Slavery Bugle,* she states: "The poor men seem to be all in confusion, and don't know what to do. Why children, if you have woman's rights, give it to her and you will feel better. You will have your own rights, and they won't be so much trouble" ("Women's Rights Convention" 4). While using terms of sympathy, she also uses an imperative—"give it to her"—to command the "poor . . . children" to take the action they oppose. In her New York address to the American Equal Rights Association on May 9, 1867, Truth is quoted as saying: "You have been having our right so long, that you think, like a slaveholder, that you own us. I know that it is hard for one who has held the reins for so long to give up; it cuts like a knife. It will feel all the better when it closes up again."[24] The imagery and simile used by Truth make the sympathy she offers double-edged. While offering understanding to the men who hold power (and earlier in the speech she specifically included African American men in that category), she also compares those men to slaveholders. She is discussing male power in this section, but by referring to the oppressors as "you" and "one," she could be addressing anyone in her audience, including white women.[25] While comparing a shift in power relations to a wound, the only aid she offers is to let it heal. In both of these cases, she uses the second person and directly confronts the group, refusing to shy away from their opposition.

Truth invokes personal identity, location, and experience, and she simultaneously draws attention to a collective class of individuals—particularly to make visible the erased perspective of African American women. She asserts the specificity of experience *and* the possibility for unity. She frequently shifts, for example, from first-person singular to first- and third-person plural. She often moves from personal experience to more generalized statements. In the *Bugle* version of the Akron speech, before the personal lines about her own work experiences, she states: "I am a woman's rights." Mabee and Newhouse place "[sic.]" after that line, implying it was a misprint (81). (With so many questionable lines in the written record of Truth, it seems odd to single this line out for "*sic*.") And indeed, perhaps she said or meant something else: "I am *for* woman's rights" or "I am a woman's rights *advocate*." The line could work in interesting ways, however, even if it is exactly what Truth meant: that she herself represents the rights of women; that her life experiences represent the ability of women to do what men can do; that with all the theoretical talk about what *might* happen if women have rights, she *is* a woman's rights.

Throughout the speech she continues to alternate between her own experiences or characteristics and more generalized statements. In the *Bugle* version, she asserts, "I have as much muscle as any man, and can do as much work as any man. I have plowed and reaped and husked and chopped and mowed, and can any man do more than that? I have heard much about the sexes being equal. I can carry as much as any man, and eat as much too, if I can get it. I am as strong as any man that is now." The quart/pint metaphor and the Eve reference follow these lines. Generalized rhetoric about "sexes being equal" is rendered specific in her own particulars. Even if those particulars are not the particulars of Frances Gage or many of the white women at the convention—her examples of equality come from her life as a slave, a working woman, a black woman—she applies them to the broader question of women's rights.

Truth locates herself, and that location is part of her authority to speak. In her September 7, 1853, speech to a convention in New York City, she articulates her authority by virtue of her birth, her citizenship, and her experiences as a slave: "I feel at home here. I come to you, citizens of New York, as I suppose you ought to be. I am a citizen of the State of New York; I was born in it, and I was a slave in the State of New York; and now I am a good citizen of this State. I was born here, and I can tell you I feel at home here" (Stanton, Anthony, and Gage 1:567). Her speech focuses on women's rights, but she locates herself first as a native New Yorker and former slave, facts that help authorize her testimony. She insists on that commonality with her audience—that she feels at home in their city—before she goes on to argue for change. The fact that she was a slave and is now a citizen ("a good citizen") already argues for the possibility of change.

Truth's emphasis on her New York citizenship is in stark contrast to the story Stowe invents of Truth coming from Africa. She has Truth say (in an encounter that took place in 1853, the same year as this speech): "Ye see, we was all brought over from Africa, father an' mother an' I" (474). Stowe not only misremembers a biographical fact, but in her eagerness to render Truth fully African, she also misunderstands a key element of how Truth presents herself to her fellow citizens.

In the years following the end of the Civil War, during intense controversy in the women's movement over whether or not to support the enfranchisement of African American men, Truth insisted on her multiple positions and did not simply or simplistically align with one side or the other. The dominant camps after the end of the Civil War held that either it was "the Negro's hour" (meaning the negro male) or that educated white women had a greater right to vote than recently enslaved black men. In either configuration, the leaders erased African American women. Many white suffragists argued that with the removal of slavery, black men and white women were politically equal, while white women were morally and intellectually superior. In a speech to the American Equal Rights Association in New York in 1867, Stanton argued: "With the black man we have no new element in government, but with the education and elevation of women we have a power that is to develop the Saxon race into a higher and nobler life, and thus, by the law of attraction, to lift all races to a more even platform than can ever be reached in the political isolation of the sexes."[26] Truth stepped outside of the seeming binary, refusing to choose between race and gender. At the same 1867 meeting, she argues for racial *and* gender equality. She locates herself as former slave, woman, and African American woman. She refutes the suffragist claim that the slavery problem had been solved, and she asserts that giving only black men the vote would leave patriarchy in place. Her opening words acknowledge that she may not be telling the audience exactly what they want to hear:

> My friends, I am rejoiced that you are glad, but I don't know how you will feel when I get through. I come from another field—the country of the slave. They have got their liberty—so much good luck to have slavery partly destroyed; not entirely. I want it root and branch destroyed. Then we will all be free indeed. I feel that if I have to answer for the deeds done in my body just as much as a man, I have a right to have just as much as a man. There is a great stir about colored men getting their rights, but not a word about the colored women; and if colored men get their rights, and not colored women theirs, you see the colored men will be masters over the women, and it will be just as bad as it was before. So I am for keeping the thing going while things are stirring; because if we wait till it is still, it will take a great while to get it going again.[27]

While her speech in New York City several years before the Civil War emphasized her citizenship in the state of New York, in this postbellum moment she opens by asserting her citizenship in the "country of the slave" at a time when many white activists wanted to forget about the legacies of slavery and the endurance of racism. To destroy slavery "root and branch" is to radically alter both the underlying assumptions upon which slavery was rooted and the legacies and consequences that continue to branch out. That radical accomplishment would mean "we will all be free." That statement about an unspecified "we" forms the transition to her argument about gender politics, although she does not leave race behind. She does not reject the "stir" about black men's rights, but she argues for continuing to agitate for the rights of all blacks and all women, "while things are stirring."

Truth repeatedly uses water imagery in her speeches at this postemancipation meeting to argue that activists have to "keep the thing stirring" and must "step in" while the water already is disturbed. In her speech the following day, she is quoted in the *National Anti-Slavery Standard* as saying, "and now then the waters is troubled, and now is the time to step into the pool" (Fitch and Mandziuk 127). This argument not to stop the political momentum also owes its imagery to the spiritual "Wade in the Water," which can be simultaneously what Moses tells the Israelites as they are to cross the Red Sea and what Harriet Tubman tells escaping slaves who must step in the river on their way to freedom. The water metaphor appears throughout her 1867 New York speeches and in multiple transcriptions, but a transcriber more familiar with African American oral traditions might have picked up such connections even more closely. This glimpse into the types of allusions made by Truth can make us wonder about other allusions that might have been lost on white reporters.

Truth is both activist and preacher, testifying in both the legal and religious sense, and she frequently uses biblical references. She invokes the Bible for authority, and she also transforms those references, using them to shift the debate. The Bible provided fuel for both reactionaries and reformers in the nineteenth century. In Akron, she counters arguments about the manhood of Christ: "And how came Jesus into the world? Through God who created him and a woman who bore him. Man, where is your part?" (*Bugle*). "Whar did your Christ come from?" she asks in the Frances Gage version. "From God and a woman. Man had nothing to do with him." In both versions, she uses the Christian story to question and debunk man's centrality. She demonstrates her knowledge of the Scriptures, and she makes them speak for her cause.

Truth invokes many other religious references that function in multiple ways. In the 1853 Woman's Rights Convention in New York City, she uses the story of Esther, a biblical queen who saves her people. "Queen Esther come forth, for she was oppressed, and felt there was a great wrong, and she said I will die or I will bring my complaint before the king. Should the king of the United States be greater? . . . The women want their rights as Esther."[28] With that simile, she uses the story to support women's rights, but it also evokes ethnic identity, for Esther was a Jewish queen whose voice prevented the genocide of her people. Truth's applications of the Bible make use of the multiple perspectives potentially available in that text.

The different versions of Truth's speeches suggest many other ways that her discourse employs multiple voices and perspectives. Her speeches always highlight her own first-person testimony, but she also uses quotations and dialogue (often in a question-and-answer format) to bring in other voices. She quotes God, Jesus, biblical characters, her mother, herself, and unnamed citizens, creating alternate voices and personae within her own voice. For example, she quotes the king in the Esther passage discussed above and later in that speech quotes both Jesus and God. The quotations here work as model ("And [the king] was so liberal that he said, 'the half of my kingdom shall be granted to thee'"), instructions ("God says: 'Honor your father and your mother'") and as a prompt for her own call-and-response ("Jesus says: 'What I say to one, I say to all—watch!' I'm a-watchin'") (Stanton, Anthony, and Gage 1:567–68).[29] She creates a conversation between God and herself about the Constitution (*National Anti-Slavery Standard,* 4 July 1863, earlier referenced in the discussion of Stetson and David's rewriting of that passage), in which God speaks not in lofty quoted lines from the Bible but in personal and concrete (though metaphoric) responses to her direct questions. In the *National Anti-Slavery Standard* report of her May 10 speech at the 1867 Equal Rights Association meeting, she quotes unnamed supporters and opponents, herself in reply, Jesus, and Mary Magdalene. If some of her quoted voices appear as authorities, it is revealing whom she constructs as having authority—Jesus seems as important as God, and Mary Magdalene is on par with Jesus, and Truth's own quoted voice is likely to be in dialogue with any of the luminaries she cites (see "First Annual Meeting" 3). Her use of multiple voices shows her understanding of multiple perspectives and her ability to invoke authority from varied sources.

Truth frequently uses songs and prayer as alternate discourses within her speechmaking. The *New York Tribune* describes the opening of one of her 1853 speeches as follows:

> At 8 o'clock, Sojourner arose and asked some person present who possessed the spirit of prayer to give utterance to it. An elderly coloured man responded to her invitation.
>
> Mrs. Truth commenced her discourse by singing a hymn beginning with
> "I am pleading for my people,
> A poor, down-trodden race."
> After the hymn was finished, she detailed much of her practical experience as a slave. ("Lecture" 6)

The article goes on to detail the specifics of her speech. The opening description tells us that her oratory quite purposefully was not speechifying alone. Not only did she mix prayer, song, and speech, but she also had a voice from the audience produce the prayer. The *Tribune* does not provide many details about the prayer and song, but they might have been marked by larger audience involvement or call-and-response as well. An eleven-verse version of this particular hymn also appears in Truth's "Book of Life," in an excerpt about an hour-long speech in Ohio followed by this "original song" (Truth and Gilbert 302). Her hymns are spiritual *and* political: they are often about slavery, escape, and struggle for freedom.

Stowe, however, does not seem to appreciate the political and liberatory elements of Truth's singing. Stowe quotes a verse that is quite politically about "the dire effects of Slavery / I can no longer stand," the struggles of a fugitive, and the hope of escaping to Canada (479). According to Stetson and David, "Stowe was struck by the immediacy of the world the singer conjured into being, mistaking Truth's lyric intensity for naiveté. Truth sang 'Away to Canada,' black poet Joshua McCarter Simpson's reappropriation of Stephen Foster's blackface anthem 'Oh! Susanna'" (89). Stowe merely calls the lyric "extraordinary" and seems amused at her guest's "simple faith" in its literal "truth," missing the deeper layers of truth (479).

Truth's singing is itself multifaceted. As in her allusion to "Wade in the Water," she draws upon African American spirituals, a tradition that often spoke in coded instructions ("The Drinking Gourd" is the Big Dipper, guiding slaves north) and veiled defiance or revolt (Moses, Egyptland, and Pharoah could also be Tubman or Turner, the South, and slaveholders; "Steal Away to Jesus" is a call to the afterlife and to physical escape in this life). To invoke this tradition invokes multiple consciousness. Truth also composes her own songs, such as "The Valiant Soldiers," sung in the voice of African American Civil War troops:

> We are the valiant soldiers who've 'listed for the war;
> We are fighting for the Union, we are fighting for the law;
> We can shoot a rebel farther than a white man ever saw
> As we go marching on. (Truth and Gilbert 126)

Even as Truth and her fellow African Americans have been oppressed by unequal laws, and even as she calls for legal changes, she also repeatedly claims the law. Here in the opening stanza she celebrates that the collective subject of her song is "fighting for the law." At the same time, she equally celebrates, with exuberance, that this lawful pursuit can include shooting white enemy soldiers. She uses the tune of "John Brown's Body," which marks the death of the white abolitionist who initiated the 1859 raid on Harper's Ferry. The same tune is used for Julia Ward Howe's 1862 "Battle Hymn of the Republic." So when Truth or the black troops themselves would sing this celebration of "the sable army of African descent," Truth's words and music would also bring those other American songs (and histories) into the listener's consciousness. Bernice Johnson Reagon's musical group Sweet Honey in the Rock performs a multiple-voiced, a cappella version of this song in a PBS documentary on Civil War songs and on a 1993 album, evidence of the enduring power of Truth's words beyond the printed page.

At the American Equal Rights Association convention in 1867, Truth directly argues for a combination of forms: "I am going to talk several times while I am here; so now I will do a little singing. I have not heard any singing since I came here" (Stanton, Anthony, and Gage 1:194). Truth's job often is to bring to her audience precisely what they have not been hearing. Further, her implication is that there ought to be a multiplicity of discourses. The multiple layers of representation from Truth's various framers seem to get in the way of analyzing her rhetoric. At the same time, those layers can serve as a powerful reminder to pay attention to multiple voices that surround and lie within her discourses. According to a letter to the editor, published near the end of her life, Truth herself apparently calls for moving beyond repeating the same old tropes: "She would never listen to Mrs. Stowe's 'Libyan Sibyl.' 'Oh,' she would say, 'I don't want to hear about that old symbol; read me something that is going on *now*'" (Truth and Gilbert 174). Studying Truth responsibly requires us to move beyond the "old symbol[s]." In her life and her rhetoric, she revised nineteenth-century constructions of race and gender. Her multiple consciousness emerged in her multiple voices and strategies. While the "old symbol[s]" of American law constructed her as voiceless and powerless, in her legal and political struggles, she both challenged and made use of the law.

PART THREE

"The Regulations of Robbers"

Harriet Jacobs's Legal Critique

"*We* Could Have Told Them a Different Story"

Slave Law and Slave Voices

It seemed not only hard, but unjust, to pay for myself. I could not possibly regard myself as a piece of property. Moreover, I had worked many years without wages, and during that time had been obliged to depend on my grandmother for many comforts in food and clothing. My children certainly belonged to me; but though Dr. Flint had incurred no expense for their support, he had received a large sum of money for them. I knew the law would decide that I was his property, and would probably still give his daughter a claim to my children; but I regarded such laws as the regulations of robbers, who had no rights that I was bound to respect. (Jacobs 187)

After Harriet Jacobs's narrator, Linda Brent, now a fugitive in New York, rejects a duplicitous offer to purchase herself, she evaluates her legal standing in the supposedly free North. Here the escaped North Carolina slave describes and reframes the legal fictions that presume to define her. Throughout her 1861 narrative, Jacobs recodes the law as criminal to undercut the legitimacy of legal practices. The keepers of the law become the outlaws, and her allegiance is to some higher law not made by white men.

Jacobs's knowledge of the law makes her critique of it all the more biting. In the example above, she reverses the positions of lawmaker and lawbreaker. She does so by rewriting the most definitive line in the most famous U.S. court ruling on slavery. In 1857, Chief Justice Roger B. Taney ruled that Dred Scott had no right to be free (despite having lived in free territory) and did not even have the right to bring a lawsuit, because African Americans had always been regarded as "so far inferior, that they had no rights which the white man was bound to respect" (*Scott v. Sandford*

407).[1] The ruling was widely condemned and helped move the nation to the brink of war. When Jacobs rewrites the line, she announces her participation in legal debates of the day. She moves beyond a mere reversal of Taney's absolute claim (asserting that African Americans *did* have rights that whites were bound to respect) and turns the tables more radically, making the lawmakers the ones without rights and placing herself in the position Taney had carved for "the white man," who could decide whether or not to respect the rights of others.[2] Her inversion exposes Southern hypocrisy and federal complicity and disproves Taney's claims of black inferiority by its very terms.

The narrative of Jacobs's life in slavery and eventual escape, published the year the Civil War began, poses a political argument that both condemns the laws of slavery and critiques dominant standards of (white) womanhood. As a literary text, *Incidents in the Life of a Slave Girl* has helped to reshape the genre of slave narrative, initially discussed primarily through male-authored texts.[3] As she has gained recognition and prominence in critical studies and course syllabi, Jacobs in many ways has come to represent "the" female slave narrator. This focus has been useful to emphasize family, constructions of womanhood, sexuality, women's community, and other issues often downplayed or treated differently by male narrators. At the same time, there is a risk of reductiveness, of using Jacobs's multifaceted text only to discuss so-called female concerns.[4] In addition to and intersecting with such issues is Jacobs's sustained legal critique, articulated on literal and figurative levels. In the crucial years before the outbreak of civil war, Jacobs engaged herself in the legal debates over human enslavement. In *Incidents,* she reframes and rearticulates legal and cultural discourses of slavery and womanhood to uncover their fictive construction. Jacobs does not merely replace fiction with truth; instead, she calls on her readers to pay attention to framing (legal and otherwise) and to put into the frame erased perspectives. Like the critical race theorists who came after her, she deploys juxtaposition and multiple consciousness to reveal the instabilities and contradictions in the law.

Using and revising the genres of slave narrative, autobiography, and domestic fiction, Jacobs creates a first-person narrator, Linda Brent, through whom she tells her story and deconstructs slave laws and ideologies of white womanhood. For Brent and for slave women more generally, fictions of womanhood are inextricably linked to questions of law. Differences that had been naturalized—dominant constructions of white women as inherently virtuous, black women as inherently unchaste—Jacobs rewrites. Such constructed differences derive less from nature, she argues, than from circumstances and legal status. Jacobs demonstrates how African American women's bodies are defined and possessed by the law, through regulations about ownership, reproduction, and sexuality. While laws in the nineteenth century attempted to limit white women to the private sphere (the domestic realm of home and family), slave women's bodies were forced into the public realm (the arena of work and economics).[5] Their sexual and reproductive bodies were an integral part of the Southern slave economy, particularly after the international slave trade was halted. They had no rights over their children, and their legal status as "property" determined their children's status. The law permitted their bodies to be "bred," raped, and sold. Jacobs exposes the ironies of her narrator's virtuous behavior being deemed criminal while the truly criminal behavior of slaveholders was safeguarded by the law. Reframing the legal fictions of her day, she exposes their history and their real impact, and she reveals the contradictions and lies embedded in seemingly neutral rhetoric.

As a multiply disfranchised subject, Jacobs writes against the dominant voices of Southern slave law and of the law itself. Antebellum legal scholars, such as her contemporary Thomas Cobb (a Georgian who wrote the fundamental Southern treatise on slave law), can frame their defenses of slavery in falsely neutral and universal terms of legal rationality and precedent while discrediting or omitting slave voices. In numerous and varied ways, the laws of slavery attempt to erase and silence African Americans, to deny their subjectivity, to say they do not exist as individuals. Laws governing legal testimony, racial identity, literacy, miscegenation, rape, and reproduction define slaves and African Americans in specific yet contradictory ways—as nonhuman, with dangerous sexuality and nonexistent subjectivity. These legal and political fictions are just that—constructed fictions—but they have tremendous power. Analyzing legal, political, and literary discourses of slavery can help deconstruct these fictions and their power (which did not vanish with emancipation).

In this chapter and the next, I will juxtapose U.S. slave law and Cobb's 1858 legal treatise with Jacobs's critique and other antislavery tellings of the law in order to expose contradictions in discourses of slavery and more broadly to demystify legal fictions. This chapter centers on the methodologies of these writers and on laws governing slave voices. The following chapter analyzes Jacobs's critique of legal fictions around sexuality, family, and motherhood. Part of the power of slave law and modern legal discourse is the appearance of neutrality and univocality. The legal system tends to make its workings and maneuvers invisible. Exposing instabilities and slippages, as Jacobs does in her narrative, helps demystify those workings, not just in slave law but in its descendants as well. Jacobs's work is a nineteenth-century example of Angela Harris's twentieth-century exhortation to "subvert [legal theory] with narratives and stories, accounts of the particular, the different, and the hitherto silenced" (255). I want to undermine the falsely "neutral" categories of slave law with narratives from Jacobs's book and with resistant readings of the laws themselves. Jacobs herself takes such an approach, by subverting the dominant discourses with multiple voices and accounts of the silenced.

"I Have Diligently Sought for Truth": Thomas Cobb and the Proslavery Rhetoric of "Objectivity"

Jacobs wrote her book in the 1850s, after Congress further federalized slavery with the Fugitive Slave Act and after the celebrated Harriet Beecher Stowe, whose literary help Jacobs had sought, questioned the ex-slave's authenticity and suggested incorporating her story in Stowe's own upcoming book. Both events helped persuade Jacobs to publish her own testimony. She completed her manuscript in 1858, the year that Cobb published *An Inquiry into the Law of Negro Slavery in the United States of America: To Which Is Prefixed, An Historical Sketch of Slavery.* In the years before the secession of the South, legal debates over slavery held particular currency. A Georgia attorney, respected legal scholar, and later a framer of the Confederate Constitution, Cobb produced the only comprehensive Southern treatise on slave law. In addition to his own credentials, Cobb was well connected in Georgia. His brother, Howell Cobb, served as governor, congressman, and U.S. cabinet member. Cobb's father-in-law, Joseph Lumpkin, was a Georgia Supreme Court justice. Cobb served nearly a decade as the court reporter for the Georgia high court and cofounded with Lumpkin the first law school in Athens, Georgia. Cobb played a key role in articulating and interpreting Southern law, producing several legal works used by lawyers, law students, and judges.[6] His articulations of slaveholding ideology express the dominant legal fictions that Jacobs counters in her narrative.

Cobb was respected and mainstream in the South and in the eyes of the Northern establishment. "We can honestly recommend Mr. Cobb's Treatise as an able, liberal, and intelligent exposition of the views now held by the leading statesmen and lawyers of the South," states the editor of the

Philadelphia-based *American Law Register* in 1858. This Northern editor praises Cobb for his reliance on the law: "Many vexed questions are examined, but always in a temperate spirit, and with reference solely to legal principles and established precedents" (qtd. in McCash 173). Cobb's treatise uses a rhetoric of legal "objectivity," positioning itself as neutrally based on law and precedent while in fact making an argument. Significantly, Cobb was not an extremist or even much of a partisan in his time—he was comfortably inside the dominant conversation.

In his treatise, Cobb defines law as linked to eternal truths. This link is articulated in his 1859 law school prospectus, in which Cobb and Lumpkin declare their intention "to teach law, not as a collection of arbitrary rules, but as a connected logical system, founded on principles which appeal for their sanction to eternal truth" (qtd. in McCash 125). Cobb's slavery treatise is cast as legal "inquiry," not political tract. The markings of a legal document lend his work a veneer of factuality. He writes, for example, not in paragraphs but in numbered sections, like a statute. Hence a reader looking up "NEGRO. mental inferiority" (one of many racist but neutrally presented subcategories in his index) would be sent to § 22 and § 31, as if these were sections of the legal code itself. This textual detail helps generate the appearance of legal authority and neutrality. The preface to his treatise asserts objectivity and fairness: "My book has no political, no sectional purpose" (x). Quickly noting and dismissing his likely bias as a Southerner, he affirms, "As far as possible, I have diligently sought for Truth, and have written nothing which I did not recognize as bearing her image. So believing, I neither court nor fear criticism; remembering that 'veritas seapius agitata, magis splendescit lucem'" [sic] (x).[7] His inclusion of Latin in this passage from the preface is another marker of authority. If we cannot join him in "remembering" the quotation or if we cannot understand the Latin, then we are that much further from *veritas*—the truth—ourselves.

Cobb's "Historical Sketch of Slavery," a 228-page preface to his *Inquiry*, traces his construction of slavery through history and across geography. Cobb constructs racial categories to suit his assertion that slavery always has existed and "negroes" always have been enslaved. His footnote to the claim that Egyptians had "negro slaves" refers readers to "a very ingenious argument by Rev. J. Priest, in his Bible Defence of Slavery, to prove that all the Canaanites were black, and that 'heathen' refers entirely to the black race." Among the Jews as well, writes Cobb, "as everywhere he is found, [the negro] was of a proscribed race." The corresponding footnote cites the Bible and translates: "The flat-nosed must refer to the negro" (xli). Racially coding slavery, Cobb links blackness to characteristics associated with enslavement. Cobb also cites scientific discourse to translate ancient cultural artifacts into modern racial facts. He footnotes "Nott and Gliddon's Types of Mankind"[8] to support his interpretation of Egyptian monuments. His assertions are cast as statements of fact: "It is . . . well agreed from these monuments, that many of these domestic slaves were of pure negro blood. . . . That they were the same happy negroes of this day is proven by their being represented in a dance 1300 years before Christ" (xliv). Words like "agreed" and "proven" suggest that Cobb is providing evidence when he is merely deploying stereotypes of the day.

The "happy negroes" construction masks the one-sided interests behind proslavery argument. Cobb claims slavery is good for the enslaved race, which physically thrives but remains mentally inferior. His racial categories are absolute, but lines prove slippery. He blends medical and demographic data to prove biological difference and to make racialized enslavement a logical solution to natural circumstances. He cites "climate and disease, which bring death to the Saxon, and health and immunity to the African" (ccxvi). Population growth proves slavery's humanity: "That their bondage has been mild is evidenced by their great and rapid increase" (ccxii).[9] "Their longevity is remarkable. Their mental development has advanced very considerably, still retaining, however, the negro characteristics, except in the case of the mulattoes, where the traits of the white parents are sometimes developed." Since Cobb defines the races so absolutely, he must bend his terms when he encounters mulattoes, often constructing them as a separate race.

Slavery also morally improves the slave, says Cobb, adding, "The improved negro, however, exhibits still the moral weaknesses of the native Ebo; his sins, if any, are theft, lust, and falsehood" (ccxii). Placing "lust" between the offenses of theft and lying foreshadows his later focus on the "lasciviousness" of the negro. While Cobb constructs a peaceful slave society and contented slave population, he also suggests threats to white power and the presence of slave agency and resistance. Itemizing these sins suggests a threat to the order he has constructed.

Cobb places himself in a discourse of reason and neutrality, and sets that discourse against abolitionist zeal. Cobb takes as a given that states have the right to keep slavery within their borders, "it being admitted by all that the Federal Government has no power to interfere with . . . the institution within the States" (ccix). States' rights trump human rights.

Citing the "infatuated zeal of many fanatics," he sets zeal against reason and puts abolitionists in the camp of zealots. "In fact," he states, claiming the realm of reason, "the history of abolitionism in the United States has been the history of fanaticism everywhere," and "in fact" any obstacles they meet "feed the flame of zeal, and more effectually dethrone the reason" (ccx). Questions of the federal role in stopping slavery—questions at that moment setting the stage for civil war—are dismissed as trivialities: "That these questions may be allowed here to rest, and be no longer used as hobbies by interested demagogues to excite sectional strifes for personal advancement, should be the sincere wish of every true American citizen" (ccxi). While Cobb asserts objectivity and "true" Americanism, anyone supporting national abolition is "interested." This constructed division places Cobb in the nonposition of neutrality and frames his book as putting all disputes to rest.

"It Is *Unquestionably* True": Alternate Readings of Slave Law?

Opponents of slavery (the "fanatics" cited by Cobb) also produced tellings of slave law. While they also claimed to be relating the truth, the discourse of neutrality was less available to them, since they argued against the legal status quo. Slavery opponents critique slave law, but they do not necessarily avoid racism or a reliance on dominant constructions of race. White abolitionist William Goodell's *The American Slave Code in Theory and Practice: Its Distinctive Features Shown by Its Statutes, Judicial Decisions, and Illustrative Facts,* published in 1853 by the American and Foreign Anti-Slavery Society and appearing in multiple editions in the U.S. and England, is a key antislavery work centering on legal discourse and practice. Goodell does not go as far as Cobb to authorize his text as legal discourse, but he does mark his work as part of the legal debate. While his evidence includes items beyond statutes and judicial decisions, such as articles, speeches, and advertisements, Goodell names his book *The American Slave Code,* as if it were a statute book, and organizes his chapters around legal categories. In his opening chapter, he sets up his project as an exploration of "the legal relation of master and slave" (15), and he repeats that quoted phrase throughout, reminding us that his is a legal inquiry.

Like Cobb, Goodell positions himself as speaking for truth, but there is never any pretense about whether his book has an argument. He may claim objectivity (i.e., fairness), but not neutrality. He opens with a letter from "HON. WILLIAM JAY TO THE AUTHOR," authorizing the book and

putting Goodell in the company of honored lawmakers. Jay positions
Goodell's book on the side of truth. On the side of fiction are novels such
as *Uncle Tom's Cabin,* but Goodell's telling is allied with mathematical fact.
"It is more easy to make than to refute a charge of exaggeration against a
work of fiction like Mrs. Stowe's," asserts Jay, "but your book is as im-
pregnable against such a charge as is Euclid's Geometry, since, like that, it
consists of propositions and demonstrations." A fictional and pregnable
telling such as Stowe's may be "true," but it is vulnerable to questions
and attack. On the other hand, "[This] book is not only true, but it is
unquestionably true" (11). For Jay, legal fact is a scientific and male world,
while fiction (though perhaps worthy) is an unstable and female world.
Not merely mathematics but specifically Euclid's geometry (named and
gendered) is invoked as a symbol of Goodell's rational and indisputable
approach.

Goodell uses irony to attack the seeming rationality of slave law, arguing that it has an internal logic based on an initial falsehood. Framing the
debate as one among men, Goodell uses the language of science, math,
and logic to critique slavery's central "axiom":

> Men may forget or disregard the rules of logic in their reasonings about
> slavery, but the genius that presides over American slavery never forgets or
> disregards them. From its well-defined principle of human chattelhood it
> never departs, for a single moment. If any thing founded on falsehood
> might be called a science, we might add the system of American slavery to
> the list of strict sciences. From a single fundamental axiom, all the parts of
> the system are logically and scientifically deduced. And no man fully under-
> stands the system, who does not study it in the light of that axiom. (105)

Whereas a critique of slave law might focus on its contradictions and irra-
tionalities, here Goodell attacks its unwavering rationality (once its basis
in falsehood is accepted). While Goodell accepts the mantle of reason
from Jay, he also exposes the danger of unwavering rationality without
acknowledgment of right and wrong. The scientific logic of slavery helps
condemn it.

One of Goodell's central references is George M. Stroud's short but
detailed work *A Sketch of the Laws Relating to Slavery in the Several States
of the United States of America,* first published in 1827 and updated in 1856.
Cobb also uses Stroud as a reference, one he attacks as abolitionist and
interested. "Of the *actual* condition of slaves this sketch does not profess

to treat," Stroud admits, insisting that in representative government "the *laws* may be safely regarded as constituting a faithful exposition of the sentiments of the people" (v). By "people" he means the people who vote, so he does not include slaves, free blacks, or white women. While Stroud critiques slave laws, he also relies on them almost exclusively to make his point and fails to turn to slave voices for evidence, context, or analysis. Stroud's goal is to "supply the proper knowledge" of slavery, and so his text is "derived from the MOST AUTHENTIC SOURCES,—*the statutes of the slave-holding states, and the reported decisions of their courts of judicature*" (viii). The laws of slavery are more "authentic" than voices of the subjects of slavery.

While Cobb—who supports slavery but claims neutrality—attacks the interestedness of abolitionist legal studies, the antislavery Stroud also shies away from such a label. Referring to himself in the third person as "the writer," Stroud assures us with the certainty of anti-Communist oaths of a century later that "he is not now, nor ever has been, a member of any *Abolition* or *Anti-slavery* Society" (ix).[10] Stroud explicitly takes a stand, declaring that slavery "is a moral, social, and political evil of incalculable magnitude." At the same time, he limits that claim—he opposes the expansion of slavery but fails to support its abolition—and he is careful to sound unbiased. "There are," he assures us, "no doubt, many humane masters and some contented slaves," and because of states' rights, "no citizen of a free state is in any degree or in any sense responsible" for the "evils" of the system (viii–ix).[11] Thus even an antislavery work must be careful not to insult white Americans who might not be culpable.

Stroud is less careful to avoid insulting African Americans. In explaining the need for a second edition of his book, Stroud says that at the time of the first edition slavery was "everywhere" spoken of as evil, "but, as it had been introduced among us during the period of our colonial dependence on Great Britain, and the number of the bond had become very great,—as, by reason of native constitution or long-continued degradation, the coloured race was manifestly inferior to the white,—it was universally felt and acknowledged that the problem of their emancipation was exceedingly difficult to be *worked out*" (vi, emphasis in original). Stroud deems slavery evil, yet he still falls back on dehumanizing constructions of African Americans, referred to here as "the bond." Though he leaves the "reason" open to debate, he treats black inferiority as an unquestioned fact. And it is "the coloured race," not merely slaves, that he finds inferior, the implication being that the cause *is* "constitution" and not condition.

Emancipation, instead of a clear goal, is acknowledged as a "problem."
His moderate approach may be a pragmatic strategy, if his aim is to avoid
alienating ambivalent Northerners, but it also permits him to leave many
assumptions of slavery undisturbed.

Suppressed Letters and Different Stories: Placing Frames at the Center

Unlike Goodell and Stroud, Jacobs targets slavery as well as racism and
patriarchy in her critique of slave law, a critique written in narrative form.
Jacobs and Cobb both claim the truth, but they have very different views
of truth-telling, objectivity, and evidence. Jacobs frames her own text—an
autobiography told by Linda Brent, a constructed first-person narrator—
with an awareness of framing and with attention to multiple perspectives.
Jacobs knows that context matters and that narratives frequently are contested. The first line of her preface promises truth: "Reader, be assured,
this narrative is no fiction" (1). Unlike Cobb, however, Jacobs does not pretend to lack purpose or agenda. She not only crafts her text with great
power and purpose but also calls attention to craft in various ways. She
often presents two different versions of something to reveal the differences
between versions, depending on the framer and her or his agenda. This
approach reveals multiple perspectives and reminds her reader to question
sources and pay attention to who is telling the story. She privileges the testimony of the oppressed in her juxtapositions, and she tells us to read all
testimony critically.

Jacobs's use of multiple perspectives often turns on multiple versions or
uses of a written text. For example, when Brent is hiding in her grandmother's attic (her refuge for seven years while she plans her escape to the
North), she writes a letter to fool her owner, Dr. Flint, into thinking that
she is already in the North. Jacobs includes both the summary of Brent's
staged letter to her grandmother as well as the text of a falsified letter with
which Flint replaces it. Jacobs presents Flint's counterfeit letter in direct
quotes and indented, so it looks real, but precedes it with a discrediting
introduction: "The old villain! He had suppressed the letter I wrote to
grandmother, and prepared a substitute of his own" (130). The letter
appears genuine, but we know it is falsified.

Jacobs is fully aware of the many layers of representation here. Flint
invents a manipulative version of the letter, and the hidden Brent—along
with the reader—is in the privileged position of knowing that his letter is

fake. The "original" letter, however, also is a construction and a manipulation, as Brent, hiding in North Carolina, pretends to write from New
York. In fact, the narrator obtains the data for her false letter by lifting
street names from a *proslavery* newspaper: "It was a piece of the New York
Herald," she writes, "and, for once, the paper that systematically abuses the
colored people, was made to render them a service" (128). Jacobs employs
the *Herald* subversively, reminding us that texts are used—that they can
be deployed, revised, and reframed for various purposes, good and bad.

Through juxtaposing different framings, Jacobs dislodges the speaking authority of those who are complicit in slavery. While status might
otherwise validate those voices, Jacobs urges us to question the source.
For example, the narrator reports a white version of her brother William's
escape before she recounts William's own version. Mr. Sands, the white
father of Brent's children (and a member of Congress), purchases Brent's
brother, supposedly with plans to free him, and takes him to the North.
Once there, the brother flees, and Brent hears two different tellings of
the escape. In this pairing of stories, Jacobs first includes the white slaveholder's rendition without comment, presented as Sands's direct words.
Then she immediately follows that version with another, in the narrator's
voice, opening with: "I afterwards heard an account of the affair from
William himself" (136). The direct quotes around the white man's story do
not lend it validity. In fact, quoting the story without interruption, like
quoting and indenting Flint's fictitious letter, highlights its constructedness. Jacobs's text clearly forces us to notice sources and speakers and to
take into account agendas and points of view. In particular, anyone implicated in the institution of slavery, including the seemingly well-meaning
Sands (who also neglects to free Brent's children), is to be viewed with
special skepticism. The conditions and events of slavery, Jacobs contends,
are best conveyed by the testimony of slaves themselves.

Jacobs also uses juxtaposition more explicitly to expose legal hypoc-
risies; for example, she will invoke the words of a law or lawmaker in contrast to what actually happens in slavery. She tells the story of a beaten
woman forced to kill herself and pairs it with the speech of a Mississippi
senator declaring that slavery is a blessing. Two short paragraphs juxtapose
two very different pictures of slavery:

> For some trifling offence her mistress ordered her to be stripped and
> whipped. To escape the degradation and the torture, she rushed to the river,
> jumped in, and ended her wrongs in death.

> Senator Brown, of Mississippi, could not be ignorant of many such facts
> as these, for they are of frequent occurrence in every Southern State. Yet he
> stood up in the Congress of the United States, and declared that slavery was
> "a great moral, social, and political blessing; a blessing to the master, and a
> blessing to the slave!" (122)

Jacobs's juxtaposing of these images forces us to see the hypocrisy of the
practices of slavery in the South. While she often employs pseudonyms,
here she accurately cites the lawmaker's name and state. She warns against
the danger of listening to one telling, like Brown's, without looking at the
material reality, or at least another telling. Jacobs's role is to keep forcing
those untold stories to the center of the frame.

In her chapter "The Church and Slavery," Jacobs uses similar tactics to
present more than one version of Christian gospel, forcing her readers to
consider who the framer is. She includes long, uninterrupted quotations
from the white clergyman who began to preach to the black community
at the same time that masters began to worry about insurrections. She
contextualizes the minister, noting the historical moment of fear over Nat
Turner, and she names him carefully and ironically: "the Rev. Mr. Pike,"
"Pious Mr. Pike," "brother Pike" (68–69). She permits him an extended
quoted sermon, with biblical language and carefully edited scriptural references. She does not interrupt his text to disagree; instead, she juxtaposes
his version of scripture with other framings.

The second minister who arrives is presented very differently. He is
never named, and his version of gospel emerges from his actions and
sentiments more than his words. Hence Jacobs includes not an alternate
sermon but a description of how this man treated his parishioners. The
juxtaposition condemns Pike more strikingly than direct attacks. Still
another version of Christian faith is the worship practiced by the African
American congregation. Jacobs includes slave-authored hymns and points
out how they differ in form from Mr. Pike's: "The slaves generally com-
pose their own songs and hymns; and they do not trouble their heads
much about the measure" (70). The content, not the measured form, of
one's worship is what matters. Jacobs not only exposes Christian hypocrisy
but also reminds us to pay attention to who is speaking (or singing).

In this chapter Jacobs calls attention to (without naming) one of the
real-life players in the politics of slavery against whom she is writing. She
derides in generic terms the Northern clergyman who visits the South and
speaks only to "the slaveholder" (who "plays his game accordingly") and

"favored household slaves." Her warning is that such a visitor must pay attention to who is framing his views and how. Jacobs then names the specific text to which she has been alluding, making her generic reference more pointed: "He comes home to publish a 'South-Side View of Slavery,' and to complain of the exaggerations of abolitionists" (74). The book in question is written by Northerner Nehemiah Adams, whose pastoral views of kindly masters and protected slaves frequently were invoked by Southern defenders of slavery.[12] Her warning about framers now is extended: The Northern clergyman listening to slaveholders should pay close attention, and the public reading that clergyman's book should be equally skeptical.

Jacobs points out the vast differences in interpretation depending on whether the particular subject or observer is in the slave community or the white population. In an early chapter, the image of New Year's Day varies sharply depending on whose New Year's is described and from what perspective. She includes a brief but vivid second-person description of the holiday for "you happy free women," but frames it on either side with explicit third-person descriptions of what for "the poor bond-woman" is "hiring-day at the south" (15–16). The contrast reveals the horrors of slavery and the vast gap between free women and slave women:

> O, you happy free women, contrast *your* New Year's day with that of the poor bond-woman! With you it is a pleasant season, and the light of the day is blessed. . . . Children bring their little offerings, and raise their rosy lips for a caress. They are your own, and no hand but that of death can take them from you.
>
> But to the slave mother New Year's day comes laden with peculiar sorrows. She sits on her cold cabin floor, watching the children who may all be torn from her the next morning; and often does she wish that she and they might die before the day dawns. (16)

The juxtaposition is powerful. Jacobs's harrowing description of New Year's Day is diametrically opposed to Adams's happy depiction of the same period. Adams claims slaveholders take care to make arrangements with the interests of the slaves in mind: "At the Christmas holidays, some of the southern cities and towns are alive with the negroes, in their best attire, seeking employment for the year to come, changing places, and having full liberty to suit themselves as to their employers. The characters and habits of all the masters and mistresses are known and fully discussed by them" (76).

Whereas Adams constructs the slaves as "having full liberty," Jacobs
uses the language of the law's punishment: "At the appointed hour the
grounds are thronged with men, women, and children, waiting, like criminals, to hear their doom pronounced. The slave is sure to know who is
the most humane, or cruel master, within forty miles of him" (15). Jacobs's
language of death contrasts with Adams's language of towns "alive with
. . . negroes," whom he describes as agents making their own choices. In
both descriptions, the slaves know about the masters, but the meaning of
the knowledge is part of the horror in Jacobs's version, not part of their
ability to "suit themselves." Unlike Adams's commentary, Jacobs's chapter
contains examples and quotations from other slaves. While Adams vaguely
references how the "characters and habits" of owners are known, Jacobs
offers specifics about what happens to those who are sold to cruel masters.
Through this implied contrast with Adams's 1854 volume and through her
more direct critique of his methodology (his reliance on slaveholder testimony), Jacobs engages herself in the current debates over competing discourses of slavery.

In addition to generalized commentary about slave women, Jacobs also
uses particular characters in her story to set up the contrasts that fill her
book. The two tellings of New Year's Day explicitly juxtapose white and
black experiences, but Jacobs later demonstrates a subtler contrast between
a constructed white telling of her Aunt Nancy's funeral and an implied
slave perspective. She provides pages of context and history, describing
Mrs. Flint's cruelty and hypocrisy toward Nancy in life and death, and
then observes: "Northern travellers, passing through the place, might have
described this tribute of respect to the humble dead as a beautiful feature
in the 'patriarchal institution'; a touching proof of the attachment between
slaveholders and their servants; and tenderhearted Mrs. Flint would have
confirmed this impression, with handkerchief at her eyes. *We* could have
told them a different story" (146–47).

Jacobs argues for multiple representations by and for African Americans—the italicized "we" who "could have" offered an alternate narrative.
The dominant narrative is represented by the quoted and discredited
phrase "patriarchal institution." She mocks what would have appeared as
"proof" of the claims of that narrative: the abusive Mrs. Flint's false gesture of sorrow. She cautions against believing interpretations that fail to
take into account multiple perspectives and silenced voices.[13] Neither story
actually is told here—whites "might have described" those images, slaves
"could have told" the travelers something different. Different, contested

framings exist even when they have not been uttered yet. Jacobs demands an active reader who will focus on that "different story," which normally remains untold or unheard, from sources likely to be unauthorized or silenced.

As Jacobs well knew, various laws worked to deny slaves a legal, political, or literary voice. They could not testify against a white person or serve on a jury. They could not vote, run for office, or petition the government. They generally were barred from learning or teaching reading and writing. Free blacks were denied many of these rights as well. State laws varied, but these basic restrictions on slave subjectivity and voice hold true throughout the antebellum South. While slavery's defenders asserted that slaves were happy, they also were determined not to let those happy slaves say a public word, whether in a courtroom, ballot box, or novel. The official line on slavery declared that slaves had no subjectivity to speak of, yet there is tremendous anxiety that there be no public arena where such a subjectivity might somehow speak. This central contradiction helps reveal the fictions underlying legal constructions of slavery.

The official story suggests that slaves had no will and no arena in which to express any such will. As it turns out, the official story was not the true story. Slaves and ex-slaves—such as Lucy Delaney's mother and Sojourner Truth, who both sued for their children's freedom—made their way into courtrooms. Numerous slaves learned to read and write and taught others to do the same, and many used their literacy in the fight against slavery, from the well-known cases of Douglass and Jacobs to individuals like Milla Granson, the Louisiana woman who taught hundreds of fellow slaves to read in her clandestine "midnight school" (Lerner 32). Such gaps between legal fictions and actual experiences occurred in various forms, and exploring these gaps reminds present-day scholars not to rely upon "official" discourses alone. Especially interesting here is the anxiety-ridden attention to detail in the official discourses designed to suppress the subjectivity that slaveholders claimed did not exist in the first place. In the following sections, to reveal the contradictions in legal discourse and to demonstrate Jacobs's role as legal critic, I will juxtapose Jacobs's rhetoric with that of legal writers and slave law in their treatment of testimony, literacy, and agency.

"His Mouth Being Closed as a Witness": Bans on Slave Testimony

Those who escaped from slavery were particularly aware of the power of testifying against the institution they left behind. In her preface, Jacobs declares: "I want to add my testimony to that of abler pens to convince the people of the Free States what Slavery really is" (1–2). The idea of "testifying" or "witnessing" is a powerful trope in African American literature. Frances Smith Foster writes that, in revising American literary tradition, African American women "were testifying to the fact of their existence and insisting that others acknowledge their existence and their testimonies" (*Written by Herself* 2). Southern laws could ban black testimony against white criminals, but by publishing her story, Jacobs testified against all slaveholders and the institution of slavery. She is bearing witness, and her book is entered as evidence.

This language of testimony, which also has religious connotations, is metaphoric. At the same time, Jacobs quite literally gives evidence of crimes—wrongs that cannot legally be prosecuted, since they were witnessed by and committed against slaves. Denied a legal voice, Jacobs prosecutes the perpetrators through her literary voice. Her book becomes a symbolic courtroom—a lawsuit for her own freedom and a criminal trial against Southern slaveholders and complicit Northerners. Whatever the law says, once someone reads Jacobs's book, her testimony is heard, making her a witness and a subject, a position slave law tries to deny.

As stated above, laws varied from state to state but consistently restricted the testimony of slaves and often extended the restrictions to free African Americans. The most absolute ban was of black testimony against whites. Restricting African American testimony against whites created the illusion of a legal white subjectivity in the absence of black subjectivity. In the narrative constructed in a court transcript, the words of various white subjects would enter the official record, but there would be official silence from African American participants. Trying to reconstruct the past is often dependent upon who has an authorized voice in written records. In concert with other restrictions, the testimony ban attempted to eliminate slave voices from the legal record.

In testimony restrictions, as in many slave laws, language frequently addressed condition and degree of blackness. In Jacobs's state, "all negroes, Indians, mulattoes, and all persons of mixed blood, descended from negro and Indian ancestors, to the fourth generation inclusive, (though one ancestor of each generation may have been a white person) whether bond or free, shall be deemed . . . incapable in law to be witnesses in any case whatsoever, except against each other."[14] Virginia's law stated: "Any negro or mulatto, bond or free, shall be a good witness in pleas of the commonwealth for or against negroes or mulattoes, bond or free, or in civil pleas where free negroes or mulattoes shall alone be parties, *and in no other cases whatsoever.*"[15] By listing all the circumstances under which an African American may speak in court, the phrasing implies that the act *creates* a right, when actually it restricts a right by silencing such a witness in any case involving whites.

The number of categories invoked—negro, mulatto, bond, free—reveals anxiety about the complications of slave society. Barring slave testimony alone would permit free blacks to testify. Specifying only "negro" might permit the testimony of mulattoes, who were increasing in number despite laws against miscegenation and partly thanks to the absence of laws against the rape of slaves. The law attempted to include every permutation to make sure the presence of African blood (which seems to be the real fear here, not simply the status of being a slave) absolutely bars testimony against whites.

Many laws, such as the Virginia testimony restriction that left its real aim until the final clause, use language and syntax to obfuscate their aims. For example, some have a preamble that claims to seek to mitigate the problems of slaves, followed by an enactment clause that further dehumanizes slaves. Such slippages reveal the contradictions in slave law and the dishonesty and anxiety in lawmakers. South Carolina, for example, enacted a 1740 measure (part of the Act for the Better Ordering and Governing of Negroes and Other Slaves) that seemed to acknowledge the problem of banning slave testimony, but its real effect was to make the ban even more restrictive:

> Whereas by reason of the extent and distance of plantations in this Province, the inhabitants are far removed from each other; and many cruelties may be committed on slaves, because *no white person* may be present *to give evidence* of the same . . . and as slaves are under the government, so they ought to be under the protection of masters . . . ; *Be it further enacted,* That if any slave shall suffer in life, limb or member, or shall be maimed, beaten or abused, contrary to the directions and true intent and meaning of this act, when no *white person* shall be present, or being present shall neglect or refuse to give evidence . . . in every such case, the owner or other person who shall have the care and government of such slave . . . shall be deemed, taken, reputed and adjudged to be guilty of such offence, and shall be proceeded against accordingly, without further proof; unless such

owner or other person as aforesaid, can make the contrary appear by *good and sufficient evidence,* or shall by his own oath clear and exculpate himself; which oath every court . . . is hereby empowered to administer, and to acquit the offender accordingly, if clear proof of the offence be not made by *2 witnesses at least* . . . (Public Laws of South Carolina 695:39, original emphasis)

The slave remains legally voiceless. The law introduces a presumption of white responsibility, but removes it with the owner's right to refute such guilt "by his own oath."[16] Acquittal is required unless *two* white witnesses testify. That new requirement actually places the slave in a worse position, equally voiceless and needing to meet a more stringent requirement—two whites willing to testify against the owner, even as the law's very premise is that these are cases in which no white is present or willing to speak. The tension between the claims of the preamble and the language of enactment reveals disquietude about the problem presented by denying slave testimony. The statute calls attention to the problem and immediately intensifies it.

Critics of slave law condemn the testimony ban for its effect on supposedly protective laws, which are rendered meaningless if no slave can testify. Goodell writes of the ban: "In the presence of such a regulation, very clearly, there can be no adequate protection of the slave under any laws framed for his benefit" (159). He cites the following section of South Carolina's 1740 slave code: "In case any person shall wilfully cut out the tongue, put out the eye, castrate, or *cruelly* scald, burn, or deprive any slave of any limb or member, or shall inflict any *other cruel* punishment, OTHER THAN by whipping, or beating with a horsewhip, cowskin, switch, or small stick, *or* by putting irons on, or confining or imprisoning such slave, every such person shall, for every such offense, forfeit the sum of one hundred pounds, current money" (qtd. in Goodell 159–60, emphasis his). The gruesome specifics suggest such treatment is common enough to warrant state action. Combined with the law denying a courtroom voice to a slave, those prohibited acts can be prosecuted only if a white person testifies. While the section opens with strong language ("whereas cruelty is not only highly unbecoming those who profess themselves Christians, but is odious in the eyes of all men who have any sense of virtue or humanity" [Public Laws 695:37]), the enactment clause hedges in revealing ways. The use of the modifier "cruelly" (italicized by Goodell) suggests there is a way to "scald, burn, or deprive . . . of limb" that is not considered cruel. The law also itemizes eight practices that are defined as "cruel" *and* permissible. Goodell places "other than" in capital letters to highlight this shift, so that the reader not mistake this list of condoned cruelties for prohibited cruelties. This specific itemizing stands in stark contrast to the general terms in which the Ninth Amendment in the Bill of Rights, aimed primarily at protecting the rights of white men, will bar the state from inflicting "cruel and unusual punishments" with no attendant list. The difference seems to be between protecting a citizen, whose rights are guarded in broad terms, and protecting the property owned by a citizen.

Goodell announces ironically that the "reasonableness" of the testimony restriction is indisputable if the relation between master and slave is to be maintained. "Allow slaves to testify," posits Goodell, "and the hitherto unimagined secrets of the Bastille would explode like an earthquake. Universal humanity would unite in one general crusade, and break down the whole fabric" (304). Although slavery advocates insist that slaves have nothing to say, their restrictions on slave voices confirm that they are as aware as Goodell that the silencing of slaves is essential to the survival of slavery. Significantly, while condemning these laws, Goodell does not himself include African American testimony. For example, while critiquing New York Congressman Vanderpool for denying slaves the right to petition the government—another form of voice or testimony denied to slaves—Goodell himself fails to let such a voice be heard. He quotes Vanderpool pontificating in Congress: "He should be ashamed of himself, if he ever could have supposed that slaves had a right to petition this or any other body where slavery exists. . . . Had *any one,* before to-day, ever dreamed that the appellation of THE PEOPLE embraced SLAVES?" (36–37). Yet Goodell includes no such petition to counter the assertion that slaves have no right to a voice in government.[17]

Stroud also quotes many sources but omits African American voices. One reason for this significant omission is that both Goodell and Stroud seek to cloak themselves with the authority and power of legal and political discourse, and since African Americans are officially excluded from those discourses, these antislavery whites may not want to risk invalidating their own authority by invoking unauthorized evidence. The silencing of African American testimony may be an effective tactic for their immediate goal of persuading a predominantly white Northern audience of the evils of slavery without challenging the deeper racial beliefs of that audience. That pragmatic strategy also has the consequence of validating the marginalization of African American voices.

Slavery advocates also cite testimony bans but toward different ends. Cobb describes these laws as justified by both condition and race. The fact that many states extend the ban to free blacks (including the free states of Ohio, Indiana, Illinois, and Iowa) is evidence for Cobb that race rightfully is the disqualifier, "showing that [the ban on testimony] is founded not only upon the servile condition of the negro, but also upon his known disposition to disregard the truth" (226). By adding "disposition" to "condition," Cobb again tries to naturalize slavery. "That the negro, as a general rule, is mendacious, is a fact too well established to require the production of proof, either from history, travels, or craniology" (233). Some of Cobb's assertions are followed by several footnotes of case references, statute numbers, legal scholars, and Latin and Greek quotations to support his claim. Other times, particularly when citing some universal "fact" about race, he simply declares that his point is common knowledge. Here Cobb invokes a variety of disciplines—history, anthropology, science—to authorize his unsupported assertion, named as fact.

In a paragraph freely mixing English and Latin, Cobb invokes the origins of common law to exclude slaves from a legal voice. "The term 'law,' according to the common law, is defined to be 'a freeman's privilege of being sworn in Court as a juror or witness'" (227). Hence, by definition the slave exists outside law itself and could never testify under the law. The law, in fact, relies upon the exclusion of slave testimony. The racism of lawmakers, combined with the absurdity of the law, leads to numerous odd distinctions. "The negro being excluded as a witness, his declarations to others, as a general rule, are of course inadmissible. There are exceptions [in which] the declarations are admissible under other rules of evidence. Thus, the declarations of a negro to a physician . . . as to the symptoms of his disease . . . are admissible . . . but his declarations as to the cause of his injury or disease [or its duration] . . . are inadmissible" (231). So a white doctor might report that a slave said she had a toothache or a miscarriage, but not that she said she had the toothache for three months or that the miscarriage was caused by a beating. Even transmitted through an authorized white voice, black testimony is severely restricted—its brief appearances remind us that it exists but attempt to keep that existence to a minimum.

Questions of who may testify can be viewed metaphorically as well.

Under the law, a slave had no voice and a white person would have to testify for her or him. African Americans were restricted in their access to testimony in other ways, and not only by slaveholders. The *New England Anti-Slavery Almanac* illustrates the white abolitionist tendency to erase the slave precisely while defending the slave:

"Things for the Abolitionist to Do,"
1. Speak for the Slave, . . .
2. Write for the Slave, . . .
"They can't take care of themselves." (qtd. in Davis and Gates iv)

While lawmakers denied slaves the right to testify in a court of law, in many ways slavery opponents denied slaves the rhetorical right to testify for themselves in the political realm. Many abolitionists, such as the New England group above, wanted to speak and write for the slave. As discussed in the preceding chapter, Sojourner Truth, although a prominent orator, had many whites writing and rewriting her testimony. Ex-slaves who did their own writing also found themselves framed by white abolitionists, as seen in Jacobs's struggle with Stowe and in Douglass's struggle with colleagues who wanted to control his voice. Douglass's chapter "Introduced to the Abolitionists" discusses—with irony not present in his first autobiography—how fugitive slaves were a welcome source of "facts" to be woven into white texts ("Mr. Garrison followed me, taking me as his text" [*My Bondage* 218]), but they were not to bear witness in any more autonomous way.[18] Goodell and Stroud amassed testimony against slavery, but it is *their* voices that we hear, as the antislavery writer remains the subject and the victimized slave the object. They critique the testimony laws but fail to subvert them.

In many ways, the desire of dominant groups to frame and speak the testimony of the oppressed group continues. In academia, politics, and art, there is often the unstated (and sometimes stated) preference for whites to do the talking—the need for a white witness to testify. In recent popular culture, for example, numerous films about black struggle, from the U.S. to South Africa, keep white subjects and testimony at the center. Although Steven Spielberg's 1997 film *Amistad* centered on Cinquez, the African who led the *Amistad* mutiny, and some of its most powerful scenes were those among the African characters, the film reverts to convention, culminating in the courtroom drama and framing John Quincy Adams as the legal and moral hero by the end. The 1989 film *Glory* frames nineteenth-century struggle (here the Union Army's all-black Massachusetts 54th) with a white voice at the center (Matthew Broderick as Colonel Robert Shaw). Shaw's voice literally tells the story as Broderick's voice-over controls the film. In filmic terms, the fictional character played by Denzel Washington might have been a more compelling focus. Historically, Douglass's sons or Truth's grandson, who served in the 54th, might have offered a revealing perspective. But the young white colonel who dies fighting on behalf of African Americans was deemed the appropriate focal point.[19]

Cultural critic bell hooks discusses the pattern of white testimony of black struggle in scholarly work. She writes, "Given the politics of domination—race, sex, and class exploitation—the tendency in this society is to place more value on what white people are writing about black people, or non-white people, rather than what we are writing about ourselves" ("Feminist Scholarship" 42). She explores how whites are seen as the authorities on issues of black culture and how that pattern is repeated in many different hierarchies. "A dimension of the oppressor/oppressed, exploiter/exploited relationship is that those who dominate are seen as subjects and those who are dominated objects. As subjects, people have the right to define their own reality, establish their own identities, name their history. As objects, one's reality is defined by others, one's identity created by others, one's history named only in ways that define one's relationship to those who are subject" (42–43).

Although the laws of legal testimony have changed, hierarchies and "structure[s] of white supremacy" still function to silence African Americans and authorize white people (hooks 43). By making visible the workings behind the testimony limitations, exposing the links between those proslavery laws and practices of the abolitionists, and acknowledging the legacy of those moves now, I hope to make it easier to see those hierarchies and silencings in operation still. Hooks's point is not that white scholars cannot write about slavery but that it is important that their work not exist at the expense of African American testimony and that scholars be aware of whose voices they privilege.[20]

Such erasures continue even in texts specifically about such denials under slavery. *Celia, a Slave*, written by historian Melton McLaurin and published in 1991, retells the true story of a Missouri slave who was purchased at the age of fourteen as a concubine for a widowed slaveowner. After four years of rape, she killed her owner, stood trial, and was executed.

Celia's 1855 trial is a compelling example of the need for the admission of slave testimony—no one else was present at the time of his final assault on her, and no one but slaves knew the extent of his abuse of her. Yet, in this literal courtroom drama, the modern historian framing the tale is vague about whether the woman at the center of the story has any voice to report. McLaurin never quotes her and never clarifies exactly how she might have taken the witness stand. Celia was allowed to testify in this case in which she was the defendant, but she could not testify against any white person, including the dead man who had threatened her, so her testimony was obviously limited.

McLaurin spends little attention on textual detail and offhandedly mentions late in the book that the trial proceedings "were summarized rather than recorded verbatim" (96). McLaurin never focuses on what she said or on how her words were circumscribed by the proceedings and the available records. The book focuses on socioeconomic context (cows per capita, for example) and on the white man as subject (after his wife's death, slaveowner Robert Newsom "needed . . . required" a sex partner, and other such observations).[21] Celia is silenced twice, by the court and by her editor a century later. Like Jacobs, Celia is an example of a slave who did resist—who stepped outside various constructions that slavery created for her (the unrapeable black woman, the content and passive slave)— but her voice disappears. A modern editor repackages her trial for modern publication, reproducing erasures encouraged by slave law.

Attempts to silence or manipulate slave voices also are subverted in various ways. One particularly unapologetic defender of slavery is Virginia journalist Edward Pollard, who published *Black Diamonds Gathered in the Darkey Homes of the South* in 1859.[22] While Pollard's descriptions are unabashedly offensive, they also reveal surprising moments of resistant slave voices emerging nonetheless. His defense of the "peculiar institution" consists of attacking what he deems the "false and libelous" testimony of abolitionists and replacing it with the "genuine" perspective of content slaves. He seeks less to eliminate and more to colonize black testimony, sparingly citing slave voices (as he constructs them) to support his points. As an example of slave "enthusiasm," he quotes a hymn sung by "Aunt Debby," who is described as a nonthreatening Mammy, a "real genuine *woolly-head*" (22), "a picture of the happy, contented, Southern slave" and "very coquettish" (25). Her lyrics, however, reveal an ironic counternarrative to his comfortable description of slave piety.

The religious element is very strong in Aunt Debby's character, and her repertoire of pious minstrelsy is quite extensive. Her favorite hymn is in the following words, which are repeated over and over again:

> "Oh run, brother, run! Judgement day is comin'!
> Oh run, brother, run! Why don't you come along?
> The road so rugged, and the hill so high—
> And my Lord call me home,
> To walk the golden streets of my New Jerusalem."

Aunt Debby's religion is of that sort—always begging the Lord to take her up to glory, and professing the greatest anxiety to go *right now!* This religious enthusiasm, however, is not to be taken at its word. (23–24)

Even in Pollard's dismissive transcription, the multilayered power of the hymn emerges. Her repeated line "Oh run, brother, run!" uses an imperative and a term of kinship. "Run" might be religious metaphor or a literal call to run away. Pollard interprets "Judgement day" as the slave's faithful (and naive) hope for heaven, but it also refers to the day of reckoning for white slaveholders who finally will be held accountable for their sins. "New Jerusalem" and "home" can be the afterlife, but they equally can refer to the North and freedom in this life. "Why don't you come along?" suggests that, if escape is being planned, "happy, contented" Debby herself is going as well as gathering others to join her. Such appeals and instructions suggest not a contented slave but an active participant in subversive acts, from wishing for freedom to inspiring fellow slaves to run away. "These songs are the articulate message of the slave to the world," writes W. E. B. Du Bois of spirituals (179). "Every tone," explains Douglass, "was a testimony against slavery" (*Narrative* 47).

Slave songs, often read by Southern whites (including Cobb) as expressions of the race's musical nature and happy disposition, frequently provided testimony of the sufferings of slavery, expressions of general liberatory encouragement, and sometimes even specific instructions toward escape. Angela Davis discusses how the dominant group failed to comprehend the implications of African American music and asserts that "black people were able to create with their music an aesthetic community of resistance, which in turn encouraged and nurtured a political community of active struggle for freedom" (*Women, Culture, and Politics* 201). With official avenues of testimony often closed to slaves, other forms of voicing emerged. Debby's brief voice rising from Pollard's proslavery tract suggests the slippages that can occur. Even under the silencings of slavery, the "different story" alluded to by Jacobs can still emerge.

"*Your* Name Could Not Be Used, You Know": Editorial Framings of Slave Testimony

Slavery allowed Jacobs no official forum for her voice. Once North, she still faced various forms of silencing. Her ability to testify in her own voice was challenged not only by slave law but also by advocates of the slave. The abolitionist trope of "speaking for the slave" in some ways encouraged silencing the slave. Jacobs, like Truth and Douglass, had a circle of associates that included white abolitionist writers. Jacobs's brush with Stowe, similar to Truth's encounter with the writer, was a struggle over representation, authority, and authorship.

As Jacobs contemplated how best to tell her story, she contacted Stowe through Amy Post, who forwarded a summary of Jacobs's story and requested Stowe's help. This contact occurred the year Stowe published *Uncle Tom's Cabin* and shortly after Truth's collaboration with Gilbert. Jacobs might have expected a similar collaboration. Jacobs also had her employer, Cornelia Grinnel Willis, write to Stowe, suggesting that Jacobs's daughter accompany Stowe on her upcoming trip to England promoting abolition. To Jacobs's surprise, the famous abolitionist doubted Jacobs's authenticity, forwarding the sketch of Jacobs's life to Willis for verification, and said that at best she might include parts of Jacobs's story in her next book.[23] While Stowe doubted Jacobs's facts about her life, Jacobs critiqued Stowe's fictions about race. As in the case of her treatment of Truth, Stowe seemed to regard Jacobs's life as an object she could possess and utilize in her own text (her upcoming *Key to Uncle Tom's Cabin*). Such issues of ownership arose in publishing as well as in slavery itself, and Jacobs was not about to hand her life over. She refused to let Stowe subsume her testimony into the *Key*, and they had no further communication.

Jacobs evidently saw the threat to her identity, autonomy, and authority in giving her story to Stowe, and such issues are strong themes in the book she decided to write. She specifically requested that Stowe not use any of her "facts," stating, "I wished it to be a history of my life entirely by itself which would do more good and it needed no romance" (235). She set her life—"a history"—against the "romance" implied by being processed into the novelist's work. She wanted to frame her testimony to give it the greatest political impact, and she believed that writing a life history would "do more good" than being written into Stowe's text. "If she wanted some facts for her book," Jacobs continued, "I would be most happy to give her some" (235). She was willing to lend the novelist "some facts" but refused to turn over her life story to "our friend Mrs Stowe" (234). She turned down the opportunity to have Stowe transform her into another statue (an option Truth did not have) and instead wrote her own testimony. Nevertheless, Jacobs's words are also framed—by her various editors and, more importantly, by herself.[24]

Various editions of *Incidents in the Life of a Slave Girl* are framed to identify and authorize the narrative—as abolitionist argument, authentic slave testimony, or part of a revised literary canon. In the 1861 title page, authority comes from biblical quotation and anonymity. The original edition was edited by Lydia Maria Child and published without Jacobs's name. Anonymity downplays the personal identity of the slave/writer, emphasizing the generic power of the argument and verifying the danger associated with writing about slave experiences.

In Jacobs's case, anonymity also was linked to the sensitive nature of her testimony. The 1861 first edition credits Child and quotes "A WOMAN OF NORTH CAROLINA" and Isaiah on the title page, but it does not name Jacobs. Jacobs herself might be the unnamed woman, making her twice an anonymous presence on her title page: she is "herself" and "a woman of North Carolina" but still unnamed. To quote an anonymous (and unraced) "woman" rather than a named authority rewrites assumptions about who appropriate authorities are. The unnamed woman, who could be a slave woman, appears before even the prophet Isaiah. Foster points out that the same quotation appears in Angelina Grimké's 1836 *Appeal to the Christian Women of the South,* so the reference also functions as a gesture to fellow abolitionists who would be familiar with the earlier work ("Resisting" 71). Both quotations challenge the reader: the first for ignorance ("Northerners know nothing at all about Slavery"), the second for inaction ("Rise up, ye women that are at ease!"). The authority for the first passage comes partly from geography—a *Southern* woman telling Northerners what they do not know. The authority for the second passage comes from the Bible—a male prophet telling passive women to listen and to act.

The book is authorized but at first glance seemingly not authored. In fact, the original copyright belongs to Child, not Jacobs, and many who read the book assumed "Linda Brent" or Child was the author. "Under the circumstances," wrote Child to Jacobs in reference to the copyright, "*your* name could not be used, you know" (letter of 27 September 1860, qtd. in Jacobs 245). Child also had Jacobs sign a paper that "in case of my death, will prove that the book is *your* property, not *mine*" (Jacobs 246). The legalisms of copyright mask Jacobs as the writer and help us trace the layers of framing. On the original title page, "LIFE OF A SLAVE GIRL" is in the largest print, followed by "INCIDENTS."[25] The phrase "WRITTEN BY HERSELF" is smaller, the same size as "EDITED BY L. MARIA CHILD." The title itself deemphasizes personal identity, focusing on "incidents," not autobiography, and "a" generic "slave girl," not a named individual. The emphasis, therefore, is on the conditions of slavery and gendered experiences under that institution but not necessarily on a unified and singular life.

One recent (and widely used) edition, on the other hand, foregrounds Jacobs's identity and presents a dual narrative: the "original" narrative written by Jacobs and the "real" and verified story presented by modern editor Jean Fagan Yellin. The modern framing is both omnipresent and masked. While Jacobs's voice is strongly asserted, issues of framing and authorization still are prominent. Yellin's edition focuses on "recovering" Jacobs and her story, authenticating the details of the narrative and the very existence of Jacobs. For years the book had been deemed a fake narrative and Brent the invention of Child.[26] Yellin's 1987 title page highlights Jacobs's name, downplays Child's, includes her own, and places a large captioned photograph as frontispiece. The 1894 photograph—with Jacobs seated, dignified, and grandmotherly (no "slave girl")—also graces the cover and binding. This image helps verify the existence of the real Harriet Jacobs and represent her as trustworthy and nonconfrontational.

The two hundred pages of Jacobs's original testimony are framed by Yellin's detailed introduction (twice the length of any of Jacobs's chapters) and a hundred pages of photographs, letters, diagrams, and notes at the end. The visuals are reproductions of nineteenth-century documents (such as an 1835 reward ad for Jacobs) interspersed with recently created documents, such as a cross-sectional diagram of Jacobs's grandmother's house. All appear in a similar gray with italicized captions, making them hard to distinguish at first. Placed after the reproduction of the original title page and before the original preface is a "Cast of Characters," compiled by Yellin but not marked as a modern insertion, which decodes the character names. Yellin translates for us, but she does not always announce those translations. Students often assume that the list of character names and their real-life counterparts was inserted by Jacobs, who significantly did *not* reveal the real names in her narrative. The original version ends with testimonials from Amy Post and a "respected colored citizen" in Boston— a white woman and a black man appear to verify Jacobs's identity and to endorse her character.[27] Yellin's version keeps those authorizers but also includes many of her own. Her notes verify Jacobs's claims, adjust her details, fill in context we do not have, and otherwise make the narrative seem like biographical and contextual "fact" more than literature or argument.

Yellin's footnotes argue that Jacobs's story is "true," though sometimes she even corrects Jacobs. For example, in a note to the chapter about Aunt Nancy, Yellin points to a seeming error, in order to point out that such errors are rare: "The assertion that Linda Brent's mother and aunt were twins is an exception to the generally striking accuracy in *Incidents* about Jacobs's family" (281). That "accuracy" has been established by Yellin's detailed work. She cites internal and external data (references to other chapters and outside records) to back up the correction. The truer version, apparently, is the Yellin version. Yellin's footnotes tend to use the real names she uncovered, rather than the character names employed by Jacobs. Through that translation, Jacobs is shown to contradict herself here, and Yellin sets the record straight. Other possibilities, such as "twin sister" as a metaphor for Nancy's closeness to the mother and her efforts to fill her place after her death ("She was my mother's twin sister," writes Jacobs, "and, as far as was in her power, she supplied a mother's place to us orphans" [144]), are set aside in the volume of verifying data.

Sometimes Yellin expounds in amazing detail, verifying and authenticating Jacobs's original details. When the narrator states that it was cold during the winter in her tiny hiding place (a claim the reader might not find controversial), Yellin footnotes "meteorological data" from that region (277). We can be confident of Jacobs's accuracy thanks to Yellin's second narrative. All this verification and amplification also helps transform this edition on one level into Yellin's new text.

Framing influences interpretation. Yellin's edition of *Incidents* is often seen as the definitive version, "the fully realized edition" according to the book jacket. A 1993 article in the *Chronicle of Higher Education* reports the new authenticity of the text, now that Professor Yellin's "detective work" has verified everything. Entitled "A Slave Girl's Authentic Life," the article implies that the life was not authentic until Yellin made it so (McMillen A9). The nature of this version affects what genre we see Jacobs's book occupying. Filled with footnotes and documents, this edition seems more history or fact rather than "literature." With the personal chronology and photographs, it seems autobiography more than argument.

Slave narratives (and African American literature itself) often are read more as sociology than art. Yellin's version is vital work, but its contours frame how we might read or teach this book. The double narrative—with Yellin verifying, correcting, or augmenting the details—makes it hard to read Jacobs's moves as literary technique, figurative construction, or political rhetoric. Jacobs offers a generic anecdote, and Yellin names the real participants. Jacobs describes the chill, and Yellin cites average seasonal temperatures. My reading of Jacobs—that she plays with framing and exposes the constructedness of various fictions—is both helped and hindered by Yellin. Yellin's references point me to useful source material, but the "factual" appearance of the form also can narrow the search and discourage attention to Jacobs's literariness. At the end of her introduction, Yellin includes a "Note on This Edition" explaining alterations in the texts, and she offers the commonly worded explanation that typographical errors from the original edition have been "silently corrected" (xxxiv). The statement reminds me to be aware of other silent reframings that might need to be called out.

"Dis 'Ere Yaller Gal's Got Letters!": Resisting Literacy Restrictions

Jacobs attacks testimony restrictions by offering her own literary testimony, by more generally asserting the value of African American voices that have been excluded, and by showing the danger of relying on a white person to speak on the slave's behalf. While calling her book "testimony" and "no fiction" (1–2), Jacobs also creates a highly crafted literary work, filled with metaphor, symbolism, allusion, and other literate markers of the world of letters. Jacobs's book, "written by herself," contradicts another legal fiction of slavery: that slaves could not read or write or teach others to do so. Many slaves, of course, did read, write, and teach. But it serves the purposes of a slave society if blacks are legally denied access to literacy, literacy becomes a marker for reason and reason a marker for humanity. That circular proposition naturalizes what is a legal constraint and functions as a convenient self-fulfilling prophecy.

Fictions of black intellectual inferiority and the nonexistence of African culture, which appear in Cobb's work, underlie restrictions on slave education. Such fictions serve to justify constraints that existed precisely because of white fear that blacks *do* possess minds. Literacy, Douglass quotes his owner cautioning, will unfit a slave for slavery: "If you learn him now to read, he'll want to know how to write; and, this accomplished, he'll be running away with himself" (*My Bondage* 92). While antiliteracy laws sought to dehumanize slaves, Douglass's 1852 "What to the Slave Is the Fourth of July?" cites those laws as proof of the slave's humanity and manhood: "When you can point to any such laws in reference to the beasts of the fields, then I may consent to argue the manhood of the slave" (286).

Cobb's study of slave law—written well after the appearance of black-authored poetry, fiction, autobiography, and oratory by writers including Wheatley, Briton Hammon, Jupiter Hammon, Olaudah Equiano, David Walker, George Moses Horton, Maria Stewart, Jarena Lee, William Wells Brown, Frances Ellen Watkins Harper, Douglass, and many others—attempts to take as an unquestioned given the mental inferiority of the black race. His entry "NEGRO. mental inferiority" in his index cites his data for this conclusion in two different chapters (352). "Averse to physical labor, they are equally averse to intellectual effort," he declares of Africans and African Americans. This assertion is revealingly ironic: Natural aversion to intellectual effort unfits blacks for education, yet the same aversion to work does not unfit them for forced labor. Cobb's generalizations continue: "The young negro acquires readily the first rudiments of education, where memory and imitation are chiefly brought into action, but for any higher effort of reason and judgment he is, as a general rule, utterly incapable" (ccii). His support consists of a long footnote quoting Northern governors who responded to a "circular" he distributed. "Circular" is a fitting term, suggesting the circularity of Cobb's reasoning and evidence gathering. Responses include: "Ignorant," "Not educated," and "Far below the whites" (cciii). He seeks conclusions about the race of negroes, not merely the class of slaves, so he generates data about free blacks. He authorizes the data that he himself has solicited by placing it in the mouths of governors.

Cobb addresses the writings of slaves in a scornful summary of an abolitionist collection of black intellectual achievements. He reinterprets this "testimony" for his own purposes: "For excellence in poetry we have Phillis Wheatley, whose productions Mr. Jefferson pronounced to be 'beneath criticism.' In composition, is Gustavus Vasa [*sic*], whose only work was a narrative of himself (by whom written, or revised we know not), which would hardly give credit to a schoolboy in his teens" (45). Legitimating his dismissal by invoking an antislavery founding father, Cobb quotes Jefferson here, not Wheatley, as more evidence that whites have a literate voice to cite and slaves do not. In questioning the authorship of the 1789 *Interesting Narrative of the Life of Olaudah Equiano, or Gustavus Vassa, the African, Written by Himself,* Cobb echoes Jefferson's nervousness in dismissing Wheatley's poetry, referring to her work as "compositions published under her name" (qtd. in Kaplan and Kaplan 188). In both cases, the literature in question evidently is poor enough to prove Africans are not intelligent, yet good enough to make the questioner wonder if someone else wrote it. Cobb mocks the "meagreness" of abolitionist volume, then he observes that most of the writers are former slaves, concluding, "The inference would seem irresistible, from the testimony of this volume, that the most successful engine for the development of negro intellect is slavery" (46). Cobb wants it both ways: Slaves are ignorant, and if one is found who is not, then that proves (irresistibly) the beneficial effects of slavery.

Serving the self-fulfilling prophecy of slave ignorance, laws placed slaves in physical danger if they pursued learning. Jacobs shows Brent breaking the law to teach an old man so that he could read the Bible. The narrator tells "Uncle Fred" the legal implications of their act: "I asked him if he didn't know it was contrary to law; and that slaves were whipped and imprisoned for teaching each other to read. This brought the tears into his eyes" (72).[28] By informing Fred of this dangerous context, she is educating her audience about the law as well. The risk of whipping is framed by descriptions of Fred's earnest religious faith. The extremity of the punishment is in stark contrast to the gentleness of this criminal accomplice.

North Carolina law by the 1830s specified different degrees of punishment for the crime of literacy, depending on the race and condition of the lawbreaker:

> Any free person who shall hereafter teach . . . any slave within this State to read or write, the use of figures excepted, or shall give or sell to such slave or slaves any books or pamphlets, shall be liable to indictment . . . and, upon conviction, shall at the discretion of the court, if a white man or woman, be fined not less than one hundred dollars nor more than two hundred dollars, or imprisoned, and if a free person of color, shall be fined, imprisoned or whipped, at the discretion of the court, not exceeding thirty-nine lashes, nor less than twenty lashes.
>
> If any slave shall teach . . . any other slave to read or write, the use of figures excepted, he or she . . . on conviction thereof, shall be sentenced to receive thirty-nine lashes on his or her bare back. (Revised Statutes 34:74, III:27)

Both laws exempt "the use of figures": apparently that use of the slave mind did not pose the threat that learning the alphabet did. Or perhaps some slaveholders were too reliant upon slaves returning with the right number of items for figures to be banned. The different penalties depending upon color and condition are revealing. A white "man or woman" is fined within a specified range and may be imprisoned, perhaps if the fine is not paid. A free black may be fined an unspecified amount *and* whipped within a specific range. A slave is whipped the highest number of lashes, on "his or her bare back." Status determines whether the offender is fined, but race determines whether physical integrity is violated. A free black could be treated as harshly as a white (subject to a fine or prison) *and* as harshly as a slave (up to thirty-nine lashes). Only a slave, however, has the bodily details so specified: Unlike the amount of the fine, the number of lashes and the bareness of the back are not left to the court's discretion. The specificity reveals not only the brutality of the punishment but also the public nature of the slave body, according to law.

Other states and, earlier, colonies had physical punishments for people of color who provided or sought learning, and the details of such laws indicate another perceived danger of slave learning, besides proof of reason. The very act of assembling to learn could be subversive. South Carolina's restrictive laws were among the earliest, first outlawing literacy in the slave code of 1740, legislation that followed the 1739 Stono Rebellion, perhaps the most extensive slave insurrection in the colonial period. That early law focused on those teaching the slaves: "Whereas the having of slaves taught to write, or suffering them to be employed in writing, may be attended with great inconveniences; *Be it enacted,* that all and every person and persons whatsoever, who shall hereafter teach, or cause any slave or slaves to be taught to write, or shall use or employ any slave as a scribe in any manner of writing . . . shall, for every such offence, forfeit the sum of £100 current money" (Public Laws 695:45). The penalty assumes a free white person with assets to forfeit. "Persons," not "slaves," are the ones penalized here. Higginbotham notes that this fine was one of the most severe in colonial law.[29]

A law passed in 1800 focused on the people of color who participated in instruction:

All assemblies and congregations of slaves, free negroes, mulattoes, and mestizoes, whether composed of all, or any of the above description of persons, or of all or any of the above described persons, and of a proportion of white persons, assembled or met together for the purpose of mental instruction, in a confined or secret place of meeting . . . shall be . . . an unlawful meeting; and the magistrates, sheriffs, militia officers, and officers of the patrol, being commissioned, are hereby directed, required and empowered, to enter into such confined places . . . to break doors, gates, or windows, if resisted, and disperse such slaves, free negroes, mulattoes, or mestizoes . . . and the officers and persons so dispersing such unlawful assemblage of persons, shall, if they think proper, impose such corporal punishment, not exceeding twenty lashes, upon such slaves, free negroes, mulattoes, or mestizoes, as they may judge necessary for deterring them from the like unlawful assemblages in future. (Acts of South Carolina 36–37)

The detailed list of targets and permutations reveals anxieties around increasingly complicated mixtures of slave and free, black and white, pure blood and mixed, who might come together, despite the law's attempt to keep people apart. The assemblage is still illegal if white persons are present, but only people of color are to be whipped. Part of the threat is the "assemblage" aspect of learning. Literacy is not merely gentle Uncle Fred reading the Bible but more threateningly political assembly. The legislature reveals anxiety about conspiracy when it specifies the illegality of instruction in a "confined or secret place." Another section of this law specifies the illegality of meeting for instruction "either before the rising of the sun, or after the going down of the same" (38).[30] Antiliteracy laws often include language about assembly, as in this statute, or pamphlets, as in the North Carolina prohibition. Learning and literacy are linked to collectivity and political action. Slavery proponents are aware—accurately— of the power and potential subversiveness of the written word.

Just as the Stono Rebellion led to repressive measures in the 1740s, Nat Turner's 1831 Virginia uprising led to crackdowns in the 1830s. In her chapter "Fear of Insurrection," Jacobs details vicious raids in her community less to describe the slaves' fears than to dissect the anxieties of the whites. She analyzes the organized raids as an exploitation of lower-class whites unaware of their own position, revealing her superior understanding of the class divisions in white society: "It was a grand opportunity for the low whites, who had no negroes of their own to scourge. They exulted in such a chance to exercise a little brief authority, and show their subserviency to the slaveholders; not reflecting that the power which trampled on the colored people also kept themselves in poverty, ignorance and moral degradation" (64). Brent calmly prepares for the arrival of the marauding soldiers, and Jacobs juxtaposes the ignorance and hysteria of the raiders with the intelligence and composure of the raided. She also contrasts the whites' uneducated dialect with her narrator's dignified language:

> "What d'ye foller us fur? D'ye s'pose white folks is come to steal?"
> I replied, "You have come to search; but you have searched that box, and I will take it, if you please." (65)

Like Stowe translating Truth's dialect to a white audience, but with a twist, Jacobs also provides interpretations to her literate readers. "'Don't won-der de niggers want to kill all de white folks, when dey live on 'sarves' [meaning preserves]," she writes, inserting a bracketed translation after the quotation (66). Jacobs plays with readers' assumptions about black ignorance and illiteracy when she depicts illiterate white characters with a dialect that evokes popular constructions of "negro" speech. That such assumptions retain currency today is evidenced in Yellin's indexing of this white speech under the heading "Black English" (296).

Much of the raid focuses on issues of literacy, revealing what the white power structure perhaps fears more than bullets. The wealthy slaveholder supervising the search does not dirty his hands with the details, except when the raiders uncover writing, which seems as important as weaponry: "If a bit of writing was discovered, it was carried to him by his ignorant followers, who were unable to read" (65). Jacobs and Brent use literacy to demonstrate superiority over the "low whites" and to expose the anxiety of Southern whites in general. "We's got 'em! We's got 'em! Dis 'ere yaller gal's got letters!" shout the raiders. Brent possesses letters, and she is a person of letters, a fact that incenses her persecutors. When the captain learns Brent can read, "he swore, and raved, and tore the paper into bits" (65). He is unnerved by her literacy, manifested by her possession of poetry, and her responses to his questions further fail to fit his assump-tions: "'Who writes to you? half free niggers?' inquired he. I replied, 'O, no; most of my letters are from white people'" (66). Her chapter details horrific abuses ("Every where men, women, and children were whipped till the blood stood in puddles at their feet"), yet Jacobs's real focus is to expose the insecurity and instability that lies behind those acts of vio-lence (64). "Strange that they should be alarmed," she writes of the white response to Turner's revolt, "when their slaves were so 'contented and happy'! But so it was" (63). Jacobs exposes the fiction of happy slaves and the fiction of confident whites in control.

Jacobs shows Brent directly resisting the literacy ban when she teaches Fred to read and when she confronts the raiders at her grandmother's house. Brent also deploys literacy during her years hiding in the garret, for example in writing the letters that mislead Flint into thinking that she is already living in the North. Jacobs critiques the way language can function to deceive and manipulate while she also makes use of such manipulation herself. She describes her hiding place with the phrase "The Loophole of Retreat." A loophole can mean an escape clause, especially in a contract or law. White characters repeatedly use such dodges in their dealings with slaves—the mistress who doesn't repay the candelabra loan, Flint not settling the same loan out of the estate, Flint claiming he's helpless because his daughter owns Brent, Sands saying Brent was always in control of the children he owned.[31] Now it is Brent, in her place of imprisonment, who finds loopholes through which to manipulate whites.[32] Loophole also denotes a slit in a wall through which weapons are discharged. The narrator uses texts to her advantage in her psychological warfare against Flint and against slavery. She writes false letters, deploys the *Herald* against itself, and uses the very book we are reading to dodge slavery and fire bullets.

"Perpetual Pupilage": No Capacity to Choose?

Literacy and testimony bans are concrete attacks on slave voices. Laws also constrained African American voices by regulating the slave's or ex-slave's legal capacity to make choices. Central to Jacobs's claim to humanity is her right to make her own choices, which she attempts to do even within her limited set of options. Brent struggles with the "choice," such as it was, to have a sexual relationship with Sands instead of Flint, and she chooses (against even her grandmother's advice) to separate herself from her children until she can bring her family north.

For the most part, Southern courts held that slaves had no voice in their own fates, even if the owner's written word willed it so. Such a recognition of humanity could destabilize the system of slavery, which depended upon slaves constructed as property; sometimes disempowering the owner was seen as the price for preserving the fiction of the nonhuman slave. These issues especially arose in cases relating to manumission. Such rulings reveal instabilities, anxieties, and complicated narratives, and they offer an interesting counterpoint to Jacobs's assertion of agency. Jacobs was unlikely to know the details of these particular cases, but she did have a complex understanding of the ideology behind such rulings.

Slaveholders feared that manumission (individual owners freeing individual slaves) would undercut the uniformity and permanence of the slave system, create a free black population, and, most threateningly, suggest the humanity of individual slaves. Manumission pointed to the relationships some owners had with slaves—many owners freed their own children, or the mothers of such children. Some states banned manumission or imposed severe conditions.[33] Some required that freed slaves leave the state; some refused to recognize the rights of ex-slaves freed in another state. Where manumission was permitted, questions arose whether freed slaves would have any legal voice, for example, the right to sue for property left to them in an owner's will. The results and the rhetoric in these cases reveal key issues around black subjectivity, definitions of citizenship, and constructions of nationhood, notions that Jacobs addresses in her narrative.

While results varied, what generally emerged was the attempt to construct slavery as the inherent, natural state of blacks or to ignore status altogether and, independent of manumission, to make race the marker of inferiority and lack of subjectivity. Taken as a whole, these cases tend to render the freed slave not a citizen, not a willful being with a voice and the right to make choices, and ultimately not a human being. The very existence of such cases, however, reveals tensions in the system. These cases emerge because there were whites who acknowledged the subjectivity of their slaves, and there were slaves and former slaves with agency and will.

In the 1858 Virginia case *Bailey v. Poindexter*, a slaveholder, instead of freeing his slaves in his will, instructed his slaves to choose between freedom and continued slavery after he died. While an owner may have the right to grant freedom, a slave does not have the legal capacity to choose, according to the judge in the case, identified as Judge Daniel:

> When we assent to the general proposition, as I think we must do, that our slaves have no civil or social rights; that they have no legal capacity to make, discharge or assent to contracts; . . . we are led necessarily to the conclusion that nothing short of the exhibition of a positive enactment, or of legal decisions having equal force, can demonstrate the capacity of a slave to exercise an election in respect to his manumission.
>
> Any testamentary effort of a master to clothe his slave with such a power, is an effort to accomplish a legal impossibility. (197)

The speaking subject of the ruling is part of the slaveholding community. Though slaveowners were a minority of whites, the voice of "we" the state is the voice of "we" the owners, who collectively own all "our" slaves. The state would need new law before it could give the slave choice—the state, not the individual owner, has the power here. The court holds: "*The master has endeavored to clothe his slaves with the uncontrollable and irrevocable power of determining for themselves whether they shall be manumitted.* And in doing so, he has, I think, essayed the vain attempt to reconcile obvious and inherent contradictions" (199, original emphasis). For this judge, "inherent contradictions" reveal not that the rules of slavery are contradictory but that slaves should be more completely denied a voice to avoid such conflicts. Daniel twice uses the metaphor of *clothing* the slave with certain powers. The image evoked is that of the unprotected, naked slave—this is the slave's inherent state and cannot be altered.[34]

An earlier case, *Bryan v. Walton,* relies on the unchanging characteristic of race, not condition, to deny black agency. Here, a free black bequeathed some slaves to his free son, who gave the slaves to a white man, who sold them to another white man. This 1853 Georgia case involves the two whites suing each other, but the legal question turns on the agency of the African American men who made the initial choices. The issue at hand is whether a free black has the right to choose to bequeath or give away his slaves, or indeed to choose any action that a white citizen might choose. Judge Lumpkin held that a manumitted African American possesses only those rights explicitly granted by the state. His definitions of citizen and state place agency in the law and make "the African" less than a child. Using allusion, alliteration, comparison, and patriotism, he constructs free blacks as perpetual noncitizens, never to have a voice of their own. Lumpkin provides a long list of holdings, waxing more biblical and poetic the more rights he denies:

> . . . We maintain, that the *status* of the African in Georgia, whether bond or free, is such that he has no civil, social or political rights or capacity, whatever, except such as are bestowed on him by Statute; that he can neither contract, nor be contracted with; that the free negro can act only by and through his guardian; that he is in a state of perpetual pupilage or wardship; and that this condition he can never change by his own volition. It can only be done by Legislation.
>
> That the act of manumission confers no other right but that of freedom from the dominion of the master, and the limited liberty of locomotion; that it does not and cannot confer *citizenship* . . . ; that the social and civil degradation, resulting from the taint of blood, adheres to the descendants

of Ham in this country, like the poisoned tunic of Nessus; that nothing
but an Act of the Assembly can purify, by the salt of its grace, the bitter
fountain—the *"darkling sea."* (198, original emphasis)

The law is supreme—over the volition of the slave, free black, and even
white master. "Statute," "Legislation," "Act," and "Assembly"—capitalized
and exalted—can "bestow," "change," and "purify," while the manumitted slave can do nothing. The word "act" emphasizes the agency of law:
The Assembly can act, the freed slave cannot.

Lumpkin constructs American citizenship as inherently white and
blacks as inherently non-American. Race outweighs status or birthplace:
Slave or free, born in Africa or America, "the African" forever has the "taint
of blood" keeping him from any citizenship rights. Lumpkin invokes
Ham (Noah's son, whose descendants are in servitude because he saw his
father's nakedness while his brothers averted their eyes)[35] and Nessus (the
lecherous centaur of Greek myth whose bloody tunic adhered to Hercules,
setting his skin on fire and leading to his death) to demonstrate the
ancientness and permanence of blackness.[36] These images contrast with
the Virginia judge who refused to "clothe" the slave with rights. Here, the
construction of the black's inherently degraded status is symbolized by
bloody and poisoned clothing that cannot be removed and by the irre-
versible sin of seeing someone unclothed. The images vary, but the notion
of permanence remains.

Lumpkin also invokes recent history to recall the founding of the state
and reiterate the whiteness of citizenship: "Our ancestors settled this
State . . . as a community of white men, professing the christian religion,
and possessing an equality of rights and privileges. The blacks were introduced into it, as a race of Pagan slaves. The prejudice, if it can be called
so, of caste, is unconquerable. It was so at the beginning. . . . Naturaliza-
tion Laws . . . do not apply to the *African.* He is not and cannot become a
citizen under our Constitution and Laws. He resides among us, and yet is
a stranger. A *native* even, and yet not a citizen" (202). State formation is a
moment of both "equality" and separation from the other, who is eternally
foreign in race, religion, and geography. "White men" alone profess Christianity and possess equality, at the expense of the *"African."*[37]

Lumpkin concludes with broader claims about America and (white)
citizenship:

Whether freedom will, in Africa, be a *reality* to the colored man and his
children or not, in the United States . . . it is worse than slavery itself. . . .

The Courts of this country should never lean to that construction, which puts the thriftless African upon a footing of civil or political equality with a white population which are characterized by a degree of energy and skill, unknown to any other people or period. Such alone, can be *citizens* in this great and growing Republic, which extends already from the Atlantic to the *Pacific,* and from the St. Lawrence to the Rio Grande. (206–7, original emphasis)

He sets the singular "African" against a collective white "population," superlative and unique, by color, character, period, and geography. They "alone" are citizens; the "thriftless African" remains foreign. Lumpkin denotes America by its form of government and vast boundaries. The very span of the Republic (newly enlarged by the 1848 Treaty of Guadalupe Hidalgo, which ended the U.S.–Mexico War by giving the U.S. a large portion of Mexican land) becomes support for the superiority of the white race and the exclusivity of citizenship.

An 1859 Mississippi manumission case, *Mitchell v. Wells,* also excludes freed blacks from citizenship and even more explicitly from legal personhood and humanity. Nancy Wells was manumitted in Ohio by her white owner and father, Mississippi resident Edmund Wells, who later died and bequeathed property to his daughter. The court found that Nancy Wells's free status in Ohio gave her no legal subjectivity in Mississippi. Judge William Harris uses language of citizenship, family, humanity, and animals to construct both free blacks and the state of Ohio itself as dangerous threats to the "family" of slaveholding states. He describes the "inferior, subordinate, subjugated" condition of the black race at the time of the adoption of the Constitution in order to give slavery national authorization.

Like Lumpkin, Harris recalls the entrance of his state into the union: "Mississippi came into the Union under this Federal Constitution as a member of this political family, to be associated on terms of political equality, comity, or courtesy with the *white race,* who *alone* by that compact had a right to be thus associated. . . . Her climate, soil, and productions, and the pursuits of her people, their habits, manners, and opinions, all combine not only to sanction the wisdom, humanity, and policy of the system thus established by her organic law and fostered by her early legislation, but they *require slave labor*" (252, original emphasis). While the state is humanized (and feminized) and "organic law" is given agency, slaves have neither humanity nor agency and exist only as labor. Like Lumpkin, Harris describes state formation as a moment of both equality and hierarchy. The equality of whites (or white, male, propertied citizens) exists at the expense of people of color, who cannot join that "political family"—they are neither political nor familial. Familial imagery contributes to the assumption of racial separation, since the legal fictions of family were entirely white (miscegenation was illegal and slaves could not legally marry).

Harris extends the language of family to his analysis of legal doctrine. A central legal principle in this case is comity (states respecting each other's laws), which Harris redefines in familial terms: "'Comity' forbids that a sister State of this confederacy should seek to introduce into the family of States . . . a caste of different color, and of acknowledged inferiority, who, though existing among us at the time of our compact of Union, were excluded from the sisterhood by common consent" (262). States are sisters, and inclusion of blacks begins to sound like a daughter bringing home an outsider. Harris quotes Cobb, who also employs familial language: "It is comity, courtesy, founded upon mutual respect, and promotive of mutual interest, the offspring of commerce and enlightenment, the handmaid of justice and of peace" (qtd. in Harris 262). Comity is thus constructed as a good daughter.

Harris sums up this definitional section by comparing comity to "courtesy, politeness, good-breeding, among families" (262). "Breeding" suggests good training and also connotes reproduction. Harris's family metaphor joins the language of sexuality, intensifying the threat of racial mixing. He declares that comity would require no duty that would "degrade a sister in the family of nations." Specifying Ohio's behavior toward free blacks, he writes, "If the sister, in violation of morality, and respect for herself, as well as her associates of the old household, will insist on the meretricious embrace, we are neither bound to sanction nor respect it, much less to receive her new associate into our immediate circle" (264). The extended metaphor suggests Ohio as an immoral daughter who embarks on an improper sexual relationship and slave states as the family that must protect itself from such pollution. Excluding freed slaves from rights in any state becomes equivalent to keeping black men away from one's (white) family members. Harris later compares Ohio's precedent to the threat of having "the chimpanzee or the ourang-outang . . . introduced into the family of sisters in this confederacy" (264).

Overall, through the language of family, illicit sexuality and animals, this ruling, described as "the high point in proslavery legal thought" by one modern legal scholar, argues that recognition of black subjectivity (even short of citizenship) would pose a danger to the state and the nation (Finkelman, *Law* 168). These dominant constructions of family, subjectivity, and nation needed to be deconstructed by Jacobs as she confronted the irrational law of slavery.

"Of Which None Exist"? The Persistent Erasures of Slave Voices

Southern lawmakers and judges nervously insisted upon the voicelessness of slaves and former slaves. Slave laws produced innumerable harmful consequences when they were officially in effect and later, when their legacies are still felt. In some ways, testimony and literacy strictures yield the most insidious contemporary effects. Such constructions attempt to write slave voices out of the record. In the constructed legal fiction—the literature of Cobb's "statute-book"—slaves had no public voice. Those laws in many ways made African Americans and their words invisible, even as Jacobs and countless others were writing and otherwise testifying. The shape of U.S. literature thereby is affected—by what was legislated out of existence and by consequent assumptions about what must not exist. Questions of authentication still persist as the authorship and authority of slave accounts still are questioned.

Despite all the testimony that does exist (in the form of slave narratives, newspaper articles, oratory, and other written and oral forms), the construction of the voiceless slave endures into the present. Representative Henry Hyde, a federal lawmaker from Illinois, released a 1991 briefing paper on his Collegiate Speech Protection Act, a bill he presented as protecting ostensibly marginalized voices on college campuses (that is, for Hyde, predominantly white males in academia under attack by the forces of so-called political correctness). In this attack on the forces of "p.c." and even deconstruction and postmodernism in academia, Hyde attacks what he constructs as the irrational extremists who make unreasonable demands on well-meaning academicians. He shares what he considers the horror story of two Harvard professors criticized for their class on the history of U.S. race relations. He reports with indignation that Stephan Thernstrom and Bernard Bailyn "were accused of racial insensitivity for, among other things, 1) reading from the diary of a southern plantation owner without giving equal time to the recollections of a slave *(of which none exist)*, 2) assigning a book mentioning that some people regard affirmative action as preferential treatment, and 3) endorsing U.S. Senator Patrick Moynihan's emphasis on the breakup of the black family as a cause of persistent black poverty" (Hyde 6, emphasis added). That little parenthetical—unsupported and untrue—erases what is estimated to be six thousand extant slave narratives.[38] The very fact that this massive erasure appears in just four words—"of which none exist"—and tucked into parentheses suggests what an easy, seemingly uncontested assumption it is. Hyde is not *arguing* that slave voices do not exist—like Cobb, he sets himself up as merely reporting the facts.[39]

Representative Hyde's phenomenal erasure of slave testimony reminds us that recovery projects remain necessary. Jacobs offers an obvious counterclaim to Hyde's erasure: She certainly remembers slavery and manages to write down those "recollections" for later generations to read. More significantly, she provides strategies for reading the falsely neutral framings of slavery for what they are, whether Cobb's "well-known facts" or Hyde's unsupported parentheses.

chapter six

Reframing Legal Fictions
of Womanhood

In *Incidents in the Life of a Slave Girl*, Jacobs deploys a slave girl's testimony along with the stories of several other women and men in order to generate multiple consciousness about the complexities of slavery. Jacobs uses these voices to challenge the fictions of race and gender that upheld the often contradictory laws of slavery in a supposedly democratic America. Slave laws regulating sex, reproduction, and family denied African American subjectivity and reveal inconsistencies and instabilities in U.S. law and society. Lawmakers simultaneously denied black subjectivity and generated fear of black sexuality, particularly in the constructions of the lascivious seductress and the dangerous rapist. The law reveals the conflict between the perceived threat of and need for African American reproduction. Slave women had no legal rights over their children, but black mothers were held to have the greatest impact on their children's fate. Legal discourse reveals white uneasiness about the risk of recognizing African American humanity (if, for example, slaves were allowed to have families, marry whites, prosecute rapists), which could threaten the principles underlying slavery.

The legal system under slavery simultaneously held that miscegenation was illegal, that there was no crime of rape against a slave, and that there could be no marriage between slaves. These laws use the frequently absurd language of legal rationality for irrational and contradictory claims. It is necessary to explode the rhetoric of rationality in legal discourses around sexuality and family, as Jacobs does, to explore how slave law both created and was sustained by contradictory constructions of race, gender, and sex. In sections on sexuality and family, this chapter first examines legal framings (through slave law and Cobb's legal treatise) and then juxtaposes those constructions with Jacobs's reframings of black womanhood. While the focus on womanhood and family helped Jacobs appeal to Northern women, she wanted more than sentimental and sisterly sympathy. Having drawn women into her story, Jacobs also deliberately makes her argument legal and federal in order to move Northerners to action. The chapter closes with analysis of Jacobs's call to activism.

"The Want of Chastity in the Female Slave": Lascivious Slaves and Honorable Statutes

Although antimiscegenation laws made consensual sex between men and women of different races illicit and illegal, the law failed to protect slave women from forced sex committed by white men, as Jacobs repeatedly reveals in her narrative. Southern law also generally failed to protect slave women from rape committed by other slaves. The rape of white women, however, was punishable by death, if the perpetrator—or the man convicted of the act—was a slave. In his antislavery *Sketch of the Laws Relating to Slavery*, George Stroud commits several pages to a chart itemizing penalty differences in Virginia criminal law depending on whether the accused is white, free black, or slave. He lists six rape-related crimes. The penalty for rape of an adult is ten to twenty years for a white perpetrator, five to twenty years or death for a free black, and death for a slave. The penalty for "attempting, by force or by fraud, to have carnal knowledge of a white female" is "death" for a slave, and "not provided for" in the case of a white male. The juxtapositions in Stroud's chart reveal in striking visual and numerical detail the relative subjectivity granted to black and white, slave or free, female or male. Justice, figured in Anglo-American legal tradition as blind, needs to know all these factors about victim and criminal before meting out allegedly neutral penalties.

Cobb's treatment of rape in his *Historical Sketch of Slavery* simultaneously denies its existence and blames slaves for interracial sex. To appear evenhanded, he cites both the "benefits and evils" of slavery throughout his treatise. He says the evils are "equally unquestionable," but undercuts each example by making it the fault of or an advantage to the slaves. Rather than addressing the rape of slave women, he shifts the causal relationship so that the "lewdness" of slave women is defined as the problem: "An evil attributed to slavery, and frequently alluded to, is the want of chastity in the female slaves, and a corresponding immorality in the white males" (ccxix). Slave women and their lack of chastity are framed as the cause, and white male immorality is merely the correspondence.

Cobb uses qualifiers and indefinite references to cloud questions of agency: "To a *certain* extent *this* is true; and *to the extent* that the slave is under the control and subject to the order of the master, the condition of slavery is *responsible*" (ccxix, emphasis added). The indefinite reference "this" denotes interracial sex, true only "to a certain extent" and defined in his previous sentence not as rape but as lack of chastity among slave women. Cobb concedes that the "condition of slavery"—not white men— may be "responsible" (responsible for what is still left indefinite), but only "to the extent" that slavery gives power to the master.

Cobb immediately readjusts by invoking another well-known fact: "Every well-informed person at the South, however, knows that the exercise of such power for such a purpose is almost unknown. The prevalence of the evil is attributable to other causes. The most prominent of these is the natural lewdness of the negro" (ccxix). Again, his references are vague: "Such a purpose" and "the evil" stand in for the interracial sex that he refuses to call rape. The charge of "lewdness" is leveled against not owners who rape but slaves who seduce. Cobb blames race, not the institution of slavery, so the flaw becomes "natural" and is attributed to African Americans as a whole: "It is not the consequence of slavery. The free negro . . . exhibits the same disposition." His evidence again relies on the pronoun "this," in a footnote declaring that the ratio of mulattoes to blacks in the North "shows this to be true." Cobb lists several numbers to imply that African American women freely seduce white men in the North. This immorality results from not only female lust, Cobb assures us, but also female cunning: "Another cause is the fact that the negress knows that the offspring of such intercourse, the mulatto, having greater intelligence, and being indeed a superior race, has a better opportunity of enjoying the privileges of domestics; in other words, *is elevated* by the mixture of blood. Her sin does not entail misfortune but good fortune on her children" (ccxix–xx).[1] Cobb's discussion of this "evil attributed to slavery" quickly becomes a "sin" committed by slave women.

Unchaste black womanhood helps preserve white womanhood, even when class threatens to prevent some white women from being true women: "It is undoubtedly true, that from this cause [i.e., white men having sex with unchaste black women] the poor white females of the slaveholding States are not subject to as great temptations and importunities as they would be under other circumstances" (ccxx). While the "want of chastity" is coded by race and gender, poor women are generally tainted as well, but African American women can help save white women from temptation. Cobb proves this point by citing data from "ignorant districts" with "few negroes" and apparently much "immorality." African American women therefore serve as a safety valve for white women's morality. Cobb's reasoning here suggests further slippage. Black women are the agents of illicit sex, he insists, but he also implies that without their presence, poor white women would be tempted into prostitution or other improprieties, suggesting that white men will seek illicit sex regardless of circumstances. Of course, Cobb never names white men in this equation, referring only to "females."

In the course of his legal analysis, Cobb acknowledges that the failure to address rape is a "defect in our legislation," but a theoretical defect only. Such "occurrence is almost unheard of," he remarks, and to whatever extent it does occur, there is the factor of "the known lasciviousness of the negro." Finally Cobb suggests a change in the law, not for the honor of African American women but "for the honor of the statute-book" (99–100). The brief slippage of acknowledging the rape of African American women, whom he has already constructed as essentially unrapeable, is quickly covered up. Having briefly entered the frame, rape is promptly brushed aside. Placed at the center is the chastity of the statute book. Cobb's legal treatise constructs personhood and subjectivity not in the slaves but in the law and the text of the law. The slippage also reveals the contradiction of constructing slaves without subjectivity but with dangerous sexuality: black women are not subjects, under this configuration, yet they can be dangerous agents against white men.

Case law erased the rape of slaves not only by white men but also by fellow slaves. The lawyer in *George v. State* argued, successfully, that the rape of a slave was essentially not rape: "The crime of rape does not exist in this State between African slaves. Our laws recognize no marital rights as between slaves. . . . The regulations of law, as to the white race, on the subject of sexual intercourse, do not and cannot, for obvious reasons, apply to slaves; their intercourse is promiscuous, and the violation of a female slave by a male slave would be a mere assault and battery" (317). The female slave in this 1859 Mississippi case was under the age of ten. The "intercourse" of slaves is deemed always already promiscuous (even in small children). The lawyer makes intercourse the subject, rather than the child, who is displaced and who is unrapeable. The reasoning is labeled "obvious," suggesting universal agreement about these constructions of race and sex.

Like the self-fulfilling prophecy about slave illiteracy, here the law refuses to recognize slaves' marital rights and then finds slave intercourse (which is legally barred from occurring in the context of state-sanctioned marriage) inherently "promiscuous." The judge (William Harris of the Ohio-as-bad-daughter ruling from the previous chapter) relies on prior U.S. cases, ancient Roman law, and multiple references to Cobb's treatise to decide against recognizing the crime of rape of a slave. Ancient law emphasizes the condition of servitude, while here the focus is on "African" slaves, adding the crucial ingredient of race. Exceptions to such precedent Harris dismisses as "founded mainly upon the unmeaning twaddle, in which some humane judges and law writers have indulged, as to the influence of the 'natural law,' 'civilization and Christian enlightenment.' . . . From a careful examination of our legislation on this subject, we are satisfied that there is no act which embraces either the attempted or actual commission of a rape by a slave on a female slave" (320). The power of legal precedent makes it easy to erase the specifics of the case. The unevenness of precedent is itself erased by dismissing exceptions as "unmeaning twaddle" and "humane . . . indulge[nce]." While using sexualized terminology (indulged, satisfied, embraces), Harris keeps his focus on "our legislation," again placing the statute book at the center and displacing any actual discourse about the circumstances of the case. Humanity and agency are in the "act" of "legislation" and not in the slave.

In an 1852 Georgia rape case in which the female was white, the result was very different. Whereas the slave is constructed as inherently promiscuous—even as a child—the white female is constructed as inherently virtuous. The Mississippi court relied upon "examination of our legislation," but the Georgia court relied upon first-person visceral reaction. In *Stephen v. State* Judge Lumpkin declares he will try to be dispassionate, even though "the crime, from the very nature of it, is calculated to excite indignation in every heart; and when perpetrated on a free white female of immature mind and body, that indignation becomes greater, and is more difficult to repress" (230).[2] As he moves through evidence and legal precedents, he concludes in increasingly first-person terms: "I would, were I in the Jury-Box, seize upon the slightest proof of resistance . . . even the usual struggles of a modest maiden, young and inexperienced in such mysteries, to find . . . that the act was against her will, and that the presumption of law was so strong, as to amount to proof of force" (239). The indignation arises not from rape, but from the idea of rape against "free white" females. Lumpkin's emotional language—"excite," "heart," "seize"—combined with the romanticized image of white seduction—"struggles of a modest maiden . . . inexperienced in such mysteries"—suggest not sensitivity to the vulnerability of women to male power but rather outrage at black male access to a white maiden. No such indignation appeared in the Mississippi case where the young girl was African American.[3]

White antislavery writers exposed the evils of slave law, although they also relied on familiar constructions of race and gender. They often invoke the image of the slave woman as the "ultimate victim," as Frances Foster describes the pattern. Further, when they do discuss rape, it is often in the context of proving the emasculation of African American men under slavery, erasing the woman. Stroud, for example, uses the generic male subject, even when the topic is rape, so the focus is on the slave husband. He quotes the Maryland attorney general: "A slave has never maintained an action against the violator of his bed" (41). The violation is against the slave husband (or his bed), not the woman.[4]

Antislavery writers may place the blame for sexual transgressions on the institution of slavery, but they retain a concern with slave "licentiousness." William Goodell's *The American Slave Code* cites the Presbyterian Synod of Kentucky, which states that the system of slavery "produces general licentiousness among the slaves. . . . Their present quasi marriages are continually thus voided. They are, in this way, brought to consider their matrimonial alliances as a thing not binding, and they act accordingly. We are then assured by the most unquestionable testimony that licentiousness is the necessary result of our system. . . . Chastity is no virtue among them" (110–11). For slaveholder Cobb, slaves (particularly women) produced "lewdness" in slavery. For abolitionist Goodell, slavery produced licentiousness among slaves. Both constructions rely upon an image of unchaste slaves.

"Do Not Judge": Reframing Legal Fictions of Womanhood

By juxtaposing such legal fictions with the experiences of Linda Brent and other slave women, Jacobs reframes legal constructions of black womanhood.[5] Whereas Cobb worries about the "honor" of statutes, Jacobs constructs the law itself as dishonorable. Throughout the narrative, she plays with the definitions of crime and virtue to expose legal ironies. While the law constructs white women as chaste, it obliges slave women to obey their masters at any cost. The narrator describes the struggle of a slave to preserve her "pride of character." Since she is a slave, "it is deemed a crime in her to wish to be virtuous" (31). Living in such a situation is worse than being a criminal: "The felon's home in a penitentiary is preferable" (31). Jacobs's chapter "Still in Prison" uses similar imagery to address the irony of Brent's freedom (from harassment and rape) as a prisoner in her grandmother's garret. She could wish her pursuer and owner, Dr. Flint, no worse punishment, "yet the laws allowed *him* to be out in the free air, while I, guiltless of crime, was pent up here, as the only means of avoiding the cruelties the laws allowed him to inflict upon me!" (121).

The law endorses cruelties against slave women and outlaws opposition to those cruelties. Brent's every action against Flint's rape attempts thus can be deemed criminal by Flint. After her child is born, Brent describes one of Flint's outbursts in legal terminology: "Then he launched out upon his usual themes,—my crimes against him, and my ingratitude for his forbearance. The laws were laid down to me anew, and I was dismissed" (61). These laws are metaphoric, but the literal law is clearly on Flint's side as well. The larger irony is that it is Jacobs ultimately who lays down the law anew by deconstructing legal fictions in the course of her narrative, which has long outlived Flint and his real-life counterparts.

Jacobs counters the dominant construction of the "want of chastity" in slave women and specifically revises the premise of white women's inherent virtue versus black women's inherent corruption. She reframes virtue as a legal construction, as opposed to racialized, naturalized fact. Viewed in the social context of nineteenth-century ideologies of womanhood and the literary context of women's domestic fiction, Jacobs radically subverts convention as she calls for revised standards that account for the experiences of black women. She admits breaking certain rules of womanhood and declares those rules ought not apply to slave women; she invokes bonds between black and white women and points out the legal differences. She critiques absolute and unvarying standards, and her style of shifting perspectives—as well as calling attention to whose perspective is authorized—helps to convey that critique.

Jacobs breaks down the divisions between women partly through her direct appeals to a constructed audience, designed to evoke "womanly" sympathy and to call for political action. "I do earnestly desire to arouse the women of the North," Jacobs announces, "to a realizing sense of the condition of two millions of women at the South, still in bondage, suffering what I suffered, and most of them far worse" (1). She both claims unity and emphasizes difference in these appeals. The audience she invokes is the stereotypical construct of the virtuous (white) woman, morally bound to feel sympathy for her suffering sisters. Whether readers live up to this fiction is secondary to playing the constructions off each other. According to Jacobs, access to "virtue" varies with legal status. White women have the protection of the law, whereas laws—and the men who make them— conspire against slave women. Black women might be as virtuous, but they face laws that prevent their exercise of virtue. White women might not be so virtuous, but they have laws protecting their virtue and their homes (constructed as repositories of white female virtue). In both cases, but for the law, virtue might be otherwise.

Emotional appeals of identification to her white sisters are sometimes followed by stark declarations of how the narrator's situation is different. She seeks sympathy from "O virtuous reader" and simultaneously declares, "You never knew what it is to be a slave." Her poetic appeal is immediately followed by the calm conclusion: "Still, in looking back, calmly, on the events of my life, I feel that the slave woman ought not to be judged by the same standard as others" (56). Jacobs uses techniques of sentimental fiction while undercutting that genre's expectations. Her sentimental appeals can become indictments. She moves between personal statements ("my life") and more generalized declarations ("a slave," "the slave girl") to make her argument both personal and political.

The bond she seeks goes beyond personal sympathy (though that is the avenue) and becomes political union as well. On the verge of confessing her sexual transgression, for example, the narrator interrupts herself, mixing legal and sentimental language: "But, O, ye happy women, whose purity has been sheltered from childhood, who have been free to choose the objects of your affection, whose homes are protected by law, do not judge the poor desolate slave girl too severely! If slavery had been abolished, I, also, could have married the man of my choice; I could have had a home shielded by laws; and I should have been spared the painful task of confessing what I am now about to relate" (54). Under different laws, she "could" have chosen differently. The "also," set off by commas and slowing the sentence, reveals that legal status and conditions of slavery separate narrator and reader. If white women possess virtue and domesticity, characteristics of "true womanhood," it is because laws create and protect those elements: their "purity" is not inherent but "has been sheltered," their "homes" are not automatically intact but "are protected by law." If allowed a "home shielded by law," the narrator would not need to be "confessing" in the first place. Jacobs uses a legal model for her appeal and subverts it. The language of confession, judgment, and pardon suggests the narrator might be casting herself as supplicant or criminal and the white women as judge.[6] While offering to confess, however, Jacobs's narrator simultaneously commands that her audience "not judge"—she sets them up as judge and undercuts their authority to render judgment.

Jacobs defers the promised confession in order to foreground her political argument before giving up these personal details. She unconventionally uses the convention of audience appeal to make sure her readers appropriately interpret the supposed transgression. The narrator still has not quite confessed when she again asks for pity and pardon, but Jacobs uses an imperative here and turns quickly to accusation: "Pity me, and pardon me, O virtuous reader! You never knew what it is to be a slave; to be entirely unprotected by law or custom; to have the laws reduce you to the condition of a chattel" (55). Laws protect the white woman and "reduce" the slave woman (who is subject to the absence of protective law and the presence of dehumanizing laws). She offers detailed specifics about what "you" (virtuous reader) "never" did ("you never exhausted your ingenuity in avoiding the snares . . . of a hated tyrant; you never shuddered at the sound of his footsteps") without quite stating what she did. Making the subject of these sentences the white reader who has not experienced those things emphasizes the differences between ignorant reader and knowing (but not quite telling) narrator.

Jacobs's focus is the experiences of slave women, but sympathetic white women also appear, and not only as readers. She tells of one "angel"-like mistress, who comes to a tragic end along with her slaves. The tale is a caution to sympathetic readers who might hope for resolution in kind individuals rather than systemic change. Jacobs narrates this episode without direct audience appeal, but its cautionary nature makes it another petition for political union because personal virtue or sympathetic individuals are not enough in the face of an evil system—and systems of slavery and patriarchy unite for this bad ending. One example of this individual's kindness is emancipating a slave the night before her wedding to a free man, "in order that her marriage might have the sanction of *law*," emphasizing the relationship's legal standing (50). While the law's sanction of marriage is a benefit to the emancipated young woman, the law's construction of marriage causes the white woman's downfall—and the consequent downfall of her unemancipated slaves. Jacobs uses the example of this white woman to illustrate intersections between race and gender hierarchy in the context of family law. Before the mistress's own marriage, "she offered to manumit her slaves—telling them that her marriage might make unexpected changes in their destiny" (50). She is aware of the legal and social implications of her marriage, but they refuse her offer. The new husband/master then claims "his property," and the free black father confronts the wife/mistress about the loss of his family. The power of the white husband in marriage, however, has superseded the power of the mistress: "I no longer have the power I had a week ago," explains the new wife (50). The ideal of womanhood is itself destroyed, as the new husband rapes the slave daughters—"she knew that her own husband had violated the purity she had so carefully inculcated" (51).

This woman is unnamed—she is first "the young lady" and then "this good mistress" (50)—but at this moment she becomes "the slaveholder's wife" (51), reflecting the two institutions that prove more powerful than her piety. The white woman who starts as a potent ally becomes a helpless victim of slavery, thanks to the laws of slavery and of marriage. Jacobs repeatedly reminds us that reliance on kind owners is no refuge from the institution.[7] They die, marry, forget promises, or otherwise fail to be effective protectors. The appeal to political action is implicit here and operates partly through invoking a limited similarity of oppression: The slave daughters and "the pious mistress" are joined in being victimized by the same man. As master or husband, he has the power to destroy their lives.

"The Condition of the Mother": Legal Framings of Family

Jacobs depicts white families as less than ideal. In describing slave families, she and other slave narrators often demonstrate a paradox: slavery hinders family, but slave families endure nonetheless. Slavery advocates, on the other hand, construct the opposite contradiction: families do not matter to slaves, but slave families are preserved. In addition, the slave-owning family is constructed as a protective surrogate family for slaves. The structure of slave law that erased families developed at the same time as family law governing white households. Nineteenth-century law was beginning to address with specificity regulations around marriage, divorce, spousal roles, and other details of white family life. Slave families, however, were outside this structure. Legal scholar Margaret Burnham writes, "In the eyes of the law, each slave stood as an individual unit of property, and never as a submerged partner in a marriage or family. The most universal life events—marriage, procreation, childrearing—were manipulated to meet the demands of the commercial enterprise" (189). Examining the legal rhetoric around family and reproduction reveals the workings of the contradictions between "white" law and slave law and between legal fictions and social relations.

Slave law held that children inherited the status of the mother—so even a white president could have children born into "negro" slavery.[8] Cobb discusses the legal principle that the "child follows the condition of mother," treating this law as one of particular historical weight: "The issue and descendants of slaves, in the maternal line, are slaves. The rule, *partus sequitur ventrem*, has been adopted in all the states" (68). In a rare translation, Cobb explains the ancient justification: "From principles of justice, the offspring, the increase of the womb, belongs to the master of the womb" (69). He includes a lengthy footnote attacking Stroud's critique of this law. "I have referred to these remarks," states Cobb, claiming to stay above the fray, "more to show the spirit in which this sketch is written, than seriously to argue the question" (68). He then proceeds for a half-page to argue the question.

In Cobb's argument, the presumption of color combines with the focus on the maternal line: "As all the negroes introduced into America were brought as slaves, the black color of the race raises the presumption of slavery, contrary to the principles of the common law, which would presume freedom until the contrary is shown. This presumption is extended, in most of the States, to mulattoes or persons of mixed blood, casting upon them the onus of proving a free *maternal* ancestor. In others, it is confined to the negroes" (67). Common law is set aside because of the specifics of African introduction into America (as told by Cobb: in reality, not all Africans in America came as slaves). Proving free male ancestors does not help prove one's right to freedom. Again, it is mothers who pass slavery on to their children.

Like Cobb, Stroud is concerned with definitions of race. While Cobb defines blackness broadly, so anyone enslaved is "negro," Stroud is disturbed that individuals who appear white are enslaved.[9] Discussing the maternal inheritance of slavery, Stroud includes a two-page footnote on the anxiety that "under this law it may frequently happen that a person whose complexion is European may be *legally* retained as a slave" (3). He cites examples of a seemingly white person enslaved, including that of a slave who gave birth to triplets, one black and two white. He discusses the case for a full paragraph, concluding: "For here are two *white* children who have been already in slavery more than ten years, and in all probability they will remain so during life" (4). The word "white" is italicized to emphasize that it is precisely the whiteness of the enslaved that is the source of the horror here. The problem is defined as enslavement of visibly white children, and the equally enslaved black child disappears. Stroud's point is to expose the absurdity and arbitrariness of slave law, but he persuades by shocking his audience with images of the enslavement of whites.[10]

Goodell also discusses the child following the mother's condition, citing Stroud. He quotes the same Latin phrase cited by Cobb, translating it as "the condition of the slave *mother* is for ever entailed on all her remotest posterity" (27). He does not italicize the Latin words, but he does place "mother" in italics to emphasize the unnaturalness of linking posterity to maternity. Cobb's translation focuses on "principles of justice" and "the womb," foregrounding the law and erasing the woman as a subject. Goodell, on the other hand, emphasizes the role of the mother. Goodell quotes Stroud's elaboration of the law: "The genuine and degrading principle of slavery, inasmuch as it places the slave upon a level with *brute* animals, prevails universally in the slaveholding States" (27). Literary critic Hortense Spillers analyzes what Goodell might mean by "condition" of the mother:

> Is it the "condition" of enslavement the writer means, or does he mean the "mark" and the "knowledge" of the *mother* upon the child that here translates into the culturally forbidden and impure? In an elision of terms, "mother" and "enslavement" are indistinct categories of the illegitimate inasmuch as each of these synonymous elements defines, in effect, a cultural situation that is *father-lacking*. Goodell, who does not only report this maxim of law as an aspect of his own factuality, but also regards it, as does Douglass, as a fundamental degradation, supposes descent and identity through the female line as comparable to a brute animality. (80)

Abolitionist legal critiques rest partly on assumptions of patriarchy. Part of the animality of slave law is the link it forces between child and mother, displacing the Western patriarchal story, what Spillers calls "the *vertical* transfer of a bloodline, of a patronymic, of titles and entitlements, of real estate and the prerogatives of 'cold cash,' from *fathers* to *sons* and in the supposedly free exchange of affectional ties between a male and a female of *his* choice" (74). Antislavery writers critique this law, but from a perspective that draws upon patriarchy and animalizes slave mothers.

The relationship between husband and wife is key to (white) family law, but under slave law that relationship has no legal existence. Cobb acknowledges that Southern law does not recognize slave marriage but claims the legal omission is of little consequence:

> The contract of marriage not being recognized among slaves, of course none of its consequences follow from the contubernial state existing between them. Their issue, though emancipated, have no inheritable blood. In trials, they may be witnesses for and against each other. Yet as the fact of cohabiting, and living together as man and wife, is universal among slaves, and the privileges of parents over children, in correcting and controlling them, are universally acceded to them, in all trials of slaves for offences committed by them, these relations are recognized by the Courts, and the merciful extenuations of the law, to the conduct of the husband and father, are extended to the slave standing in the same condition. (245)

While slaves are prohibited from testifying against whites, they can be forced to testify against a spouse, a relation protected for whites in the legal system. Cobb claims that the "universal" respect for slave families leads to courts recognizing family rights not actually included in the law. He specifies only by referencing the conduct of "husband and father," constructing the slave defendant as male, and he provides no cases to support his claim.

Cobb addresses the separation of families as an unfortunate legal possibility that, like rape, never happens. His language becomes increasingly absolute as he constructs the fiction of slave families preserved by the good will of good masters: "That the marriage relation between slaves is not recognized or protected by the law, is another evil. . . . In practice, public opinion protects the relation. The unfeeling separation of husband and wife, is a rare occurrence. It never happens when both belong to the same master" (ccxxi). He later names it the "unnecessary" separation of families, allowing of course for *necessary* separations, and says that the former "rarely if ever" occurs. His main concern is that the law not fasten a vicious husband on the owner of the wife.

> How far this contubernial relation between slaves may be recognized and protected by law, is a question of exceeding nicety and difficulty. The unnecessary and wanton separation of persons standing in the relation of husband and wife, though it may rarely, if ever, occur in actual practice, is an event which, if possible, should be guarded against by the law. And yet, on the other hand, to fasten upon a master of a female slave, a vicious,

corrupting negro, sowing discord, and dissatisfaction among all his slaves;
or else a thief, or a cut-throat, and to provide no relief against such a nui-
sance, would be to make the holding of slaves a curse to the master. (245–46)

The subject is the owner, who is protected from being helpless before the
marital rights of slaves, lest slaveholding become a "curse." Cobb allows
that some limited protection might make sense, but "how much farther
the lawgiver may go, requires for its solution all the deliberation and wisdom of the Senator, guided and enlightened by Christian philanthropy"
(246). The important actor is "the Senator," whose Christian charity
decides the fate of slave families.

As forcefully as he denies the separation of spouses, Cobb also denies the
separation of child from parent: "The young child is seldom removed from
the parent's protection, and beyond doubt, the institution prevents the
separation of families, to an extent unknown among the laboring poor of
the world" (ccxvii). The institution is humane *and* superior to systems of
white labor. The footnote supports this vast declaration by giving one personal example: "On my father's plantation, an aged negro woman could
call together more than one hundred of her lineal descendants. I saw this
old negro dance at the wedding of her great granddaughter" (ccxviii). Here
as elsewhere, Cobb constructs slaves as content and even dancing. Exact
numbers of family separations are impossible to ascertain, since slave families had no legal standing and official records did not mark their existence
directly. Slave narratives are rife with examples, such as Douglass's descriptions of his separation from his mother. Herbert Gutman generates some
numerical data in his studies of the family under slavery. For example,
records in Mississippi and Louisiana during and after the Civil War show
that more than 20 percent of partners in slave marriages registered by the
army and Freedman's Bureau had previously been married elsewhere.
Those previous unions were dissolved by slave sales or moving (126–30).

In addition to the fate of black families, Cobb addresses the incorpo-
ration of slaves into white families. He offers this summary: "Southern
slavery is a patriarchal, social system. The master is the head of his family.
Next to wife and children, he cares for his slaves. He avenges their injuries,
protects their persons, provides for their wants, and guides their labors. In
return, he is revered and held as protector and master" (ccxviii). The unstated subject of this last passive sentence is wife, children, and slaves—all
subordinates in the white man's family. Cobb presents as fact a romanticized
domestic vision of the protection offered by slavery: "As a social relation,

negro slavery has its benefits and its evils. That the slave is incorporated into and becomes a part of the family, that a tie is thus formed between the master and slave, almost unknown to the relation of master and hireling, that in consequence even the young spendthrift experiences a pang in sundering a relation he has recognized from his infancy, that the old and infirm are thus cared for, and the young protected and reared, are indisputable facts" (ccxvii–viii). In this story, which relies upon the Mammy construct, slave families are unharmed, their inclusion in white families protects them, and white offspring grow up to love the black women who raise them.

At the same time, according to Cobb, an evil resulting from the interracial closeness of slavery harms white children: "The imbibing by children of the superstitions, fears, and habits, of the negroes, with whom they are necessarily, to some extent, reared. The negro is not yet more than semi-civilized" (ccxx). White children are "necessarily" raised with and by slaves. Citing the complications of familial situations in the South, however, also has the effect of humanizing the slaves to some degree. The white children are doing the "imbibing," but the blacks are marked with power and influence in Cobb's nervous statement. The comment suggests the ways that black culture did affect white culture, and it indicates the way that such influences were rewritten.

"A Hearthstone of My Own": Reframing Familial Fictions

Jacobs demonstrates that, despite their legal erasure, slave families survived, though often in altered forms. Her redefinition of family is linked to a redefinition of womanhood and reformulation of domestic fiction. She subverts the marriage plot, the expectation that the story will end with male/female domestic union. Family is privileged, but husband is not; motherhood is valued, but marriage is omitted. While the last chapter of *Jane Eyre* opens with "Reader, I married him," Jacobs offers no such hope of domestic closure. "Reader," opens her penultimate paragraph, "my story ends with freedom; not in the usual way, with marriage" (201).[11] She dethrones marriage as the goal, replacing it with legal and physical freedom and family outside of marriage, and she questions the compromised nature of this freedom.

The final chapter's climax is not a marriage contract but a bill of sale.[12] The legal record of Brent's freedom yields not personal triumph but political outrage: "'The bill of sale!' Those words struck me like a blow. So I

was *sold* at last! A human being *sold* in the free city of New York! The bill
of sale is on record, and future generations will learn from it that women
were articles of traffic in New York, late in the nineteenth century of the
Christian religion" (200, original emphasis). In the chapter called "Free at
Last," she is instead "*sold* at last!" Jacobs locates the geographic, religious,
and temporal moment of this outrage to direct possibilities for political
action. Instead of celebrating the personal resolution, she forces her readers to redirect anger at the still-existing political situation. Fellow women,
human beings, and Christians should rise up, for the sake of individuals
and for the historical record. The narrator finally is free from slaveholders,
which, surprisingly, "is not saying a great deal." She is "as free" from their
power "as are the white people of the north," who, under the Fugitive
Slave Act, are still implicated in slavery (and who are likely her primary
audience). Brent still lives with racism and class division. She still lives in
a position of servitude, even if constructed as grateful service to the
woman who purchased her. Laws of slavery no longer directly bind her,
but God as well as "love, duty, gratitude, also bind me to her side" (201).
These are not the bonds of slavery, nor are they bonds of matrimony: here
is a happy ending not quite in terms of domestic union and not quite
happy. Hers is a lesser version of slavery (she is bound because paid for)
and an altered version of marriage (she is bound by love, duty, and a bill
of sale). Because of this economic status, the final image of her life is one
of domesticity denied: "I do not sit with my children in a home of my
own. I still long for a hearthstone of my own, however humble. I wish it
for my children's sake far more than for my own" (201). Domestic motherhood more than marriage is the goal, and that goal is both achieved and
frustrated.

Marriage is mentioned—and dismissed—early in the book, and its
denial is the result of legal, not romantic, factors. In the chapter "The
Lover," Jacobs assures us that Brent loved a man with "all the ardor of a
young girl's first love," though the chapter never names him or details their
interactions. We do, however, learn the details of the laws of slave marriage and family. Brent halts the story of her romance with a freeborn
carpenter with a reminder of her legal status: "But when I reflected that I
was a slave, and that the laws gave no sanction to the marriage of such, my
heart sank within me" (37). North Carolina law did not outlaw such marriage but gave it no protection. Possibilities of love are thus constrained by
legal formulations. If she did marry, Brent would remain in her owner's
complete control, "for the husband of a slave has no power to protect her"

(38). The hierarchy of husband-over-wife is a legal construct and means nothing in the slave context. She does not dismantle that hierarchy here; she bemoans its absence.

Since marriage under Flint's ownership is not an option, she quickly considers and rejects the other option: "My lover wanted to buy me, but I knew that Dr. Flint was too willful and arbitrary a man to consent to that arrangement" (37). While she opens the chapter with the sentimental language of "the tendrils of the heart" (37), she ends with stark delineations of her lack of options. Brent finally rejects any hope of marrying this man for legal reasons. "There was no hope that the doctor would consent to sell me on any terms," she states, and she further reasons that even if her lover "could have obtained permission to marry me while I was a slave, the marriage would give him no power to protect me from my master. It would have made him miserable to witness the insults I should have been subjected to. And then, if we had children, I knew they must 'follow the condition of the mother'" (42). Legal and economic realities outweigh any other concerns. She quotes directly the law that guarantees slaveowners the children produced by slave women, whether through marriage to free men, marriage to fellow slaves, forced "breeding," or rape.

Jacobs exposes in no uncertain terms the motivation of such a regulation when Brent later does have children. Even though the father is white, Brent cannot ignore Flint's threat to sell her child: "I knew the law gave him power to fulfill it; for slaveholders have been cunning enough to enact that 'the child shall follow the condition of the *mother*,' not of the *father*; thus taking care that licentiousness shall not interfere with avarice" (76). Jacobs's succinct analysis names the law for what it is, a cynical intersection of gender, sex, race, and economics. Her reframing exposes the legal fiction. Cold legalistic language is followed by her decoding the real motivation: the desires of licentious and avaricious men. This appearance of the law precedes the birth of her daughter, and Brent expresses particular sorrow at that circumstance: "When they told me my new-born babe was a girl, my heart was heavier than it had ever been before. Slavery is terrible for men; but it is far more terrible for women" (77). Her daughter will face the same gender oppression she herself faced under slavery. The notion of a child following the mother's condition has a particular resonance for daughters: like their mothers, they can be raped. Jacobs quotes the law yet again, in the "Fugitive Slave Law" chapter, pointing out the complications of this irrational federal act, newly passed and intersecting with existing irrational laws, for residents of a so-called free state. In a list of cruel results of this new federal law, she cites as the worst example that "many a husband discovered that his wife had fled from slavery years ago, and as 'the child follows the condition of its mother,' the children of his love were liable to be seized and carried into slavery" (191). She both emphasizes the power of family and exposes the obstacles to family. She articulates the contradictory fact that the law for slaves stands in the way of family and that some version of family—a version that whites might recognize—*does* powerfully endure.

Slave women are denied the legal status of mothers and at the same time are central figures as mothers in Jacobs's text. Jacobs depicts multiple representations to show both that slavery threatens the exercise of motherhood and that motherhood endures. While Brent's struggle for successful motherhood is central, Jacobs offers other examples of motherhood denied. She juxtaposes denials of black motherhood with images of protected white motherhood to demonstrate the legally imposed differences and to suggest a chance for unity. Brent's childless Aunt Nancy has a chapter to herself, presenting a tragic example of obstacles to womanhood. The chapter opens with her questionable marital status: "This aunt had been married at twenty years of age; that is, as far as slaves *can* marry. She had the consent of her master and mistress, and a clergyman performed the ceremony. But it was a mere form, without any legal value. Her master or mistress could annul it any day they pleased" (143). The simple statement of marriage is followed by numerous qualifications. The owners do not annul the marriage, but practices of slavery have the same effect. Their home—"the use of a small room in an outhouse"—is immediately disrupted: "On the wedding evening, the bride was ordered to her old post on the entry floor."

Nancy's maternal status is equally disrupted. When Nancy married, Mrs. Flint was childless, but the mistress's maternal status clearly is the priority: "She was expecting to be a mother, and if she should want a drink of water in the night, what could she do without her slave to bring it? So my aunt was compelled to lie at her door, until one midnight she was forced to leave, to give premature birth to a child. In a fortnight she was required to resume her place on the entry floor, because Mrs. Flint's babe needed her attentions. She kept her station there through summer and winter, until she had given premature birth to six children; and all the while she was employed as night-nurse to Mrs. Flint's children" (143). White motherhood flourishes, at the expense of black motherhood. Eventually, "Dr. Flint declared it was impossible she could ever become the mother of a living child" (143). Nancy's own premature infants die even as she feeds the healthy Flint children.

Jacobs offers other examples of African American motherhood deferred or interrupted. When the narrator explains that her mother's mistress and her mother were "foster sisters" (both nursed by the grandmother), she adds: "In fact, my mother had been weaned at three months old, that the babe of the mistress might obtain sufficient food" (7). The role of "mammy" outweighs the role of mother. Such examples are meant to evoke sympathy and action from Jacobs's readers and serve to expose the fiction of the white family unit as a protective surrogate family to the slave. While Cobb offers that fiction as fact ("That the slave . . . becomes a part of the family, that a tie is thus formed between the master and slave . . . are indisputable facts"), case studies such as Nancy's directly dispute his claims.

In addition to black motherhood denied, Jacobs also describes surrogate figures who are strong symbolic mothers but who significantly are not the literal mother of the person they nurture. There is no legal motherhood under slavery (except to the extent that maternal status determines the child's fate; there are no positive rights of motherhood), so literal maternity is not all-important. The grandmother and other women frequently fulfill mothering roles to Brent and others who are not their literal children. When Brent's mother dies, the grandmother tries to take her place: "She promised to be a mother to her grandchildren, so far as she might be permitted to do so" (10). Assertions of surrogate motherhood are generally tempered by legal and practical limitations. The grandmother is permitted some obligations of motherhood—she helps provide food and clothing for her surrogate children—but she has no legal rights over them. Nancy, whose literal motherhood is destroyed by slavery, can serve as a symbolic mother: "She was my mother's twin sister, and, as far as was in her power, she supplied a mother's place to us orphans" (144). This statement is one of the seeming errors cited by Yellin in her footnotes, as discussed earlier. The factual readjustment may be useful, but the editorial reframing also diminishes the rhetorical impact of Jacobs's statement. Since literal motherhood is being put aside, other literal identities may also be questioned here. Linking Nancy so closely to the absent mother may have metaphoric rather than biologic meaning here. She can supply "a mother's place," despite the destruction of her biological maternity, within the limits of "her power." The destructiveness of slavery and the strength of black motherhood are jointly emphasized through these non-literal examples.

While motherhood is a central issue for women here, men as fathers are fairly absent (especially if black) or malicious (if white). Slave fathers have no legal status, and the status of white fathers is as owner not parent. Of Dr. Flint, the narrator states, "I had seen several women sold, with his babies at the breast. He never allowed his offspring by slaves to remain long in sight of himself and his wife" (55). His legal position—owner of mother and children both—is far more relevant than his biological relationship. The image evokes the master-mistress-slave-child matrix that again exposes the lie of the white family welcoming slaves into its fold. Another mother of Flint's children is depicted as being punished precisely because she revealed his parental status: "When the mother was delivered into the trader's hands, she said, 'You *promised* to treat me well.' To which he replied, 'You have let your tongue run too far; damn you!' She had forgotten that it was a crime for a slave to tell who was the father of her child" (13). Legal positions supersede parental relations: more important than father and mother, he is owner, and she is constructed as criminal. The real criminal is Flint, but not in the eyes of the law.

Sands, less culpable than Flint, still is implicated in slavery and finally is referred to by his legal, not familial, position. He is named as Brent's friend (never lover—that term is reserved for the black man she loves), then as the father of her children, and finally as slaveholder and master of her children. When she does refer to his biological relationship to them, she usually indicates her skepticism, sometimes through quotation marks. At the celebration following the purchase of the children, the narrator describes Sands with careful and distancing language: "The father was present for a while; and though such a 'parental relation' as existed between him and my children takes slight hold of the hearts or consciences of slaveholders, it must be that he experienced some moments of pure joy in witnessing the happiness he had imparted" (107). He is "the" father, not "their" father, and a "slaveholder"; his "relation" is technical and legal more than emotional or familial. After Sands marries, Brent refers to her own children as "Mr. Sands's slaves" and analyzes the relationship: "I knew too well how lightly slaveholders held such 'parental relations.' If pecuniary troubles should come, or if the new wife required more money than could conveniently be spared, my children might be thought of as a convenient means of raising funds" (137–38). The legal and economic relationships dominate. Gender, race, and law intersect to determine the configuration. Because Brent is black and a slave, and because Sands's legal relationship is slaveholder, there is no option of a "family" relationship from the outset.

Jacobs compares Sands and Flint to undercut the attempt simply to contrast good and bad masters, who, under the law, have complete power. After Brent's children are purchased, Sands (who is as shifting and unstable as his name) claims he "never intended to claim them as slaves," and Flint (who is as hard and inflexible as his name) says "the contract [of sale] is not legally binding" (138). Both men are playing with words and with the law. "So, then," concludes the narrator, "after all I had endured for their sakes, my poor children were between two fires; between my old master and their new master! And I was powerless. There was no protecting arm of the law for me to invoke" (138). She points out their legal positions and their ability to play games with the law. Flint hides behind the age of her legal owner (she belongs to his daughter, who technically cannot agree to the children's sale) and Sands claims her children were always free (though he has not freed them yet and sends them where he wants), leaving Brent legally powerless. As their mother and a slave, she has infinitely less legal power over their fates than does their legal owner (whether father or not). What Sands constructs as a paternal action—sending his daughter to the North to be educated—the narrator recasts as the equivalent of a slave auction.

Another significant parental issue (in pragmatic and symbolic terms) is that of naming, which has legal, familial, and other rhetorical implications. Jacobs's fictitious names, such as Sands and Flint, are carefully chosen, and she also pays attention to the politics of naming in other ways. Unlike the unnamed "lover," Mr. Sands has a name but never a familiar name or term of affection—only a title and last name. Eventually he loses even that name and is referred to by his legal relationship to Brent's children: "my children's owner." When the narrator's children are first born, naming them is a social and legal issue: "Always it gave me a pang that my children had no lawful claim to a name" (78). Instead of providing them with a legally meaningful paternal name, she gives her children her own last name, which derives from her own father's nonlegal name.[13] "When my baby was about to be christened, the former mistress of my father stepped up to me, and proposed to give it her Christian name. To this I added the surname of my father, who had himself no legal right to it; for my grandfather on the paternal side was a white gentleman. What tangled skeins are the genealogies of slavery! I loved my father; but it mortified me to be obliged to bestow his name on my children" (78). Naming her child raises issues of that child's parentage and of slave "genealogies" more generally. These threads must trace natural as well as legal descent, since those lines are not always identical for slave families. Part of Brent's shame is having to give her own last name to her children, instead of that of a husband. The narrator echoes these concerns at the birth of her second child: "It was a sad thought that I had no name to give my child. His father . . . was not unwilling that he should bear his name; but he had no legal claim to it; and if I had bestowed it upon him, my master would have regarded it as a new crime, a new piece of insolence" (62). The legal owner has more power than even the white father. Instead of naming a child being a legal right, such an act becomes a "crime."

Jacobs simultaneously encourages white readers to identify with slave mothers and challenges them with their ignorance about slave women's experiences. "O reader, can you imagine my joy?" the narrator asks in a fairly conventional aside, upon her reunion with her son. The response comes not from a sympathetic reader weeping over the page, however, but from Brent reminding the reader of their differences: "No, you cannot, unless you have been a slave mother" (173). Jacobs moves between identification and distinction: "She may be an ignorant creature, degraded by the system that has brutalized her from childhood," she says, emphasizing what might seem the most distancing characteristics of the bond-woman, "but she has a mother's instincts, and is capable of feeling a mother's agonies," she concludes, invoking more essential notions of motherhood (16). Slave women have "a mother's instincts," but they also face legal and material obstacles that no white woman can imagine.

Brent makes choices with which no free white woman easily can identify. The narrator tells us her choices are for her children's sake, and she arouses her audience by asserting the absolute and invariable nature of motherhood even as she points out that her white Northern readers cannot fathom what it means to be a slave mother. She wants to reclaim motherhood for black women, but she wants to redefine it first. It may be absent a traditional family structure and absent a father. It may be absent a home or even the ability to live in the same place. Jacobs focuses on those absences, but she also reveals what is present. Motherhood within slavery is not permitted a legal definition or frame. Jacobs's goal is to put slave motherhood in the frame in the first place, to make it visible.

To begin to place it in the frame, Jacobs constructs motherhood as central to Brent. The relationship with Sands is described as being for the sake of Brent's as-yet-unconceived offspring. That decision is linked to legal issues. She is concerned that the children, who will be the legal property of her owner, not also be the offspring of that owner and thus even more vulnerable. "I shuddered to think of being the mother of children that should be owned by my old tyrant. I knew that as soon as a new fancy took him, his victims were sold far off to get rid of them; especially if they had children" (55). Other legal or economic possibilities might be available if the father is not the owner: "Of a man who was not my master I could ask to have my children well supported; and in this case, I felt confident I should obtain the boon" (55). Other turning points, such as her decision to escape, also are described as the result of prioritizing her children's welfare: "I could have made my escape alone, but it was more for my helpless children than for myself that I longed for freedom" (89). "Nobody respects a mother who forsakes her children," admonishes the grandmother (95). Brent decides to leave the Flints, the narrator states, when she sees that her children are to be endangered: "But now that I was certain my children were to be put in their power, in order to give them a stronger hold on me, I resolved to leave them that night. . . . Nothing less than the freedom of my children would have induced me to disregard [my grandmother's] advice" (95). Jacobs presents her first-person narrator as an agent, but she also links those moments of activism to acceptable female-coded goals such as motherhood. Actions taken by Brent that seem contrary to ideals of white womanhood—initiating a nonmarital relationship, running away and separating herself from her children—are rendered more acceptable by constructing them as promaternal actions.

As part of her analysis of legal constructions of family, Jacobs makes juxtapositions across national boundaries to contrast American slave families with the English poor.[14] Without dismissing English suffering, she argues that key legal differences make it far better to be toiling in British fields than American ones. Jacobs acknowledges the oppressive living and work conditions for the poor in England. She refuses, however, to equate these circumstances with slavery. "I felt that the condition of even the meanest and most ignorant among them was vastly superior to the condition of the most favored slaves in America," she asserts (184). Even the "most favored" of the enslaved—such as those belonging to the "pious mistress" in Jacobs's cautionary tale about kind owners—are at the mercy of the inhumane laws of slavery. Her emphasis on legal rights is expressed through a description of the domestic setting and whether the law protects or victimizes the family: "Their homes were very humble; but they were protected by law. No insolent patrols could come, in the dead of night, and flog them at their pleasure. The father, when he closed his cottage door, felt safe with his family around him. No master or overseer could come and take from him his wife, or his daughter. . . . There was no law forbidding them to learn to read and write; and if they helped each other in spelling out the Bible, they were in no danger of thirty-nine lashes" (184). The actual lived conditions might vary among slaves, and some might be "the most favored" (184), but the legal possibility of flogging or rape or other governmentally approved practices made the conditions of the family under slavery utterly unique and unlike poverty or any other set of oppressive circumstances.

Indicting a Nation:
The Fugitive Slave Act and a National Call to Action

The comparison with England intensifies Jacobs's condemnation of the U.S. as a nation for its complicity in slavery. Throughout her narrative, Jacobs details the violence that slavery does to family and womanhood, and she shows her narrator and other African Americans resisting that violence rhetorically and physically. Beyond depicting the resistance of fellow slaves, she also must call for action from her broader audience. Her primary readers are neither slaves nor slaveholders but rather Northerners, particularly white women. Such women have no direct responsibility for the crimes of slavery, but Jacobs seeks to make them understand their accountability nonetheless. Her focus on family and womanhood helps to "arouse the women of the North to a realizing sense of the condition of two millions of women at the South" (1). Her focus on the laws of slavery helps to center her attack on the institution itself and not just on the individual perpetrators.

The link between the law and the nation is clarified through her focus on federal policy, specifically the Fugitive Slave Act of 1850. Jacobs makes references to it throughout the book, and she also dedicates one chapter to this federal law that made national the slave status of fugitives from the South and that made it illegal to aid an escaped slave, even in "free" states. Part of the federal Compromise of 1850 that was supposed to help keep the union together, its enactment marks a crucial moment in U.S. slavery and in the fight for abolition. After this moment there can be no pretense of slavery as the South's isolated "peculiar" issue.

As noted earlier, Jacobs shows this new federal law working in concert with Southern laws of slavery, and she highlights the destructive impact on African American families in the North: "Many a husband discovered that his wife had fled from slavery years ago," making her subject to the Fugitive Slave Law (even if her seemingly successful escape was years before the law passed), "and as 'the child follows the condition of its mother,' the children of his love were liable to be seized and carried into slavery" (191). In the federal logic of slavery, a mother's indelible status is passed on to her children even in the ostensibly free North. Jacobs invokes the crimes of this federal law to include Northerners in the responsibility for slavery. "Free soil" means nothing if a fugitive can be captured anywhere and returned to slavery, particularly when legal and financial incentives encourage Northerners to pursue fugitives.

Jacobs often uses animal imagery, particularly that of human bloodhounds, to indict Northerners using this law. Whereas slave laws tried to dehumanize slaves, she describes slavery itself and slave-catchers as animals. After a detailed narration of Flint's harassment of Brent and of his fathering of many slave children, Jacobs asserts: "Reader, I draw no imaginary pictures of southern homes. I am telling you the plain truth. Yet when victims make their escape from this wild beast of Slavery, northerners consent to act the part of bloodhounds, and hunt the poor fugitive back into his den, 'full of dead men's bones, and all uncleanness.' Nay, more, they are not only willing, but proud, to give their daughters in marriage to slaveholders" (35–36). Jacobs never permits slavery to be an individual problem or even a Southern one. In her analysis, the entire nation is responsible. That responsibility is symbolized by the image of giving one's daughters to slaveholders. She is accusing the Northerners of being quite literally in bed with the agents of slavery.

Some of Jacobs's indictments of the North come as direct second-person admonishments: "Surely, if you credited one half the truths that are told you concerning the helpless millions suffering in this cruel bondage, you at the north would not help to tighten the yoke. You surely would refuse to do for the master, on your own soil, the mean and cruel work which trained bloodhounds and the lowest class of whites do for him at the south" (28). Jacobs sometimes invokes class difference when she talks of whites doing the dirty work of slavery, suggesting that her constructed audience might be made up of whites of a better class who ought to be above such mean work. Here she argues for the validity of "truths" about slavery and the necessity for Northerners to take action. Her argument clearly is directed against the complicity of Northerners who actively support the institution or who simply refuse to believe the truth about it.

In addition to generic examples, Jacobs cites personal experience under the Fugitive Slave Act. In the chapter named for the law, Brent goes to New York with Mrs. Bruce's infant. "I had but one hesitation, and that was my feeling of insecurity in New York, now greatly increased by the passage of the Fugitive Slave Law" (190). Invoking a complex model of white motherhood, the narrator praises Mrs. Bruce for endangering her own child for a fugitive slave: "But how few mothers would have consented to have one of their own babes become a fugitive, for the sake of a poor, hunted nurse, on whom the legislators of the country had let loose the bloodhounds!" (194). The hunted nurse and white babe are both fugitives here. More culpable than bloodhounds are the "legislators of the country" (not just the South) who created the situation. Jacobs quotes Mrs. Bruce in response to a proslavery relative who "told her she was violating the laws of her country; and asked her if she was aware of the penalty. She replied, 'I am very well aware of it. It is imprisonment and one thousand dollars fine. Shame on my country that it is so!'" (194). Guilt belongs to the nation, not the individual who breaks this unjust law. Jacobs has a virtuous and sacrificing white Northern woman articulate the specific penalty and the condemnation of that penalty to help persuade her white Northern audience to take action. If this model Northerner can defy this unjust law, even at the risk of her own infant, then Jacobs's readers can consider challenging it as well.

Like other slave laws, the Fugitive Slave Act resulted in the irony of the guiltless being treated as criminal. There was no escape, under this nation-wide law: "I was subject to it; and so were hundreds of intelligent and industrious people all around us. . . . What a disgrace to a city calling itself free, that inhabitants, guiltless of offence, and seeking to perform their duties conscientiously, should be condemned to live in such incessant fear, and have nowhere to turn for protection" (191). The protection of the law is denied to these guiltless inhabitants, while the power of the law belongs to the bloodhounds and other animals of slavery: "I dreaded the approach of summer, when snakes and slaveholders make their appearance. I was, in fact, a slave in New York, as subject to slave laws as I had been in a Slave State. Strange incongruity in a State called free!" (193). The city and state are only "called" free, and Jacobs exposes the fiction of that naming.

The reality of life under the Fugitive Slave Act led to various forms of activism: "This state of things, of course, gave rise to many impromptu vigilance committees. Every colored person, and every friend of their persecuted race, kept their eyes wide open. Every evening I examined the newspapers carefully, to see what Southerners had put up at the hotels. I did this for my own sake. . . . I wished also to give information to others, if necessary; for if many were 'running to and fro,' I resolved that 'knowledge should be increased'" (191–92). Quoting the Bible, Jacobs invokes a higher law than that of the white man. Her activism and her very existence in New York are deemed illegal, but in her narrative that activism is authorized by religious references. The list of examples also tells the reader that activism can involve simply pursuing and providing information—ventures that she and her reader are involved in right now.

Jacobs particularly indicts Massachusetts for its hypocrisy under the Fugitive Slave Act. Describing a moment in the 1840s, she jumps back and forth in time to invoke a well-known episode (during the 1851 *Sims* case) when officials put chains around the courthouse to prevent the rescue of a fugitive slave: "The Fugitive Slave Law had not then passed. The judges of Massachusetts had not then stooped under chains to enter her courts of justice, so called. I knew my old master was rather skittish of Massachusetts. I relied on her love of freedom, and felt safe on her soil. I am now aware that I honored the old Commonwealth beyond her deserts" (187). The reference is brief and more metaphoric than explanatory. Jacobs expects some knowledge—and responsibility—on the part of her readers. Earlier references to that state as a safe haven also foreshadow what becomes of it under the federal law: "Even in that dark region, where knowledge is so carefully excluded from the slave, I had heard enough about Massachusetts to come to the conclusion that slaveholders did not consider it a comfortable place to go to in search of a runaway. That was before the Fugitive Slave Law was passed; before Massachusetts had consented to become a 'nigger hunter' for the south" (131). The state itself is personified so it can be held personally accountable: It consented and became a "nigger hunter." Jacobs's blunt language indicts the North more generally, for if freedom-loving Massachusetts can take this path, then no Northern state can be trusted.

Jacobs's legal focus helps reveal the North's complicity in Southern slavery, but she also condemns the North for its own legal manifestations of racism, including legally sanctioned segregation. Brent rides in segregated train cars and steam boats, stays in segregated hotels, and describes racist work rules and work places. She indicts the arbitrariness of racist policy in the North and thus broadens her argument against racism: slavery is its most grotesque form, but subtler manifestations must be exposed as well. For example, the narrator questions legal and social meanings of racial identity when she notes the discrimination her son Benny suddenly faces at his Boston workplace: "One day they accidentally discovered a fact they had never before suspected—that he was colored! This at once transformed him into a different being" (186). Boston had long rejected slavery,[15] but in the 1840s many of its trades remain closed to African Americans, relying on the same arbitrary racial categories. Laws and practices of racial discrimination often pretend there are easy lines drawn between who has rights and who does not, and Jacobs questions the ease of such distinctions. The Americans—including Irish Americans—at the printing press find it "offensive to their dignity to have a 'nigger' among them," she reports, adding, "after they had been told that he *was* a 'nigger'" (186). Their offendedness seems absolute, but the lines between categories are blurry. The son's quoted status is clearly a label, a newly discovered "fact," and not an essential identity. The story of the discovery of Benny as black points to the arbitrariness of racial identity. The story also tells us that the enemy is not only slavery in the South but also racism in the North.

Jacobs's examples of Northern racism serve her call for activism. When Brent thinks more money can buy a better seat on the train to New York, her Northern friends explain: "O, no. . . . They don't allow colored people to go in the first-class cars" (162). The narrator compares this affront to treatment in the South: "Colored people were allowed to ride in a filthy box, behind white people, at the south, but they were not required to pay for the privilege. It made me sad to find how the north aped the customs of slavery" (162–63). Northern complicity is again conveyed through animal imagery. After this "first chill" to her optimism about the "free" states, she encounters more examples of segregation and racism. Even when Jacobs describes Brent overcoming segregation policies, she uses that very escape (in this case because she was serving as nurse to a white woman) to condemn the regulation: "Being in servitude to the Anglo-Saxon race, I was not put into a 'Jim Crow car,' on our way to Rockaway, neither was I invited to ride through the streets on top of trunks in a truck; but every where I found the same manifestations of that cruel prejudice, which so discourages the feelings, and represses the energies of the colored people" (176). Her description makes the exception she benefitted from sound little different from slavery. Her conclusion makes the connection between external practices and internal reactions.

Her action proposals generally target free Northerners, calling on them to take action against slavery for their black sisters in the South. At the close of this chapter, she also specifically calls for action among fellow African Americans, using first-person singular and plural. After describing her persistence in the face of racist treatment at the Pavilion Hotel, she reveals her triumph in quiet, general terms: "Finding I was resolved to stand up for my rights, they concluded to treat me well." She does not stop at example, however. She goes on to declare: "Let every colored man and woman do this, and eventually we shall cease to be trampled under foot by our oppressors" (177). The "we" is clearly African Americans, slave and free. While her imperative is indirect ("let"), the statement clearly is a call to action. Throughout her narrative, whatever the construction of her various readers, Jacobs challenges those readers to hear her voice and to act.

Interrogating antislavery legal analysis, Cobb's legal rhetoric, and laws around slave subjectivity and sexuality helps expose the legal fictions that present themselves as fact. Jacobs offers first-person testimony about the evils of slavery and a cogent critique of the legal fictions undergirding slavery and racism. Reading her narrative alongside the legal texts and principles she undermines reveals the erasures and instabilities of the law, particularly in its constructions of race and gender. Her analysis forces us to rethink definitions of family, sexuality, motherhood, and the nation itself. Such an analysis helps us read slavery and its legacies. An examination of slave law and its critiques opens up for discussion the legal fictions constructed around slavery that in many ways continue to inform present-day legal constructions of race.

Epilogue

chapter seven

Confronting the Legacies

Decoding Modern Rhetorics of Race

The contradictions of slavery run deep and have a long history in this nation. Even before the Pilgrims landed at Plymouth Rock in their escape from European oppression, European ships were bringing enslaved Africans to the American continent.[1] At the same time that the Founding Fathers were writing about "life, liberty, and the pursuit of happiness," many of them also were fathering slaves. In the same breath as they spoke of equality and morality, nineteenth-century legal scholars and judges also spoke of African Americans as aliens and animals. Even as American law constructed slaves as mindless, voiceless, and passive, American slaves read, wrote, taught, and resisted. Analyzing discourses of slavery and resistance can help reveal the embeddedness of race in U.S. law. Such an exploration also reminds us to interrogate the seeming rationality and neutrality of modern legal discourse that also may obfuscate racism and sexism today.

This epilogue centers on how to apply the previous chapters' reading strategies (including juxtaposition, reading for silences, and deconstructing framing) to contemporary texts to analyze suppressed voices of racism and resistance. At the dawn of the twenty-first century, amid claims that civil rights and feminism are things of the past, political retrenchments often are cast in terms of progress. Rhetorics of racism are couched in the language of "color-blindness." Any number of modern policy debates facing the U.S. today can be read for how they both feature and veil race: repeals of affirmative action (in the guise of "civil rights" initiatives), retreats from voting rights, immigration restrictions, "English only" efforts, welfare "reform," death penalty debates, "Three Strikes, You're Out" and other criminal (in)justice initiatives, the ever-expanding (and increasingly African American) prison population, policies around new reproductive technologies—and the list continues. Here I focus on just one category of contemporary public policy that reveals constructions of race and gender: state reproductive interventions. I will center on efforts to impose the contraceptive Norplant on certain women, but these arguments might apply to other reproductive cases and other policy issues.

Intersections of race and gender are particularly crystallized in debates over the family and in reproductive policy. From sterilization policies to Margaret Sanger's birth control crusade to the notorious and still-quoted 1965 Moynihan Report, issues around birth control, "illegitimacy," and the family often have been informed by racialized and racist notions. Beginning in the 1990s, legal and legislative attempts to impose the long-term, surgically implanted contraceptive Norplant—attempts that sometimes announce race but more often obscure racial intentions—reveal constructions of race and gender that recall nineteenth-century notions of simultaneously erasing women's agency and placing blame for social problems on black female sexuality. I juxtapose these issues in order to demonstrate that they are not random moments with accidental similarities but rather part of a continuum.

In pointing to the multiple legacies of slavery and its constructions, this chapter is intended to be suggestive, exploring certain examples as a way of opening a dialogue about future scholarly and activist work. By juxtaposing different moments from the past and present, I seek to generate a politics of comparison, to examine the present in a particular historical context. Locating these constructions in a specific moment and context is crucial, because when an isolated image is pulled from its context, many of its powerful subtexts can go unexamined. Placing these images next to each other is not an attempt to say that modern situations are "the same thing" as slavery. Nor does this juxtaposition argue that slavery is the direct or unique cause of modern circumstances. Solely blaming long-dead slaveholders would wrongly exonerate current participants in racism. Simplistically relying on such images can create distortions: Using a problematic shorthand and invoking nineteenth-century labels without context can displace responsibility and obscure details of contemporary power relations.[2] This epilogue examines how modern legal and political discourses use, update, translate, and transform constructions of race and gender that emerged during slavery. Keeping these contexts in mind can help decode what happens today in law, policy making, and political rhetoric.

The images that emerge from slavery are not uniform, and it is precisely their contradictions that help reveal the distance between those fictions and the complex social realities. Defusing modern uses of the contradictory images discussed in the preceding chapters requires identifying the tropes, their ideological origins, and the power relations that they mask. Patricia Hill Collins examines constructions and representations of African American women in the past and present as related to ideology, power, and oppression. In *Black Feminist Thought,* she argues: "The controlling images of Black women that originated during the slave era attest to the ideological dimension of Black women's oppression. . . . From the mammies, Jezebels, and breeder women of slavery to the smiling Aunt Jemimas on pancake mix boxes, ubiquitous Black prostitutes, and ever-present welfare mothers of contemporary popular culture, the nexus of negative stereotypical images applied to African American women has been fundamental to Black women's oppression" (7). The images often construct African American women as happy in their powerlessness and deserving of their circumstances. Collins writes, "These controlling images are designed to make racism, sexism, and poverty appear to be natural, normal, and an inevitable part of everyday life" (68). They also make these things seem the fault of African American women—not only inevitable but also of their own doing. As nineteenth-century laws simultaneously stripped slaves of subjectivity and constructed them as dangerous, modern uses of these images dehumanize African American women and make them agents who actively produce their own pathology.

Placing the modern manifestations of such moves next to the absurdity of nineteenth-century legal fictions (like Cobb blaming slave women for interracial sex) helps expose the workings of these constructions and helps reveal these things as not inevitable but produced through eliding discourses. Breaking down the impact of these images, especially when they appear in the "neutral" framework of legal discourse, requires contextualization, multiple perspectives, and interdisciplinary approaches.

"The Tangle of Pathology":
Using Slavery to (Mis)Place Blame and Construct Matriarchy

A highly publicized and much-analyzed statement of federal policy on race, reproduction, and family emerged more than three decades ago and continues to be invoked today. In 1965, Daniel Patrick Moynihan, then an assistant secretary in the Department of Labor under President Lyndon B.

Johnson, produced a short (and unsigned) government report entitled *The Negro Family: The Case for National Action.* In the midst of the Civil Rights movement, this report articulated the theory of black matriarchy, linked this "pathology" of female dominance to slavery, and blamed it for the ills of the African American community in the present. The women constructed in this report combine many of the "controlling images" that Collins discusses: the motherhood elements of the Mammy image with the uncontrolled sexual elements of the Jezebel image, the inappropriate power of the matriarch and the economic dangers of the welfare mother. Moynihan's narrative can be displaced with other images and voices of women under slavery—including the narratives of Jacobs and Truth, African American women who challenged such constructions of black womanhood when they appeared a century earlier. Moynihan's framing of black "pathology" also must be undercut with stories about family structures ignored or erased by the report and with causes of poverty other than self-perpetuation—such as racism, discrimination, and other social, economic, and political factors.

The Moynihan Report shaped debates over slavery for years to come and still is revived in policy discussions today—debates about African American families, "welfare mothers," "illegitimacy," and reproduction.[3] The textual appearance of *The Negro Family: The Case for National Action* gave it the weight of neutral governmental fact. While the document has come to be known as the "Moynihan Report," it was initially released as a government document with no personal author listed, only arms of the state: OFFICE OF POLICY PLANNING AND RESEARCH / UNITED STATES DEPARTMENT OF LABOR. The front cover did not even cite those authors: It was a black cover with THE NEGRO FAMILY in huge, outlined, white-on-black capital letters, one word per line, alternating left and right justification (so the appearance is jagged, unstable), covering three-fourths of the page, with THE CASE FOR NATIONAL ACTION in much smaller white-on-black letters through the middle of the page. The image suggests the authorless booklet will shed white light on this unstable black problem called the Negro family.

The "fact" of inherently unstable African American families is written into history, and the act of writing that story is obscured. The booklet is filled with footnotes and multitudinous graphs, tables, and quotations. As with Cobb's document a century earlier, authority here comes from people already in power, not from those who are the object of the study.[4] The charts and graphs, which appear on almost every page, visually present government-gathered data on matters such as "FERTILITY RATES FOR NON-WHITE WOMEN," "ILLEGITIMACY RATIOS," and "DISTRIBUTION OF EVER-MARRIED NEGRO FEMALES," often centering on dangers of overfertile, undermarried black women.[5]

Moynihan's basic thesis regarding black America is that, rather than racism or economics or some other societal structure, "the *fundamental* problem is that of family structure" (emphasis added).[6] The flaw in family structure ultimately boils down to female dominance,[7] and Moynihan uses the language of sickness to describe the problem. In the section called "The Tangle of Pathology," he writes: "In essence, the Negro community has been forced into a matriarchal structure which, because it is so out of line with the rest of the American society, seriously retards the progress as a whole, and imposes a crushing burden on the Negro male and, in consequence, on a great many Negro women as well" (29). The structure may have been "forced" on the community, but now matriarchy is the agent that "retards" and crushes black individuals, particularly males. The passive-voice phrase "has been forced" may allude to slavery, but since slavery is now gone, blame can be located with the modern "Negro community," which chooses to retain that misaligned "matriarchal" structure. After briefly mentioning housing segregation—a public policy problem that government might appropriately address—Moynihan immediately shifts the problem to the sickness of the group again: "The children of middle-class Negroes often as not must grow up in, or next to the slums, an experience almost unknown to white middle-class children. They are therefore constantly exposed to the pathology of the disturbed group and constantly in danger of being drawn into it" (29–30). "Slums" contain pathological, "disturbed," and dangerous individuals. Moynihan mentions other possible contributing factors, such as white crime and white hostility, but again quickly recenters the blame: "Nonetheless, at the center of the tangle of pathology is the weakness of the family structure. Once or twice removed, it will be found to be the principal source of most of the aberrant, inadequate, or anti-social behavior that did not establish, but now serves to perpetuate the cycle of poverty and deprivation" (30). Pathology, meaning disease and disorder, is repeatedly used to describe the status of black families and in particular the illness and aberration of matriarchy. In order to construct this image of sickness, a healthy norm is constructed for white families and juxtaposed to "the" black family. Two single-sentence paragraphs set up the contrast in stark terms:

The white family has achieved a high degree of stability and is maintaining that stability.

By contrast, the family structure of lower class Negroes is highly unstable, and in many urban centers is approaching complete breakdown.
(5, boldface in original)

The singular "white family"—without class markers or other modifiers—is defined as uniformly stable and is given credit and agency for achieving that status; "Negroes," however, are modified by "lower class" (though not compared to "lower class" white families) and generalized as ranging from "highly unstable" to "complete breakdown." Moynihan uses boldface here, so the "Negro family" paragraph is visually darker and stands out as the problem.[8]

Moynihan also explicitly relies on essentialist notions of male and female natures to make his point. In bemoaning the unmanning of African American men in slavery and Reconstruction, he writes, "The very essence of the male animal, from the bantam rooster to the four-star general, is to strut." But such behavior was discouraged in the black male: "The 'sassy nigger' was lynched" (16). This sentence—written in the passive voice and omitting a reference for the quoted phrase (which allows him to use a racial epithet without taking responsibility for it)—leaves out the lyncher and helps permit Moynihan in his larger argument to place blame more squarely on the African American women who usurp what should be male power.

Under Reconstruction, according to Moynihan, the black male suffered the brunt of restrictions: "Keeping the Negro 'in his place' can be translated as keeping the Negro male in his place: the female was not a threat to anyone" (16). The Jim Crow policies of segregation did impact women as well as men, but Moynihan erases that history with an unsupported assertion of a gendered public sphere: "The male was more likely to use public facilities, which rapidly became segregated once the process began, and just as important, segregation, and the submissiveness it exacts, is surely more destructive to the male than to the female personality" (16). From Jacobs confronting segregated facilities to Rosa Parks instigating the Montgomery bus boycott, there is more than adequate evidence of African American women subject to and resisting Jim Crow, but Moynihan's approach requires deemphasizing commonalities between men's and women's encounters with racism.[9]

Moynihan's report constructs the African American community as blameworthy, lessening government responsibility for societal ills. This strategy is useful for the state, especially during a period of intense pressure for state action to right the wrongs of institutionalized racism. In a later article referring to his own findings, Moynihan more explicitly constructed the ills of the black community as deserved: "There is one unmistakable lesson in American history: a community that allows large numbers of young men to grow up in broken families, dominated by women, never acquiring any stable relationship to male authority, never acquiring any set of rational expectations about the future—that community asks for and gets chaos. Crime, violence, unrest, disorder . . . are not only to be expected, they are very near to inevitable. And they are richly deserved."[10] In a fund-raising letter twenty-seven years later, Moynihan introduces the same passage with this boast: "I claim no gifts of prophecy . . . [but] I could just as easily have written these words in 1993." The 1993 letter asks for reelection contributions to help the senator continue his efforts for welfare reform. "Dear Senator Moynihan," reads the insert that is to be returned with the donation. "It's time America hears the truth about Welfare." In the quoted passage, agency rests with the specific "community" for "allow[ing]" the dysfunctional patterns to exist. The dysfunctionality is immediately gendered. The problem is defined as what happens to the "young men" who are denied "male authority" and are instead subject to families "dominated by women." The community is not named as black until the body of the letter begins, and it becomes clear the topic is black America and problems of welfare (two completely intertwined issues for Moynihan).

The construction of deserved sufferings continues today and is often authorized by Moynihan's claims. In 1989, the *New Republic* declared, "Nearly 25 years after Daniel Patrick Moynihan was pilloried for saying so, *it is universally accepted* that black poverty is heavily the *result* of family breakdown" (Kondracke 18, emphasis added). The "universally accepted" causal shift articulated here—making African Americans the cause of their poverty—takes the onus off of the state to address those economic circumstances (and uses rhetoric similar to that of Cobb, who frequently invoked the "well-known fact"). By placing responsibility first on the past and then on the "pathology" within the black community, Moynihan removes from responsibility the power structures and the "white world" of the present: "Three centuries of injustice have brought about deep-seated structural distortions in the life of the Negro American. At this point, the present tangle of pathology is capable of perpetuating itself without assistance from the white world" (*Negro Family* 47). Racist oppression is reframed

ironically as "assistance" and then is done away with by Moynihan's
rhetoric. Generalized "injustice" is replaced by "distortions" in the singular "life of the Negro American," so that societal oppression becomes individual abnormality and then illness. That "pathology" is described with
agency, as it is "capable of perpetuating itself." The white world is quite
literally excused from the cycle, made by Moynihan into an innocent
bystander. Ironically, Moynihan's use of slavery is part of what allows this
shift of responsibility away from the "white world." Blame for current
social problems is shifted backward to nineteenth-century systems, which
damaged black individuals, and then forward to twentieth-century black
individuals, who perpetuate the problems themselves, skipping twentieth-
century white individuals and institutions in the process. This transfer-
ence of responsibility is part of what makes Moynihan's thesis so attractive
to later commentators and policy makers.

Some of the power of Moynihan's report comes from the way it managed
to frame the debate, so that even those who disagree with him often respond in terms of matriarchy and family dysfunction. Some of Moynihan's
critics dispute his data and conclusions but leave intact the assumptions of
"matriarchy" and "illegitimacy" as pathology. Angela Davis analyzes how
much of the scholarly work on slavery in the 1970s was directed at discrediting Moynihan's "Black Matriarchy thesis," often leading to an overly
dismissive view of African American women's power under slavery. It is
important to critique Moynihan's thesis without being bound to accept
his terms.

Davis and Collins both disprove Moynihan's findings and analyze the
gendered implications of his underlying assumptions. Collins writes: "The
image of the matriarch is central to interlocking systems of race, gender,
and class oppression. Portraying African-American women as matriarchs
allows the dominant group to blame Black women for the success or failure of Black children. Assuming that Black poverty is passed on intergen-
erationally via value transmission in families . . . diverts attention from the
political and economic inequality affecting Black mothers and children
and suggests that anyone can rise from poverty if he or she only received
good values at home" (74–75). Davis criticizes Moynihan's conclusions as
well as his premises and methods. Focusing on the complexity of family
life under slavery and the diversity of gender roles, she also critiques
responses to Moynihan that simply denied matriarchy by asserting male
dominance. She suggests that the theory of matriarchy emerged from the
slaveholders' emphasis on maternal lines (the child follows the condition

of the mother), but she argues that it is simplistic to translate that legal rule (which had nothing to do with female power or dominance) into matriarchy. Davis is also careful not to insist on the image of the subordinate wife instead. She suggests that some form of family did survive and that slave families contained diverse gender roles and elements of sexual equality. Most of all, she argues for more research that does not erase slave women or rely on stereotypes. Her own work on slavery contains analysis from researchers as well as testimony from slaves, especially women. It is only through these multiple voices that simplistic images like those proposed by Moynihan can be displaced.

Placing Moynihan next to nineteenth-century texts helps to reveal how he relies on fictions of slavery for his background. Tellings of U.S. slave law, including Goodell's critique of slavery (discussed in chapter 5), can reveal the sources of some of the cultural and legal fictions upon which Moynihan is drawing. "If we can account for an originary narrative and judicial principle that might have engendered a 'Moynihan Report,' many years into the twentieth century," writes Hortense Spillers, "we cannot do much better than look at Goodell's reading of the *partus sequitur ventrem:* the condition of the slave mother is 'forever entailed on all her remotest posterity'" (79). Spillers links Moynihan to the nineteenth-century text and then takes apart the arguments behind both abolitionist Goodell and Democrat Moynihan, concluding that both finally conflate "mother" and "enslavement," seeing the link to the maternal as the source of degradation.[11] Like some abolitionists who professed opposition to slavery but in some ways furthered racial tropes, Moynihan presents himself as a liberal policy maker and social scientist with the interests of the African American community at heart. Reading Moynihan next to Goodell helps to reveal the contradictions in both writers.

The arguments of the Moynihan Report need to be countered with alternative narratives about slavery and about contemporary poverty, narratives that shift the focus to the complexities of social, economic, political, and institutional causes and not just sociological "pathology." It is important to include a range of testimony, including the voices of those Moynihan presumes to describe. The report's declarations about slavery took hold partly because there were not many alternate narratives about slavery with wide availability (and certainly not published and distributed by the government). Reading Moynihan alongside Jacobs's autobiography, for example, makes it impossible to take seriously his attack on the too-weak black family and the too-strong black mother.

Jacobs depicts strong women and the centrality of motherhood, but her picture is quite different from the "pathological" "matriarchy" that Moynihan invokes. Narrator Linda Brent exemplifies the complexities and paradoxes of life under slavery. Slavery dismantles family, and yet the black family endures. Instead of showing the dysfunctional families featured in Moynihan's report, Brent describes the strength of her extended family, even as she details how slavery harmed them. Instead of the reductive gender roles conjured up by Moynihan, Jacobs offers complex portrayals of black women and men (including Brent and her grandmother, mother, father, uncle, brother, and children), who are simultaneously disempowered and resistant. She depicts immense obstacles to the slave family and to the survival of the family without reinscribing traditional roles (or their inverse). The power of such a narrative can help displace the fictions constructed by Moynihan's governmental facts.

"Can Contraception Reduce the Underclass?": Blaming Black Female Sexuality (Again)

Race has always played a key role in U.S. reproductive policy. White feminists, while placing a priority on reproductive rights, generally have failed to address the role of race in reproductive issues. Meanwhile, Moynihan's thesis about "the Negro family" endures in many forms, especially in debates over race, family, and reproduction. Anxiety about black reproduction permeates his report, and his argument rests largely on such data as fertility rates and numbers of "illegitimate" births. While Moynihan directly invokes images of slavery to make his argument about African American families, often the traces of gender and race constructions emerging from slavery are less immediately visible. In this section, I examine contemporary reproductive policy, particularly through proposed uses of the contraceptive Norplant. Race has been omnipresent yet erased in legal and political narratives about Norplant. The legal texts that obscure race issues can be countered with alternative narratives and diverse voices. It is important to expose stories that appear within those texts and push at the margins or peek through in other ways, in order to displace what seems like the neutral voice of law.

Norplant, a five-year contraceptive implant, was released for use in the U.S. after being tested outside of the country for years, primarily on "Third World" women, raising troubling questions about whose bodies get experimented on for whose benefit.[12] Within the U.S., African American bodies have frequently served for white America's experiments. In his study of slave law, Goodell discusses the use of slave bodies for medical research. One nineteenth-century newspaper item read: "To planters and others—wanted, 50 Negroes, any person having sick Negroes, considered incurable by their respective physicians, and wishing to dispose of them, Dr. S. will pay cash" (87). Renowned doctor J. Marion Sims (who has a speculum and a gynecological position named after him) gained worldwide fame when he developed a treatment for fistulas (tears between the vagina and bladder) by experimenting on slaves, whom he repeatedly opened and sutured whenever he had a new idea.[13] He bought these women for these experiments, but even modern references to his work refer to the women as having "agreed" to them (Wertz 101). White women of the privileged class were the eventual beneficiaries of his medical innovations.

Black bodies were the terrain for medical experimentation in the twentieth century as well. In 1932, the notorious Tuskegee syphilis experiment began. Six hundred African American men were lured by promises of treatment for "bad blood" and left to suffer and die while doctors from the U.S. Public Health Service gathered data from watching the disease progress unchecked. The experiments often included painful procedures, disguised as treatment, while the men were denied penicillin or any other real treatment. This lasted several decades, ending only in the 1970s.[14] These and other moments in American medical history confirm the need for attention to the costs of "advances" in medical science.

Once introduced to the U.S. as the first significant new contraceptive in a generation, Norplant might have been such an advance, a positive medical development offering women another reproductive health option. Because of Norplant's characteristics, however, as a long-term and passive form of birth control (once implanted, its effectiveness does not depend on user behavior), there was immediate speculation about what groups of women *ought* to use it. Drug users, teenagers, welfare recipients, African Americans—all these groups were named by policy makers and the press as ideal targets for Norplant. At the same time, because of its limited availability and its cost—more than $500—Norplant has not been particularly accessible for women who want it, which is ironic, since it has been suggested for many women who have not asked for it. These ironies surface in many ways. The Native American Women's Health Education Resource Center found, in analyzing use of Norplant in the government-run Indian Health Service, that Norplant was not available in some areas and over-promoted in others. Where it was heavily promoted, Native American women were being implanted at high rates and with little or no information about side effects and dangers (69).

Ironies frequently emerge in discourses around Norplant. Some expressions of slave law (including Cobb's language of "benefits," for example, or restrictive statutes that appeared to expand rights) sounded like the intention was to benefit slaves. Such confusions between rights and restrictions continue in modern policy expressions. Norplant proposals tend to conflate compassion and coercion, choice and control. For example, shortly after Norplant's introduction, California governor Pete Wilson proposed making the surgical procedure "available" to teens and possibly "mandatory" for drug users.[15] There is a quick and easy slippage between those two ideas, despite the fact that access and coercion are very different policy positions. A Republican legislator in Kansas introduced one bill making Norplant a term of probation for fertile women who commit drug crimes and another offering a $500 "incentive" to women on Aid to Families with Dependent Children (AFDC) who "choose" to be implanted. He said the latter "empowers female public assistance recipients" (Patrick 11A). The bills died, but only after receiving nationwide attention. Louisiana lawmaker David Duke used comparable for-their-own-good language to talk about his proposal, which would have similarly "persuaded" low-income mothers to stop reproducing. Duke was quoted as saying, "I support any kind of contraceptive for welfare recipients. Norplant, eggplant. Anything" (Barnett 8–9).

Even without the participation of former Ku Klux Klan Grand Wizard Duke, we easily can anticipate how such policies would have a disproportionate effect on low-income women and women of color. Immediately after Norplant was approved for use, the *Philadelphia Inquirer* called for public policy innovations that would encourage African American women in particular to use Norplant to help "reduce the underclass." The article uses the words "black," "poor," and "dysfunctional" fairly interchangeably, implying the terms are synonymous ("Poverty and Norplant: Can Contraception Reduce the Underclass?" 18A). Echoing Moynihan, the article briefly mentions other approaches to addressing poverty, such as education, but immediately rejects those ideas: "But it's very tough to undo the damage of being born into a dysfunctional family." As in the Moynihan Report, the assumption is that white families are functional while black families are hopelessly damaged. Since the cycle is constructed as self-reproducing, the *Inquirer* can only envision a halt to reproduction as a cure. The editors admit they might be "raising the specter of eugenics" but say it would be a worse offense not to draw "the logical conclusion." Logic, not race, is described as directing their argument.

Many proposed policies are not racially explicit in their terminology but clearly target certain groups of women.[16] If being on welfare triggers Norplant imposition, for example, the effect is bound to be class-based.[17] In addition, the "welfare mother" trope is quite explicitly linked to African American women. According to Collins, "Essentially an updated version of the breeder woman image created during slavery, this image provides an ideological justification for efforts to harness Black women's fertility to the needs of a changing political economy" (76). If Norplant is linked to drug use (or rather, institutional awareness of suspected drug use), it will affect a skewed population. African Americans are more likely to be prosecuted for drug use than white Americans, independent of usage rates, and women of color, low-income women, and battered women already are disproportionately prosecuted under laws penalizing drug use by pregnant women.[18] Institutionalized racism in the criminal justice system and in the health care system guarantee that such disparities would occur under a Norplant regulation as well. Such a regulation could always appear "race-neutral," however, making it difficult to strike down as discriminatory. The "official" invisibility of issues such as race, class, and gender make them difficult to address. Official voices can always deny their presence. An examination of the details of one particular Norplant case demonstrates how this denial works.

In January 1991, a California judge sentenced a twenty-seven-year-old woman to contraceptive surgical implants as a term of her probation. Norplant had been approved for use in the U.S. only days before the sentence. The "facts" of the case seem clear: A parent abuses two of her children and agrees to birth control as a term of her punishment. The legal system and the media deemed the following details relevant: Defendant Darlene Johnson was a single mother, was pregnant, and already had four children. She was on welfare. She was African American. She smoked and drank coffee. She had prior convictions. She was living with a man to whom she was not married. But such a narrative, which may evoke familiar tropes, does not adequately or accurately tell the story. Why does the narrative get written in these terms? Who determines that the above information is factual, relevant, or should have any bearing on Johnson's penalty?

No matter how many such details are amassed, we cannot recover a single "authentic" version of Johnson's story. What I address here is how the "facts" of the case were constructed and framed to make this sentence seem a rational and legal condition of probation. In the transcript of this courtroom drama, the "criminal" and the "public" are defined and classified in significant ways. The defendant is redefined not only as committing a particular crime but also as being a particular kind of person—a bad mother and irresponsible reproducer, evoking both Jezebel and a distorted Mammy image. The court must construct itself as the distributor of ungendered, uncolored, objective justice. In this case, Superior Court Judge Howard Broadman presents himself as the neutral transmitter of justice. Examining in the texts of this case the various moments of slippage—through metaphor, metonymy, redefinitions, role changing, pronoun shifting, and other rhetorical moves—will help displace the appearance of neutrality.

A repeated pattern with pregnancy-related policy in general (in the nineteenth century and today) is the contradictory attempt to erase women while female bodies are precisely the focus. Such policies obviously single out women, and they disproportionately impact particular groups of women. Broadman's Norplant order appeared during a climate of increasing attempts at reproductive interventions by the state, both promoting and restricting maternity. In addition to proposed abortion regulations, there are also attempts to place the state in women's uteruses through actions ranging from workplace "fetal protection" policies and the prosecution of pregnant drug users to forced cesarean sections and coerced contraception.[19] Legal scholar Dorothy Roberts argues that the tendency in such policies to separate the interests of the fetus and the mother is not a new phenomenon but has its roots in the treatment of pregnant slaves.[20] Women of color are particularly targeted by various reproductive policies, and their bodies are particularly singled out as the site for blame.[21] Exploring this case involving the imposition of Norplant will help illuminate how the female body—and, more specifically, the black female reproductive body—is constructed in legal discourse. The Johnson case has its own particulars, but it also fits into a larger trend of the state exercising control over African American women's reproduction.

An examination of the larger context of race-linked reproductive policy and an analysis of the particular texts indicate that race, gender, and class certainly intersect in the Johnson case, although Broadman vehemently denies any such suggestion. He defends his sentence and himself against outside criticism that his decision is "sexism or anti-feminist."[22] Other judges also have denied such charges. A Washington, D.C., Superior

Court judge was accused of sexism when he sentenced a pregnant African American woman to special, additional jail time for a check forgery conviction, saying he wanted to keep her fetus safe from possible cocaine use during her pregnancy. This judge responded to the charge of sexism by admitting gender-specific treatment but then immediately erasing the gender-specificity of the criticism. "It is true that defendant has not been treated the same as if she were a man in this case. But then a man who is a convicted rapist is treated differently from a woman" (*U.S. v. Vaughn*). The individual woman—Brenda Vaughn—becomes the unarticled, generic, and genderless "defendant," her economic crime of check forgery is paralleled to the violent crime of rape, and a uterus-specific penalty is justified by a nonparallel comparison.

Broadman on the other hand constructs his defense by simply pointing to the impossibility of defending himself against such charges: "There is no way in which to prove one is not a misogynist or a sexist, and I am outraged at any such suggestion. This Court in a proper case with appropriate technology would make a similar order against a man." He makes a fairly safe claim here, since he never will encounter any such "proper case" with a man. He similarly defends himself against the charge of racism: "Once again, there is no way to prove that one is not a racist.[23] I can say that I do not see color. It is my job to not see color" (T3 23). Race and gender become invisible. Ungendered, uncolored reason is all that remains. That fiction—the American myth of gender- or color-blind justice—is at the core of many cases in recent decades that turn back the clock on civil rights.

The texts of the Johnson case help reveal how that fiction of neutrality is sustained. In this instance, Broadman relies on various framing devices to help justify his sentence. The authorizing procedures built into the legal system qualify certain players to define facts. For example, the format and appearance of the official court transcripts are crucial in establishing legitimacy and apparent objectivity. In the official format for all these transcripts, every line is numbered, and the text is boxed into the right three-quarters of the page by an outlined rectangle, creating a container of ordered facts. That literal frame boxes in the official texts of the proceedings. What falls outside that frame does not appear as authorized "fact." Because these rules are standardized, they become invisible and unnoticed. The standardized format, with the weight of the state behind it, makes the legal transcript appear as a factual, nonsubjective account. The official documents privilege the court's interpretation while appearing as a noninterpretation.

The name of the case appears on the first page of each transcript, set off in its own box: THE PEOPLE OF THE STATE OF CALIFORNIA, Plaintiff, vs. DARLENE JOHNSON, Defendant. Readers of this document presumably can tell where they fit ("people") and whom they are against (Darlene Johnson). Throughout the transcripts, the way the characters are labeled reveals who has authority. The judge—the main interpreter—appears unnamed throughout the dialogue of the court transcripts, labeled only as "THE COURT," rendering invisible the agent of power. The other players cannot be named in any comparable manner. Johnson appears anonymously in the dialogues as "THE DEFENDANT," and the attorneys are listed by honorific and last name. In this way, alone metonymized into "The Court," Broadman comes to represent not an individual but institutional and state power. He is the institution. And it is institutional, governmental, documentary fact the System seeks. Who better to define those facts than "The Court"?

Courtroom rhetoric announces who has the power to define facts and construct identity. A piece of Johnson's identity deemed relevant is that she is pregnant. We learn her reproductive status because Broadman wants Johnson to stop smoking: "You should quit —," he states, "you know, you're pregnant. You got real problems with these children." He will order her to stop smoking later, at the sentencing hearing, but he plants the seeds now. A smoking prohibition is not the only preview of what is to come: "I'm also going to try and think, and I'd like the minutes to reflect, of some special probation conditions for this lady who beat her children severely" (T1 3). Broadman is not merely trying to intimidate Johnson. He is speaking for the record, for the minutes, to create the paper trail. That paper trail helps authorize him and helps document Johnson's knowledge and alleged "consent." The written transcript is the goal of Broadman's performance here. And this particular piece of the paper trail will be used later at the sentencing hearing to justify his "special" conditions.

In the next proceeding, Broadman announces (speaking as The Court): "She can smoke after she has the baby. I just didn't want her to smoke while she was pregnant" (T2 4). So prenatal, maternal-inflicted, fetal damage is defined as the problem to be eliminated—not fetal damage from second-hand smoke or infant damage from a smoke-filled nonuterine environment, concerns that might lead to regulating the habits of those surrounding Johnson. If Broadman were to keep Johnson in prison until after the birth, he might need to impose various controls on the habits of her guards and fellow prisoners and on the prison environment itself (if fetal health were the real goal). The problem is defined carefully so that the solution is one that Broadman has the power to enact.

Women's bodies (and in particular, the bodies of low-income women of color) become the battlegrounds over which many social problems are fought because there is something frighteningly enforceable about a uterus-based policy. The goal for the criminal justice system becomes not necessarily punishment or deterrence—or even the production of docile subjects—but rather a solution within the state's parameters to control. In this way, power works to legitimate itself: it assigns itself tasks it can handle.

The justification for the smoking ban is implied: tobacco can harm an existing fetus. To justify the more aggressive element of this reproductive sentencing—implants to prevent future fetuses—certain facts must be more actively constructed, such as the alleged safety and simplicity of Norplant. This contraceptive is not just a drug but a five-year implant, several small rods inserted surgically under the skin in the upper arm, constantly releasing progestin into the woman's body. It has side effects including heavy bleeding, mood swings, nausea, dizziness, headaches, abdominal discomfort, and hair loss, and it is not recommended for women with certain medical conditions, including diabetes, high blood pressure, high cholesterol, and heart conditions (see Barnett for a fairly comprehensive—and long—list of side effects and contraindications). To discontinue use, a physician cuts away built-up tissue and surgically removes the rods. A woman cannot simply stop use on her own.[24] When Broadman describes Norplant, however, he defines it very simply: "It's a thing you put in your arm and it lasts for five years" (T2 6). Johnson momentarily has agency: *you* put it in *your* arm. No mention of surgery, doctors, the cutting away of tissue.

Johnson's first and only question recorded in this transcript is, "Is it harmful to the body?" (T2 7). Johnson leaves herself out of this question, asking generally about "the body"—neither her body nor women's bodies but the generic body. She asks a factual question and gets two "facts" as a response. Broadman, capable in the rhetoric of legal evasion, answers: "It's FDA approved. It's not experimental." His rhetorical displacement does not answer her question, but it sounds like a "No." The received "fact" is that it is not harmful. One arm of the state invokes another (the federal Food and Drug Administration) to convince Johnson that the device is safe. The lessons of DES, the Dalkon shield, silicon breast implants, and other "safe" products for women should remind us that Broadman's two-sentence answer is no answer at all. Nevertheless, his nonresponse enters the transcript as the factual answer and is the end of the discussion.

A court transcript reads like a dialogue, but participants do not have equal power to speak. Any real questioning of the "facts" established by the judge can be contained, since it is the judge who is authorized to answer such questions. The only other questioning of Norplant in this proceeding is a tentative inquiry from the defense attorney: "Your Honor, may I ask, I'm not fully familiar with—is it reversible?" (T2 7). The answer places agency back in the audience: "You just take the thing out." Obviously, the attorney will not remove it, but using the second person erases the fact that this is a surgical procedure requiring a physician who will administer local anesthesia, make an incision, and cut away built-up tissue before removing the implants.[25] In fact, the judge never mentions the word "surgery." But the attorney is satisfied: "Fine," he states. And the judge, protesting too much, asserts: "This is not forced sterilization. That went out in the forties" (T2 8).[26]

The reference reminds us that the state did officially permit the involuntary sterilization of various groups it deemed undesirable, but Broadman attempts to place such governmental excess firmly in the past. Disproportionate uses of sterilization—sometimes coerced, sometimes without informed consent—continued well after the forties and into the present, but Broadman's legal fiction does not acknowledge this fact. In the most famous case on the matter, *Buck v. Bell,* the Supreme Court upheld the forced sterilization of "mental defectives," declaring: "The principle that sustains compulsory vaccination is broad enough to cover cutting the Fallopian tubes. . . . Three generations of imbeciles are enough."[27] The Supreme Court rejected forced sterilization in 1942 but never overturned *Buck v. Bell.* The practice continues in some states, only less overtly. In some cases, "consent" has been obtained from non-English-speaking women who are given a form to sign when they are about to give birth, for example, or by a state offering to cover expenses if the surgery is done in conjunction with an abortion.[28]

The court transcript constructs certain stories about the past and about Johnson in order to justify Broadman's sentence.[29] Challenging Broadman's terms would require changing the stories, which would have to be processed though the transcript again. Broadman clarifies his response about the nature of Norplant to make sure Johnson understands that the "you" who can take the thing out is not actually Johnson herself. Adding not a doctor but a judge to the equation, he states: "But don't take it out unless you come back and say, 'Judge, here's my story.' Because you beat your kids, and you beat your kids inappropriately. So you shouldn't have any kids until we get you squared away and find out what's going on, right" (T2 8). "My story" will not exist for Johnson unless and until that story is told to "Judge." Some collective legal "we" must first "square" her away, put her story in the box of the transcript, before that story becomes valid, becomes fact. It is ironic that Broadman would ask Johnson to tell him her story in some hypothetical future when in the present he has denied her a voice in telling that story. To whatever extent that story exists in this script, it is predominantly through his words. In this glimpse of potential testimony, Broadman literally speaks for Johnson, putting his summary of her words in quotes and even naming himself in the constructed quotation.

While The Court in this document gives The Defendant permission to go to a doctor, in a later transcript the ability to object on medical grounds is moved further away from Johnson or even her doctor: "In the event that it is, in fact, not safe for her due to some contraindications and a trained physician so testifies, the Court will appoint an independent physician witness and set the matter for hearing, and, thereafter, the Court would issue an appropriate ruling after hearing all of the facts and the applicable law" (T3 23). This public discourse about Johnson's private body must be filtered through authorized voices. Subjectivity and agency belong to "the Court," not the woman, and her private reproductive status is literally a matter of public record. Her reproductive choice and testimony about her own body must be filtered not only through a doctor but also through a physician witness, a hearing, a listing of the "facts," and an "appropriate" ruling. The medical reality of Norplant's effect on Johnson's body has to be transformed and transmitted into another court transcript. Since the court has the final word, the medical testimony could in fact be set aside and the Norplant order upheld. Or, accepting the medical objections, the court presumably could order some other form of birth control that would be "safe" (perhaps sterilization or abstinence?). The important thing, apparently, is that the change not be motivated by Johnson's unauthorized voice alone.[30]

Many women not in the criminal justice system also have faced obstacles to having Norplant removed. They were not being sentenced for a crime, but as low-income women who had used public funds to obtain Norplant (often after being pressured to "choose" Norplant in the first place), they were still considered by doctors and agencies as not qualified to decide for themselves when they wanted the device removed. Listening to the voices of such women provides an alternate narrative to Broadman's legal voice and various political and medical voices promoting the method as safe and reversible. ("You just take the thing out," says Broadman [T2 7], and "become fertile again," says the *Philadelphia Inquirer* ["Poverty" 18A]). A 1995 study of young, low-income, mostly African American women in South Carolina, all of whom had requested early removal because of side effects, reveals the difficulties they faced in having their voices heard.[31] Several women report having their objections to Norplant invalidated. "They don't jump to take it out but they sure do want to put it in," observes one woman, who had experienced unacceptable levels of bleeding while on Norplant (469). "I was still having heavy bleeding," she reported, "and they said, well, it takes a little while, so I went for a year. . . . It didn't get no better. I mean, who wants to go 19 days' worth of bleeding?" (469) Many women in the study describe a struggle between how they know they felt and how medical staff tried to make them feel: "They look at you like you are stupid and they make you feel that way too," states one woman. She had to call repeatedly to request removal and observes: "They can't tell you how you feel but they can make you think they know how you feel. . . . They don't know what it's like to have that thing in there and they don't care what harm it does" (469). Another woman endured side effects for more than two years but still faced resistance when she wanted the device removed and skepticism about her reasons: "When I called them to talk to the doctors to take it out, they did not want to take it out at all. They gave me some kind of stuff about, you keep it in there, this happens to everybody. . . . It made me feel like I was trying to lie about how I was feeling" (468).

Even when doctors obliged, they continued to dismiss the women's concerns: "When he took mine out, he criticized the reason why I wanted to get it taken out" (469). Echoing the way Broadman maintained control over Johnson's Norplant decision, one woman reports that her doctor "didn't say that I would have to go through all these procedures before *he decided I didn't like it*" (469, emphasis added). Whether or not she liked it was up to a doctor to decide, and only after certain procedures were met.

Public funding of Norplant insertion (which ought to imply greater reproductive choice) means that the state has an economic interest in these women not removing the implants. One woman in the South Carolina study concludes that "they push the Norplant" for women who already have had a child "so you won't be coming back," but such calculations depend upon the women keeping Norplant: "If they can spend $200 over the long run of 5 years to have it put in now, that will save them over the long run" (469). Medicaid often pays for insertion but requires proof of medical necessity before covering early removal. "I believe that the reason they were so hard about taking it out," asserts one woman, "is that they were thinking it was just some story to . . . get Medicaid to pay" (469). The official "story" is that Norplant is safe and reversible, and a Medicaid recipient's experience to the contrary is therefore a manipulative "story" to illegitimately use more Medicaid funds.

The reluctance to remove the implants is all the more pernicious given that many women are pressured to accept Norplant in the first place. One woman in the South Carolina study reports that "they just kept hassling me" to use Norplant immediately after she gave birth: "I really did not want it but after I had my baby, they came in my room and asked me to look at the [educational] movie. . . . They put mine in the day I had my little girl" (468). Another was encouraged to take advantage of the Medicaid support for insertion: "They were telling me, 'What you gonna do for birth control? Are you gonna get a Norplant? It's good. . . . Medicaid will pay for that to go in'" (468). A common observation is that the medical personnel and the instructional video (developed by Wyeth-Ayerst Laboratories, the company distributing the drug) emphasize the benefits of Norplant and downplay the side effects. Women resent being kept from that vital information: "I think they should educate you more. I mean, we're young but we're not stupid" (468).

Other women have testified to similar experiences. Yvonne Thomas, an African American woman from Baltimore, describes the difference between the stories told about Norplant and her actual experience of the drug: "They told us this and they told us that about the Norplant and I'm going through all these changes and I'm trying to have it removed."[32] Like the women in the South Carolina study, she found the medical staff denying her words and her experiences: "Then they tell me that it's not putting me in bed, as if they know how I feel on the inside of *my* body." Thomas also concludes that her status as a low-income mother receiving public assistance and using a public clinic led to the reluctance to remove the device. "I feel like because I'm a social service mother that's what's keeping me from getting this Norplant out of me." Echoing Moynihan's constructions from three decades earlier, the perception of over-reproductive "welfare mothers" endures in today's reproductive policies. Women are blamed for their poverty and that of their children,[33] and if they succumb to pressure to use Norplant, they are blamed when they want the device

removed. Thomas sums up her struggle to have the implants removed:
"That's how they make me feel, like *'you got this Norplant you keep it.'*"

A month after being sentenced, Johnson challenged the Norplant order,
but she had to do so within the confines of the same system that sentenced
her in the first place. Not surprisingly, that system privileges Broadman's
version of the facts. The language used in that version contributes to a construction of Johnson as nonsubject, dangerous agent, and foreign entity.
Antebellum judges handed down rulings that framed slaves and former
slaves with similar constructions, denying African Americans subjectivity,
even as they were defined as threats to the state.[34] Broadman distances
Johnson much more subtly, through metaphor and other indirect comparisons. In the Motion to Modify Sentence, Johnson's lawyer argues against
the Norplant order, citing data from Norplant's inventor and a Norplant
researcher. He specifies that Johnson's own medical situation makes her
unsuited for Norplant: she has high blood pressure, diabetes, asthma, and
a heart murmur, making Norplant an inappropriate and even dangerous
contraceptive for her. Instead of responding to the specific information,
Broadman interrupts and shifts the discussion by invoking a surprising—
and revealing—metaphor: "THE COURT: It just happened that I'm reading a book about the making of the atomic bomb. And the great debate
the scientists had about whether the bomb should be used, that question
about whether, you know, is it the scientist's right to tell Truman to use
the bomb or not to use the bomb. Is that parallel?"

If we accept Broadman's "parallel," some frightening equations emerge.
Male Scientist is still Male Scientist; White Male Judge becomes White
Male American President; the contraceptive is the bomb; the African
American woman becomes Japanese civilians; and the black reproductive
body becomes the land and more specifically enemy territory. Such a metaphor erases Johnson as an agent while it constructs her as the enemy of the
people and hyperbolizes her threat to the community. It renders her foreign, alien, inanimate, nonindividual, and expendable. The easy use of this
chilling comparison reveals who has what kind of authority and agency.
The Lawyer tries to invoke the Scientist to authorize the claim actually
being made by the Woman, but the Judge outranks them all.[35] This reference to an earlier and supposedly resolved debate is expected to authorize Broadman's dismissal of the doctor's arguments. And it seems to
work: The *defense* attorney responds with: "That scenario occurred to me
as well."[36] Broadman successfully constructs consensus around this nonparallel "parallel."

Johnson's case, emerging in the very same moment as Norplant itself, helped set the stage for Norplant debates throughout the 1990s. The fact that she challenged the order reveals her agency, even as the constraints of the legal record make it difficult to hear her voice and to imagine her in terms other than the ones constructed by Broadman. We must strain to hear her words through the public record (for example, when her testimony is filtered through her defense attorney or when she asks Broadman the most salient question about the device he is prescribing from the bench: "Is it harmful . . . ?" [T2 7]). One way to hear alternate narratives is to listen to the voices of other women who faced Norplant decisions, such as the young women in the South Carolina study. Their voices offer revealing insight into the pressures to use Norplant, the often debilitating side effects, and the obstacles to having it removed. Women in other countries have expressed a collective voice against overpromotion of unsafe contraception when they have organized protests against Norplant trials. For example, "under pressure from women's groups, the Brazilian government rescinded its authorization for Norplant testing in 1986" (Roberts 125). Since white activists have tended to construct reproductive freedom as access to abortion and birth control, it has been hard for mainstream U.S. feminism to hear such voices here and abroad.

Norplant continues to surface in policy discussions and courtrooms around the country, although increasing health problems and multiple lawsuits have made it less popular a solution than newspapers and judges first imagined. Even if Norplant itself is declining in use, the policies and discourses around this technological innovation help to predict what may come next. Roberts concludes that the "leading candidate for Norplant's immediate replacement" is Depo-Provera, an injection that provides contraception for several months, producing some similar side effects as Norplant without any option to remove the drug once it is injected (144). Researchers are also developing new "contraceptive vaccines," and methods not now imagined may be on the horizon. The experience with Norplant reminds us that, in a nation accustomed to regulating African American women's bodies, new advances in reproductive technology might not be used to enhance reproductive freedom for all women. The birth control movement, sterilization policies in the twentieth century, and birth control restrictions dating from the late nineteenth century reveal elements of social engineering, eugenics, and racism.[37]

Postbellum antimiscegenation regulations had reproductive control as a central aim. Legal configurations under American slavery in the nineteenth century and going back to the 1600s constructed black female sexuality as dangerous and colonized African American women's bodies for reproduction. Then, it was in the state's interest to have African American women reproducing, benefitting owners by increasing their "stock" and boosting the economy as a whole. Those policies also used the seemingly factual, neutral reasoning of "The Law" to enforce state control over black reproduction. Now, the state perhaps thinks it has too many black babies and often tries to step in with the opposite goal, still using economics as a justification.[38] These are not identical moves, but modern reproductive policies bear the legacy of such earlier constructions of gender, race, and reproduction.

Feminist theory and activism ought to present a challenge to such policies. Like nineteenth-century activists who shaped a women's movement centered on white, middle-class women's interests, contemporary feminists have tended to advocate a narrow configuration of "reproductive rights" that erases African American women's experiences of reproduction and reproductive controls. While abortion rights have taken center stage in the mainstream movement, to many women, the right to have children on their own terms, or the right to have fully informed health care options— or access to health care at all—are more salient issues.[39] Problems emerge not from the defense of abortion rights but when activists see abortion rights as the only issue and fail to imagine other concerns. Problems also occur when feminist activists and theorists fail to acknowledge the role that race and racism have played in the history of reproductive policy in the U.S. I would endorse Roberts's thesis that taking race, racism, and the experiences of African American women into consideration forces us to reimagine reproductive liberty.[40] Interrogating the modern and historical roles of gender, race, and class in reproductive policy and practices can help complicate feminist approaches to these legal issues. Such complications are necessary to create a more responsible and effective feminism.

This epilogue begins to analyze modern legacies of nineteenth-century constructions of race, gender, and slavery. Study of how these issues function in the nineteenth century matters precisely because these constructions endure in various forms today. This endurance can be seen in explicit evocations of images from slavery and in more indirect reliance on those constructions. Directly invoking slavery and its constructions poses the danger of doing so without enough context, responsibility, and acknowledgment of the multiplicity of perspectives—for example, by looking at only one small part of a larger picture or a particular trope without acknowledging the social relations that that construction obscures. It is important to expose and complicate these moves, such as when Moynihan blames a contemporary black matriarchy, supposedly born under slavery, for modern economic and social problems. Even more difficult to address is the reliance on constructions from the nineteenth century without explicitly naming the tropes. A central example is the endurance of the image of dangerous black sexuality without acknowledging that construction as a legacy of slavery, as in policies and presumptions around reproduction. Those moves need to be called out, deconstructed, and defused.

There is no formula to identify where and how the legacies of slavery and its constructions emerge. Three centuries of North American slavery certainly left their mark on modern law and culture. It is crucial that participants in law, literature, and other disciplines acknowledge the historical context of slavery while not allowing the enduring constructions of slavery to obfuscate modern responsibilities. One of the ways to achieve this balance is to be aware of the multiple voices establishing and challenging fictions of slavery. Feminist theory is one possible entry point to this approach, but it must be a consciously antiracist feminist theory that itself takes a range of perspectives into account.

Critical race theory offers an approach that uses multiple perspectives and keeps race at the center. In order to examine slavery and its aftermath, to have African American women at the center and not the margins, to step outside of polarized thinking, it is necessary to acknowledge and emphasize a multiplicity of voices. In addition to multiple voices, it is important to examine multiple genres and periods. In academia, that can mean juxtaposing texts from different perspectives in our scholarship and our syllabi, not for any false sense of evenhandedness but precisely to displace the seemingly neutral authority of any single text. Canonical literature must be taught alongside texts not always recognized as part of the canon—such as slave narratives and abolitionist tracts—and along with documents often not even considered texts, such as court cases and statutes. By the same token, in legal work (whether academic or political), traditionally legal texts can be read using the tools of literary analysis and alongside texts other than official legal documents. Such an approach includes analyzing law alongside literature, juxtaposing the antebellum moment with the turn of the millennium, anthologizing multiple versions of the "same" text, and devising other strategies for reading the inevitably partial records of history and literature.

The previous chapters used the strategy of multiple consciousness to read nineteenth-century law, literature, and black women's resistance. Truth's multiple voices can be heard when she speaks in different discourses and from different positions. Jacobs confronts the discursive dilemmas of slavery: the power of forbidden literacy, of manipulating language, of the tricks of discourse. She is a victim of such moves (when the two men who own her and her children play with law and with words, for example), and she deploys discursive power herself (writing fake letters, publishing her testimony), transforming it even as she uses it. Both are aware of their multiple locations: as African Americans, women, slaves, mothers, Christians, activists, Americans. To erase some of this complexity—to see Truth as suffragist only, or Jacobs as slave narrator only, for example—silences some of the multiple voices generated by these women.

The law tries to erase multiple consciousness and create one perspective, that of a law with personhood, agency, objectivity, and the only voice. It is necessary to expose those legal utterances as not neutral, as unstable and oxymoronic, and to replace that model of one voice with multiple voices.

This epilogue applies these approaches to some recent texts and events, but with every passing year the cited examples become older and newer examples surface. Each new illustration contains the traces of earlier patterns. The theory and method articulated here can be applied to whatever comes up next, in Congress, in the courts, in the so-called court of public opinion, in the next controversial state ballot initiative, and in countless other venues. Many legal and political issues likely to continue to have currency in the coming decades have racial undercurrents and racially disparate impacts but are presented as race neutral. Ultimately, I am arguing for radical skepticism about claims of neutrality (in legal and political discourses and in academic scholarship) and for multiple (but situated) consciousness as a counter to false univocality. We need to examine multiple discourses, perspectives, and periods simultaneously and critically, and we need to dissect how texts and stories are framed. My entry point into this approach is the textual record of slavery and resistance, but the ultimate goal is to rethink how we read the present.

notes

Chapter One

1. See Wheatley's *Collected Works* for the poems and letters making up her public voice, for example, in exchanges with the secretary of state for North America (the earl of Dartmouth) and General George Washington. For the stories of Freeman and Terry, see Kaplan and Kaplan, *The Black Presence in the Era of the American Revolution* (237–41 and 244–48). Truth's 1850 narrative (Truth and Gilbert, *Narrative of Sojourner Truth*), combined with the recent biography by Painter *(Sojourner Truth: A Life, a Symbol),* details her activism. Jacobs's and Delaney's autobiographies (*Incidents in the Life of a Slave Girl,* 1861, and *From the Darkness Cometh the Light,* 1891) are the primary sources for their stories of legal resistance.

2. The Smithsonian Institution, located in the nation's capital, is the National Museum of the United States (so designated in 1858), and its National Portrait Gallery houses the likenesses of "distinguished Americans." Truth's calling card hangs next to portraits of Frederick Douglass and Lucretia Mott; all three were active in a range of political efforts. They are displayed in the abolitionist section of the Civil War floor of the gallery, highlighting certain categorizations. Each is written up for abolitionist activities, but mention of their feminist efforts is omitted. Around the corner is Harriet Beecher Stowe, and nearby are public officials, including Abraham Lincoln. The particular configuration of this display might change over time, but these particular details—in terms of what is emphasized and what is downplayed—still record agendas and priorities of a particular moment.

3. Painter analyzes Truth's photographs as key elements of her self-fashioning that could operate outside of literacy. "Truth could not write, but she could project herself photographically. Photographs furnished a new means of communication—one more powerful than writing. They allowed Truth to circumvent genteel discourse and the racial stereotype embedded in her nation's language" (*Sojourner Truth* 198).

4. In "Sixteenth Century Scholars as Agents of Conquest," Jed quotes Daphne Marlatt: "What is fact? (f)act. the f stop of act. a still photo in the ongoing cinerama" (10).

5. I avoid saying "women and blacks" because that phrase tends to erase African American women, who occupy both categories. Black women could not vote (after the Fifteenth

213

Amendment passed) because they were women; black women could not testify (primarily in the antebellum South) because they were black.

6. The 1850 Fugitive Slave Act and the 1857 *Dred Scott* ruling are two key federalizing moments in the 1850s. Even as the abolitionist movement grew and Americans in the North became increasingly uncomfortable with slavery, the federal government further enshrined slavery as a federal institution.

7. Deborah Gray White's *Ar'n't I a Woman?* offers a probing analysis of these constructs, especially the contrasting uses of the Mammy and Jezebel images. She writes, "The image of Jezebel excused miscegenation, the sexual exploitation of black women, and the mulatto population. It could not, however, calm Southern fears of moral slippage and 'mongrelization,' or man's fear of woman's emasculating powers. But the Mammy image could. Mammy helped endorse the service of black women in Southern households, as well as the close contact between whites and blacks that such service demanded" (61). White sees both images as ideological strategies that serve social and political purposes. In *Black Feminist Thought*, Patricia Hill Collins examines how such images are updated today.

8. Several legal scholars discuss legal constructs as narratives or stories. See, for example, Berry's *The Pig Farmer's Daughter and Other Tales of American Justice* and Peggy Cooper Davis's *Neglected Stories: The Constitution and Family Values*. Both works call attention to the constructions of race, gender, and sexuality underlying the dominant stories recognized by the law from slavery time to the present. Both Berry and Davis also insist that we rethink the dominant narratives and pay closer attention to stories that have been neglected, marginalized, or erased.

9. "Critical race theory" emerged as a label in the late 1980s, forming partly out of interest in and discontent with critical legal studies. *Critical Race Theory: The Key Writings That Formed the Movement* (Crenshaw et al.) details the history of the movement and includes foundational writings from as early as the 1970s. Many writers acknowledge the work of earlier thinkers, such as Frederick Douglass, but such nineteenth-century writings are not commonly labeled as examples of critical race theory.

10. "Multiple consciousness" builds upon W. E. B. Du Bois's term "double consciousness," which he used in *The Souls of Black Folk* in 1903 to describe the duality or "twoness" of being simultaneously "an American, a Negro; two souls, two thoughts, two unreconciled strivings; two warring ideals in one dark body, whose dogged strength alone keeps it from being torn asunder" (3). While Du Bois sees race creating a duality for African Americans, Harris and other feminist theorists of color examine what can happen when there are more than two vantage points or categories of identity. Du Bois sees double consciousness as a painful reality, not a consciously chosen strategy, but this splitting also makes the African American "gifted with second-sight in this American world" (3) and can emerge in literature and politics, for good or for ill: "Such a double life, with double thoughts, double duties, and double social classes, must give rise to double words and double ideals, and tempt the mind to pretence or to revolt, to hypocrisy or to radicalism" (142). Matsuda echoes his approach in her discussion of the multiple consciousness of a woman of color in law school: "This bifurcated thinking is not unusual to her. She has been doing it throughout her schooling—shifting back and forth between her consciousness as a third-world person and the white consciousness required for survival in elite educational institutions. . . . This constant shifting of consciousness produces sometimes madness, sometimes genius, and sometimes both" (*Where Is Your Body?* 5).

11. Among these scholars are Gayatri Spivak, Abdul JanMohamed, and Henry Louis Gates Jr., who read texts against codes of power; and Matsuda, Patricia Williams, and Derrick Bell, who juxtapose legal theoretical voices with marginalized voices (237).

12. "Items of evidence," wrote Marshall, "do not, of course, 'stand alone,' or exist in alien juxtaposition" (qtd. in Crenshaw and Peller 285. Marshall is quoted from *Richmond v. Croson*). Crenshaw and Peller write, "Just as the defense attorneys directed the jury's consideration from the reel-time of the video to the disaggregated stills of the L.A. police and Rodney King, the Court freeze-framed each element of the Richmond setting and isolated them from their meaning-giving context—the history of racial subordination in Richmond, Virginia, the former capital of the Confederacy and one of the central sites of 'massive resistance' to desegregation orders in the 1960s" (288).

13. The high court sapped the power of the Voting Rights Act in the 1995 ruling *Miller v. Johnson*, a case that arose in Georgia, which has a long history of disfranchising African American voters. While the government still can shape voting districts in different ways to benefit many types of interests, conscious efforts to increase the participation of racial minorities now can be singled out and challenged as segregation. In 1996, California voters approved Proposition 209, which sought to dismantle civil rights policy throughout the state but ironically (and strategically) called itself the California Civil Rights Initiative and deployed the misleading language of evenhandedness, neutrality, and antidiscrimination. Other states have followed suit.

14. Of the available terms, I often identify myself as "white," despite problems with that constructed racial label. There is no box on ethnic-data forms for the multiplicity of my background, Italian-Chinese-Armenian-French. I usually choose the "white" box not to erase my cultural and ethnic background or the immigrant status of my grandparents but rather to acknowledge my access to white privilege, by virtue of my skin color and class position.

15. In this essay, hooks aims simultaneously to encourage cross-cultural scholarship and to remind scholars that their work does not appear outside existing relations of power. The problem is not that people from the dominant group produce such scholarship but that often their work is granted more authority. "When we write about the experiences of a group to which we do not belong," she writes, "we should think about the ethics of our action, considering whether or not our work will be used to reinforce and perpetuate domination" ("Feminist Scholarship" 43).

Chapter Two

1. The speaker of Samuel Taylor Coleridge's 1798 poem "Rime of the Ancient Mariner" is a sailor who killed an albatross, considered a symbol of good luck on the sea, and who, as punishment, must wear the dead bird around his neck and tell everyone he meets the story of his offense.

2. M. Benjamin Constant, speech in the French Chamber of Deputies, 17 June 1820 (qtd. in Whittier 265). Massachusetts poet John Greenleaf Whittier wrote "The Slave-Ships" in response to the *Rodeur* incident. He plays with images of light and dark, in the closing lines linking the eventual blindness of the last sighted sailor with his crimes: "O'er a world of light and beauty / Fell the blackness of his crime" (127–28).

3. Conneau's letters to Mayer, now reprinted in a 1976 edition of Conneau's original

manuscript, probably were not available to Hayden when he read the 1928 reprint of Mayer's edition of Conneau's journal.

4. The *Amistad* (which means "friendship") was transporting illegally kidnapped Africans between ports in the Caribbean in 1839 when the fifty-three captive Africans mutinied. They kept two of the Spanish slavers alive to navigate the ship. At night, the sailors steered westward, and the ship finally was boarded by the USS *Washington* off the coast of Long Island. The Africans were imprisoned, and several different parties leapt into the legal morass: the Spanish sailors demanding return (and prosecution) of their "merchandise," the U.S. naval officers suing for "salvage" rights to the human "property" they captured, U.S. President Martin Van Buren worrying about the political fallout among his proslavery supporters, and abolitionists fighting for the Africans' freedom and for the political capital that such a story could generate. The case reached the Supreme Court in 1841 and was successfully argued by John Quincy Adams (see *U.S. v. Amistad*). The Mendian leader of the mutiny was Sengbeh Pieh, who was called Cinquez in Spanish and Cinqué and other names in the American press. Sengbeh Pieh and the other survivors eventually returned to Africa. I use the Spanish version of the African name here because that is the form Hayden uses.

5. In addition to the *Amistad* case and the 1841 *Creole* revolt, Melville most closely draws upon the events and texts of the 1805 *Tryal* mutiny. American captain Amassa Delano published his own account of the event along with translated documents, including Cereno's legal deposition, in his 1817 *Narrative of Voyages and Travels*. Melville plays with the dates, names, and events to produce his story.

6. "Delano took to Negroes, not philanthropically, but genially, just as other men to Newfoundland dogs" (84), but after the revolt, "their red tongues lolled, wolflike, from their black mouths" (102). Another polarity of animal similes occurs when Delano observes a woman with her child and offers a generalization about "negresses," stating that they are "unsophisticated as leopardesses, loving as doves" (73). He is certain that he is observing "naked nature" in this scene, again revealing how unaware he is of the Africans' masquerade and of his own constructions of race.

7. Virtually forgotten for decades, the *Amistad* case in recent years has garnered much attention, from historians and literary critics as well as filmmakers and composers. In addition to Spielberg's 1997 film, writer Thulani Davis and composer Anthony Davis collaborated on an opera based on the revolt. The revival of this story also has produced controversy. Writer Barbara Chase-Riboud charged that Spielberg's film appropriated elements of her 1988 novel about the *Amistad* case, *Echo of Lions*. The case settled out of court, and Chase-Riboud ultimately dropped the charges, but it seems fitting that a plagiarism controversy surrounded this story. Tellings of slavery, slave revolt, and the Middle Passage often raise issues of authorship, authenticity, and appropriation.

8. There have been many detailed studies of *Benito Cereno* (see among others Sale, *The Slumbering Volcano;* Stuckey, *Going through the Storm;* and Sundquist, *To Wake the Nations*), and certainly there are crucial differences between that story and "Middle Passage." Hayden's poem in many ways more radically unsettles and implicates the reader. Here I want to emphasize the contrast with Spielberg's representation: Both historical poet Hayden and canonical novelist Melville depict a white vantage point, but they do so precisely to call attention to problems of framing and perspective.

9. In a volume with poems dedicated to kings, lords, and reverends, Wheatley also

includes a verse "To S.M. a young African Painter, on seeing his Works" (114–15). Her 1774 letter to Occom thanks him for his support of the rights of "the Negroes" and uses biblical language to link the enslavement of the Israelites and the enslavement of Africans in America. Calling attention to the hypocrisy of slaveholders ("our Modern Egyptians") who are also revolutionaries crying for their own liberty, she concludes: "How well the Cry for Liberty, and the reverse Disposition for the Exercise of oppressive Power over others agree,—I humbly think it does not require the Penetration of a Philosopher to determine" (177).

Chapter Three

1. From Truth's address to the American Equal Rights Association, 9 May 1867, as quoted in *History of Woman Suffrage* (Stanton, Anthony, and Gage 2:193). "Pettifoggers" are petty and unscrupulous lawyers.

2. In *Where Is Your Body?* Matsuda writes: "The struggle against racism is historically a struggle against and within law. The hard-won victories of that struggle demonstrate the duality of law: law as subordination and law as liberation" (52). Matsuda describes this seeming contradiction as one that can be theorized: "Scholars of color have attempted to articulate a theoretical basis for using law while remaining deeply critical of it" (24). Analyzing this duality can help reveal the contradictions already embedded in the law.

3. In 1850, Truth collaborated with Olive Gilbert to produce a narrative of her life, which appeared in multiple editions in the years to follow. The 1828 emancipation date in the subtitle is one of many errors that entered the textual record. Beginning in 1875, the narrative was appended with the "Book of Life," which included letters, articles, speeches, and other documents collected by Truth and compiled by her later editor, Frances Titus. In the following chapter, I will examine the textual details (and complications) of her life story in more depth. Unless otherwise noted, references to the *Narrative* are taken from the 1991 Schomburg reprint of the 1878 edition, which includes the original 1850 text but is framed by Titus's introduction and arrangement of the "Book of Life." See Painter, *Sojourner Truth* 107, for a photograph of the original 1850 title page.

4. See Higginbotham, *A Matter of Color* 139–48, for detailed analysis of these debates.

5. The Declaration of Independence states: "But when a long Train of Abuses and Usurpations, pursuing invariably the same Object, evinces a Design to reduce them under absolute Despotism, it is their Right, it is their Duty, to throw off such Government." Lucy Delaney, who won her freedom through a combination of escape and lawsuit, describes her resistance to enslavement in the language of independence and government. In *From the Darkness Cometh the Light* she writes, "My mother had so often told me that she was a free woman and that I should not die a slave, I always had a feeling of independence" (26). She describes her refusal of a particular whipping (which leads to the threat of sale that finally is the catalyst for her departure): "I rebelled against such government" (27).

6. Truth and Gilbert, *Narrative of Sojourner Truth* 41. The details of Truth's departure are drawn from her 1850 narrative (although the date comes from her later biographers [see Painter, *Sojourner Truth* 23]). The textual complications of this collaborative life story will be discussed in the following chapter. The rhetoric here is interesting. When Dumont confronts her with having run away, she responds: "No, I did not *run away;* I walked away by day-light, and all because you had promised me a year of my time" (43), making it clear

that she left because he broke their contract—and that she could play with language and the letter of the law as well as he.

7. In "Speaking in Tongues," Henderson uses the image of a black woman on trial as a metaphor for the role of the African American woman writer, who has to testify about her identity and prove herself to various jurors and spectators. She uses Zora Neale Hurston's character Janie, on trial at the end of *Their Eyes Were Watching God,* as her point of departure. "The challenge of Hurston's character is that of the black woman writer—to speak at once to a diverse audience about her experience in a racist and sexist society where to be black and female is to be, so to speak, 'on trial'" (148). The metaphor might apply more broadly to African American women as public figures, seizing public discourse in any form, not only writing.

8. See Higginbotham 143. Additional laws were passed in the early 1840s (when New York slavery had nearly ended) to protect free African Americans from abduction, including *"An act more effectually to protect the free citizens of this State from being kidnapped, or reduced to Slavery"* (Northup 254). Solomon Northup, "born a freeman" in New York (3), was kidnapped and sold as a slave. His kidnappers were prosecuted under the laws of the 1840s, but escaped conviction (248). The title of Northup's 1853 narrative tells some of the story: *Twelve Years a Slave: Narrative of Solomon Northup, A Citizen of New-York, Kidnapped in Washington City in 1841, and Rescued in 1853, From a Cotton Plantation near the Red River, in Louisiana.* The narrative, whose editor was lawyer David Wilson, includes details of the unsuccessful legal proceedings.

9. For example, in *An Inquiry into the Law of Negro Slavery,* Cobb argues, "The young child is seldom removed from the parent's protection, and beyond doubt, the institution prevents the separation of families, to an extent unknown among the laboring poor of the world" (ccxvii).

10. Liberia had been founded only a few years earlier by the American Colonization Society, whose goal was to remove free African Americans from the U.S. to Africa. Many African Americans, including Douglass and African Methodist Episcopal (AME) Bishop Richard Allen, denounced these efforts as racist and refused to give up their right to remain Americans. David Walker wrote in his 1829 *Appeal:* "Let no man of us budge one step, and let slave-holders come to beat us from our country. America is more our country, than it is the whites—we have enriched it with our *blood and tears. . . .* And will they drive us from our property and homes, which we have earned with our *blood?*" (65).

11. Stowe's sentimental/political novel again offers a contrasting depiction. When fugitive slave Eliza Harris meets Mary Bird, a senator's wife, they connect through the common experience of losing a child: "The woman looked up at Mrs. Bird, with a keen, scrutinizing glance, and it did not escape her that she was dressed in deep mourning." Eliza's perceptiveness activates Mary's empathy. "'Ma'am,' she said, suddenly, 'have you ever lost a child?'" Mary bursts into tears, and Eliza is able to tell her story to an understanding audience (the weeping Mary and, presumably, the weeping reader) (*Uncle Tom's Cabin* 149).

12. Stetson and David, *Glorying in Tribulation,* 70. In *Fanaticism; Its Sources and Influence,* Vale repeatedly casts their project as one of truth-seeking: "When Isabella was thus informed, that a formidable book was coming out against her and Matthias, by Mrs. Folger, aided by all the Christians, she exclaimed, with much energy, (for she is really very energetic and not very timid,) 'I have got the *truth,* and I know it, and I will *crush* them with the *truth*'" (2:116). Truth's desire to tell the truth is in the context of others not only

lying about her but also trying to suppress her statements. Vale details the Folgers' witness tampering: "Mr. B. Folger frequently sent for Isabella before the trial, and was extremely anxious to suppress her information" (2:118).

13. As discussed in the last chapter, in "The Difficult Miracle of Black Poetry in America," Jordan marvels that a poet could emerge from the displacement of the Middle Passage and slavery: "A poet is somebody free. A poet is someone at home." Given the reality of slavery, "How should there be Black poets in America?" (252). A poet by definition is at home (this is the common assumption that Jordan articulates: "A poet is African in Africa, or Irish in Ireland, or French on the Left Bank of Paris, or white in Wisconsin" [252]), and African American poets must rewrite that definition. A preacher or orator perhaps is by definition and by design not at home. She must travel, seeking a changing audience to save and to persuade.

14. The 1896 Supreme Court ruling upheld Louisiana's segregated trains and established the doctrine of "separate but equal," inviting the widespread passage of Jim Crow laws. "Separate but equal" remained the law of the land until *Brown v. Board of Education* in 1954.

15. In an 1867 letter to the editor, Stanton quotes Truth dissecting the irrationality of voting restrictions: "What a narrow idea a reading qualification is for a voter! I know and do what is right better than many big men who can read. And there's that property qualification! just as bad. As if men and women themselves, who made money, were not of more value than the thing they made. If I were a delegate to the Constitutional Convention I could make suffrage as clear as daylight" (Stanton, Anthony, and Gage 2:926–27). Truth again envisioned herself as a legal actor.

Chapter Four

1. The documents of women's suffrage reflect the marginalization of African American women in the movement. For example, in *African American Women,* Terborg-Penn points out that several African Americans organized the integrated South Carolina Woman's Rights Association in 1870. Nevertheless, she notes, the *History of Woman Suffrage*—the multivolume history assembled by Stanton, Anthony, and Matilda Gage and used by modern scholars as a central reference for the early women's movement—dates the beginnings of the South Carolina movement as 1890, when the white-organized South Carolina Woman Suffrage Association was founded (110). African American women were organized and involved throughout the country from the earliest periods of activism, and their efforts repeatedly were marginalized and erased in similar ways. Since modern historians rely on such "official" histories, the erasures endure.

2. Carby's groundbreaking study *Reconstructing Womanhood* exposes the racial subtexts of the ideology of true womanhood and analyzes the critiques posed by African American women writers, including Jacobs. In *Women and Sisters,* Yellin uses the "Am I Not a Woman and a Sister?" motto and motif—depicting an "exposed and enchained" slave woman appealing for help—to explore the problems of how white antislavery feminists regarded and used their African American "sisters" (xv). Yellin discusses Truth and Jacobs as ex-slaves who use and critique the cult of true womanhood as a cultural construction with race-based underpinnings. She acknowledges the problems in transcriptions of Truth's words, but she nevertheless relies on those transcriptions to make her argument about Truth's

discourse. The representations of Truth by white women writers often rely upon her physical appearance and its constructed variance from "the norm" to deny Truth's personhood
and womanhood. This pattern is one of Sanchez-Eppler's conclusions in *Touching Liberty,*
which analyzes the rhetorics of nineteenth-century feminism and abolition. She posits that
feminist and abolitionist discourses are structured by problems of representing or having a
body, because "for both women and blacks it is their physical difference from the cultural
norms of white masculinity that obstructs their claim to personhood" (29). Sanchez-Eppler
explicitly addresses issues of race, but she seems to limit her discussions to the discourse of
white feminists and white abolitionists without acknowledging the marginalization of
African American activists and their rhetoric.

3. In "Ecce Homo, Ain't (Ar'n't) I a Woman, and Inappropriate/d Others," Haraway
argues that Truth's multiple identities and discourses may offer a point of departure away
from the falsely unified humanism of patriarchal and racist society. She cites one of Truth's
reporters, who attempted to transcribe her but said he might as well try to report the seven
apocalyptic thunders. That reporter then quoted Truth speaking literally and metaphorically about what "colored folks [are called upon] to clean up after." Haraway suggests:

> Perhaps what most needs cleaning up here is an inability to hear Sojourner Truth's
> language, to face her specificity, to acknowledge her, but *not* as the voice of the seven
> apocalyptic thunders. Instead, perhaps we need to see her as the Afro-Dutch-
> English New World itinerant preacher whose disruptive and risk-taking practice led
> her "to leave the house of bondage," to leave the subject-making (and humanist)
> dynamics of master and slave, and seek new names in a dangerous world. This
> sojourner's truth offers an inherently unfinished but potent reply to Pilate's skepti-
> cal query—"What is truth?" She is one of Gloria Anzaldúa's *mestizas,* speaking the
> unrecognized hyphenated languages, living in the borderlands of history and con-
> sciousness where crossings are never safe and names never original. (98)

Haraway calls on us to critique the false specifics of Truth's transcriptions—generalizations
in the *"guise* of the specific"—and instead attempt to confront Truth's specificity more
directly. She urges us to confront Truth's multiple locations and languages, her disruptions
and her crossings.

4. I have had similar experiences teaching the texts of Truth's speeches over several years,
painstakingly explaining how the *Anti-Slavery Bugle* article about Akron is more reliable
than Gage's colorful but problematic version (penned twelve years later), only to have students insist that the Gage version of Truth "just sounds like her" or "is so much more
authentic," often because of details such as dialect that I thought we had problematized. I
wasn't surprised by Painter's anecdotes, but I was surprised that after nearly three hundred
persuasive pages, she found herself forced to cede to a symbol: "The symbol we require in
our public life still triumphs over scholarship" (*Sojourner Truth* 287).

5. In *Glorying in Tribulation,* Stetson and David take on the controversy around the
most famous line from Gage's version of the speech, but then they critique those who critique its presence. "It has been argued that Truth never said 'Ain't I a woman.' This is a
surprising argument, since both the *Tribune's* phrase 'She said she was a woman' and the
more awkward 'She said I am a woman's rights' reported by the *Bugle* can be reasonably
understood as affirmative restatements of this question, and 'What is a woman' was certainly
the speech's theme" (118). In examining both internal evidence and the larger context of

gendered abolitionist imagery, they defend the substance, if not the wording, of the line, and they do so far more convincingly than anyone else. (Other defenses usually rest on evidence-shunning emotional refusals to relinquish this famous line. In her "Coda" to *Sojourner Truth*, Painter relates that in conversation, a scholar who had just finished reading the manuscript of Painter's Akron chapter joked, "I think she said it. It sounds like her." "That's not funny," replied Painter [283–84].)

6. In 1852, Douglass argued against the effectiveness of mere moral suasion, saying the conflict would come to blood. Truth reportedly responded, "Is God gone?" or "Is God dead?" (Mabee and Newhouse 83–88; Stetson and David 131–35; Painter, *Sojourner Truth* 160–62). Painter critiques the mythic proportions attained by the line, and Mabee and Newhouse focus on whether the word was "gone" or "dead." Stetson and David place the debate in its specific historical context and analyze how the confrontation was manipulated by white abolitionists. The abolitionist press, threatened by Douglass's independence, seizes this moment of Douglass seemingly put down by a black woman. Stetson and David point out how the accounts begin shifting the terms of the debate to gender, so that Truth's political challenge becomes a challenge to Douglass's manhood: "The white abolitionists' accounts, if not the event, reverberate with the hidden anxieties of power, saturated as always with those of race and of gender" (133).

Truth came to reject Garrisonian nonresistance. But the symbolic value of the quotation proved stronger than history, and "Is God dead" is even engraved on Truth's tombstone (thanks to one of her editors, Frances Titus, who edited her words even in the grave). "In canonizing this phrase from an instance of black-on-black conflict, white people in the nineteenth century awarded transcendent value to the concept of black non-resistance" (Stetson and David 135). In this insightful discussion, Stetson and David probe the real significance of the exchange and the uses to which it was put by those who make the official records (which are printed in newspapers, reprinted in anthologies, and literally etched in stone).

7. Endeavoring to find "true" accounts from those who have been marginalized, other writers also have found they sometimes need to write those accounts themselves. Jordan makes a similar move in "The Difficult Miracle," discussed in an earlier chapter. A decade before Jordan, Alice Walker in her essay "In Search of Our Mother's Gardens" also found the need to rewrite literature to find the black maternal ancestry that she knows is implicit in the history of creative expression, a history we must reenvision in order to hear stifled voices, to read quilts and gardens (figuratively and quite literally). She rewrites an African poem, replacing male nouns with female ones, warning us only that this is "my paraphrase of Okot p'Bitek's great poem" (234). She invokes Wheatley as a tool to rewrite Virginia Woolf, who, five decades earlier, had instructed (white) women to rewrite the history of women and literature, a story so repressed that she had to make up the story of Judith Shakespeare. Walker quotes directly from *A Room of One's Own* but fills the excerpts with brackets instructing contemporary readers to "insert 'black woman'" where Woolf saw only white, to "add" slavery and racism where Woolf saw only patriarchy. Woolf writes of the gifted girl "thwarted and hindered by contrary instincts," and Walker intrudes with "[add 'chains, guns, the lash, the ownership of one's body by someone else, submission to an alien religion']" (235). Walker does not reject Woolf's reasoning, but she pushes it further, makes it say things it ought to have said, calls attention to what is not in the frame. This move is not identical to Woolf's call for rewriting literary history to replace the empty shelves she

sees, nor is it identical to Jordan's or to Stetson and David's rewriting of African American women, but each example reminds us of the need for innovative and literally creative scholarship when we try to write about those who could not write freely.

8. The *Anti-Slavery Bugle* article appeared on June 21, 1851, unsigned, with the title "Women's Rights Convention" (subsequent references to the *Bugle* version of the speech refer to the entry in the bibliography under that title). Painter attributes this article, which consists of a short paragraph of introduction and a long paragraph in Truth's voice, to white abolitionist editor Marius Robinson, with whom Truth stayed during the convention. According to Painter, "Her friend and host, Marius Robinson, was used to her way of speaking and was also serving as secretary of the convention" (*Sojourner Truth* 125).

9. See Finkleman, "*Prigg v. Pennsylvania* and Northern State Courts." William Story was not particularly involved in politics, but he did edit a collection of his father's legal writings.

10. In addition to Story's *Sibyl*, Stowe finds another statue that Truth resembles. Her opening description posits that Truth must have been "as fine a specimen of the torrid zone as Cumberworth's celebrated statuette of the Negro Woman at the Fountain. Indeed, she so strongly reminded me of that figure, that, when I recall the events of her life, . . . I imagine her as a living, breathing impersonation of that work of art" ("Sojourner Truth" 473). Stowe constructs an inanimate product of a male artist as the original and Truth as the imitation, a simile. Truth becomes a regular at the Stowe household, but she remains a fetishized object. Still statuelike, she would "sit among pictures and ornaments," among fellow objects, "the object of attention both to parents and children" (478–79).

Truth's grandson, who appears in Stowe's narrative as an afterthought ("I should have said that she was accompanied"), is similarly objectified. He is the "fattest, jolliest woolly-headed little specimen of Africa that one [apparently one who is white] can imagine" (479). He has no voice, only inappropriate giggles, in a description that echoes the young black characters in *Uncle Tom's Cabin*. He is transformed into "the little black Puck of a grandson" (479) and "our little African Puck" (474)—diminutized, foreign, nonhuman, and "our[s]." Stowe's intended readers are sympathetic white Northerners who cannot quite identify with the objects of their sympathy. And that "we" joins together to possess this black child, undercutting the abolitionist message with language of ownership and objectification.

11. Truth's height is frequently invoked, as in the palm-tree image. Such references need not be disempowering. In Truth and Gilbert's *Narrative*, Truth is quoted using height symbolically to represent the power she felt when seeking her son's freedom: "I felt so *tall within*—I felt as if the *power of a nation* was with me!" (45). In Stowe's version, however, the reference becomes more concrete and physical: "I tell you, I stretched up. I felt as tall as the world" (477).

12. References to clothing often have been used to derail feminist argument. Coverage of the women's movement in the 1970s, for example, sometimes focused obsessively on bra wearing (sometimes actually listing who at a meeting was and who was not wearing a bra) and on the myth of bra burning instead of on substantive issues. Stowe's outlook on feminism may have changed in later years, but in this glimpse she seems dismissive of the women's movement.

13. "Some writers, in quoting Gage's report of what Truth said, covered up Gage's error by arbitrarily altering the figure of thirteen children to five, without giving any hint of uneasiness about doing so" (Mabee and Newhouse 75).

14. "With an Introduction by Jeffrey C. Stewart" (1991); "Edited and with an Introduction by Margaret Washington" (1993); "Edited with an Introduction and Notes by Nell Irvin Painter" (1998). In 1991 and 1998, Gilbert's name did appear in the small-print Library of Congress Cataloging-in-Publication Data. Such choices have pragmatic consequences, such as whether a database search for Truth or Gilbert as author will produce the edition.

15. See, for example, Sundquist, "Nat Turner, Thomas Gray, and the Phenomenology of Slavery" (in *To Wake the Nations*), and Wood, "Nat Turner: The Unknown Slave as Visionary Leader."

16. Versions of his revolt are told in proslavery Southern newspapers and in Northern papers, including the abolitionist *Liberator* (which argued that this revolt is exactly what they had been predicting as the inevitable result of slavery). African American writers, including Jacobs, refer to his revolt in their narratives. Another first-person narrative by the same title appeared in 1967, when Southern white novelist William Styron published his fictional *Confessions of Nat Turner* to both acclaim and attack.

17. "Mr. Garrison followed me, taking me as his text" (218); "I was a 'graduate from the peculiar institution,' Mr. Collins used to say, when introducing me, '*with my diploma written on my back!*'" (219); "I was generally introduced as a '*chattel*'—a '*thing*'—a piece of southern '*property*'—the chairman assuring the audience that *it* could speak" (Douglass, *My Bondage* 220). Truth's concerns might have been different, but Douglass's pointed description is still instructive.

18. Gilbert has nearly a page in Truth's voice, comparing God's ability to work and her own: "It seems that God cannot do as much as *I* can; for *I* can bear the sun at noon, and work several days and nights in succession without being much tired" (107, emphasis in original). By the end of the long quoted passage, Gilbert seems to forget to maintain Truth's first person: "As it regarded the worship of God, he was to be worshipped at all times and in all places; and one portion of time never seemed to *her* more holy than another" (Truth and Gilbert, 107–8, emphasis added).

19. A sampling of collections in which Truth has appeared: *Black Women in Nineteenth-Century American Life; The American Negro: His History and Literature; Norton Anthology of Literature by Women; Norton Anthology of African American Literature; Nation under God: A Religious-Patriotic Anthology; Black Sister: Poetry by Black American Women, 1746–1980;* and *The Faith of Our Fathers: An Anthology Expressing the Aspirations of the American Common Man.*

20. Slave narratives often highlight issues of naming. In *Incidents,* Jacobs (who took her father's surname, which came from "a white gentleman") discusses the complications of naming her children: "What tangled skeins are the genealogies of slavery! I loved my father; but it mortified me to be obliged to bestow his name on my children" (78).

21. Higginbotham cites several cases in which defendants challenged their treatment in courtrooms where all whites were referred to with honorifics and African Americans were referred to by their first names (*Shades* 137–38). From another arm of government, during the Vietnam War, the all-white Albany, Georgia, draft board initially granted a deferment to Preston King with a letter using the title "Mr." When the board discovered the draftee was African American, the deferment was denied, and every subsequent correspondence used his first name alone, even after King protested (see "Call Me Mister!").

22. Truth frequently had her grandson or a friend act as amanuensis, producing letters

written in the first person from Truth's perspective. They often were signed "Sojourner Truth," without indicating that they were written down by another (creating a record of documents in different handwritings all signed with the same name).

23. Pro-Lincoln abolitionists tell one story, emphasizing how receptive the president was to this ex-slave, while others make the president less of a hero, often through subtle changes in the direct quotations of the story. See Mabee, "Sojourner Truth and President Lincoln." In the 1960s, in "Sojourner Truth: The First Sit-In," Harlowe constructs the encounter as the first American sit-in, emphasizing that Truth had to sit in Lincoln's office "quietly and resolutely" for several hours before he finally came out to see her (173). African Americans sometimes were barred from the White House, and Truth once was refused entry to a public reception there.

24. *New York Evening Post,* 9 May 1867. Similar versions, with variations, appeared in the official proceedings of the convention; *New York Daily Tribune* (10 May 1867); *National Anti-Slavery Standard* (1 June 1867); and Stanton, Anthony, and Gage (2:193–94). See Mabee and Newhouse, *Sojourner Truth: Slave, Prophet, Legend* 178–79.

25. Mabee and Newhouse limit the possibility of this interpretation when they reprint the speech with bracketed insertions: "You [men] have been having our right[s] so long . . ." (179). While the insertions might provide some clarity, they also remove some of the interesting ambiguity in the passage.

26. Stanton, Anthony, and Gage 2:188. As representative feminist icons, Stanton and Truth still make the news. Controversy erupted in 1997 when a massive sculpture depicting Stanton and other white suffragists was to be moved to the U.S. Capitol Rotunda (from its more marginalized place downstairs in the crypt, after years of lobbying by feminist groups) and African American women's organizations argued that the sculpture erased the role of black women in the struggle for suffrage and should include the figure of Truth.

27. Stanton, Anthony, and Gage 2:193. The text is taken from the convention proceedings.

28. Ibid. 1:567. See also Berlant's discussion in "The Queen of America Goes to Washington City" of Frances Harper's use of the story of Esther in *Iola Leroy.*

29. As usual, different versions reveal variations. The *New York Daily Times* report of 8 September 1853 has the same overall content but not any of the direct quotes that appear in the *History of Woman Suffrage* version: here the king and God speak only in paraphrase. Such a difference could suggest that an eager transcriber inserted the quotations. But the *Times* also had a particular structure in mind for the piece, one that would highlight the boisterous behavior of the audience. Their version interrupts Truth every few sentences with a bracketed insertion of her hecklers' words and behavior. It is possible that with so many inserted quotations, the *Times* reporter chose to omit Truth's use of quotations. See "Woman's Rights Convention" 1.

Chapter Five

1. Scott sued for his freedom in 1846 under Missouri law after having lived in the free state of Illinois and the free territory of Wisconsin. Settled Missouri law held that once an owner took a slave into free territory, that individual slave became free. By the time the case reached the U.S. Supreme Court, however, it became an opportunity to make far-reaching claims about slavery and race. In *Scott v. Sandford,* Taney wrote a strikingly partisan and

proslavery decision, while using rhetoric that suggested he was merely reporting well-known facts. Taney declares a long history of African American inferiority, rooted before the Declaration of Independence, and supports his claim by asserting: "This opinion was at that time fixed and universal in the civilized portion of the white race. It was regarded as an axiom in morals as well as in politics, which no one thought of disputing, or supposed to be open to dispute; and men in every grade and position in society daily and habitually acted upon it in their private pursuits, as well as in matters of public concern, without doubting for a moment the correctness of this opinion" (407). Any white citizen not holding this opinion is thereby excluded from the "civilized portion" of humanity. For a detailed analysis of the ruling and its impact, see Fehrenbacher.

2. Jacobs anticipates Foote's rewriting of the same passage in the 1879 spiritual narrative *A Brand Plucked from the Fire*. In fighting for her right to preach the gospel, Foote finds herself struggling against not only racism but also the sexism of African American men of the cloth. She writes a letter stating her side of the story and finds her document ignored. "Why should they notice it?" she asks ironically. "It was only the grievance of a woman, and there was no justice meted out to women in those days. Even ministers of Christ did not feel that women had any rights which they were bound to respect" (207). Over a decade after the *Dred Scott* ruling was overturned, Foote employs another radical reversal of its terms, this time to indict sexism.

3. See, for example, Braxton's article on *Incidents* as a redefinition of the genre. Stepto takes male narrators and especially Douglass's 1845 book as his starting point in his influential study of African American narrative. Starling's pioneering work *The Slave Narrative* asserts that it is Douglass's book that "stands for the entire genre" (xvii). Foster's ground-breaking study *Witnessing Slavery* by her own account "seriously slights slave women's narratives" (xxii). Foster focuses on Jacobs and other women writers in her later study *Written by Herself.*

4. Some readings concentrate on one element at the cost of reducing the complexity of Jacobs's approach. For example, in *Touching Liberty,* which centers on constructions of the body in feminist and abolitionist rhetorics, Sanchez-Eppler emphasizes Jacobs's focus on sexual experience, arguing that sexuality and childbirth "are" this slave narrative (84). While interesting and provocative, her reading also deemphasizes other concerns in Jacobs's book.

5. The notion of a gendered public/private split is linked to the idea of separate spheres. This ideological construct emerges from various cultural and legal fictions and masks race and class assumptions. For specific analysis of nineteenth-century laws, see Burnham, "An Impossible Marriage." For general analysis of separate spheres ideology, see, for example, Rosenberg, *Beyond Separate Spheres.* For an analysis of "the legal order and the public/private split," see Taub and Schneider, "Women's Subordination and the Role of Law." An often-quoted legal expression of this idea—merging civil, natural, and divine law—comes from the 1873 Supreme Court ruling *Bradwell v. Illinois:* "The civil law as well as nature itself, has always recognized a wide difference in the respective spheres and destinies of man and woman. Man is, or should be woman's protector and defender. The natural and proper timidity and delicacy which belongs to the female sex evidently unfits it for many of the occupations of civil life. . . . The paramount destiny and mission of woman are to fulfill the noble and benign offices of wife and mother. This is the law of the Creator" (141–42).

6. Cobb also published *The Supreme Court Manual* (1849), *A Digest of the Statute Laws*

of the State of Georgia (1851), fifteen volumes of Georgia Supreme Court decisions, and *The Code of the State of Georgia* (1861).

7. Cobb's quotation asserts that "truth, the more it is stirred up, the more it will shed its light." *Splendescit* means to render clear and bright, perhaps suggesting a whitening of truth as well.

8. Josiah Nott and George Gliddon were prominent scientists who, along with Dr. Samuel Morton, promoted the theory of polygenesis. Political and legal defenses of slavery and racism increasingly invoked scientific discourses in the nineteenth century, drawing upon "objective" and quantifiable "fact" for evidence. In *An Inquiry into the Law of Negro Slavery*, Cobb often invokes science as a body of facts undergirding law and history. His science sometimes appears in animal analogies: "It is a fact, well known to entomologists, and too well established to admit of contradiction, that the red ant will issue in regular battle array, to conquer and subjugate the black or negro ant, as he is called by entomologists" (8). As black ants go, he implies, so go black humans. The authority of unnamed "entomologists" confirms the scientific validity of his claim. Cobb further details that some slave ants, "on account of the form of their mouth, have not the physical ability either to prepare habitations for their family, to procure food, or to feed them" (9). The comparison implies that human slaves are equally incapable, according to laws of nature and of the state, of caring for their families or functioning as anything but slaves.

9. Such reasoning still appears today. Citing population growth figures, a recent book review asserts, "American slavery turned out to be unique in its capacity to sustain human life. . . . The reasons for that astounding growth are debated. . . . By the 19th century slaves were given ample food, adequate housing and medical care that was extraordinary by contemporary standards" (Maier 9).

10. Cobb nonetheless declares: "Stroud's 'Sketch of the Law of Slavery' is and was intended only as an Abolition pamphlet" (x).

11. While Stroud excuses the "free states" from any blame for slavery, many activists, including Jacobs and Douglass, take the opposite approach (especially after passage of the Fugitive Slave Act) and hold the entire nation responsible for its role in upholding Southern slavery. In one famous speech, for example, Douglass explicitly defines his subject as "AMERICAN SLAVERY," not Southern slavery, and he concludes with this unambiguous indictment: "For revolting barbarity and shameless hypocrisy, America reigns without a rival" ("What to the Slave Is the Fourth of July?" 285, 288).

12. Unlike most Southern apologists for slavery, in *South-Side View of Slavery*, Adams expresses concern for possible abuses, but generally he sets the reader's mind at rest. He tends to structure his impressions by replacing slave testimony with white testimony. For example, he describes what appears to be a heartbreaking auction but then talks to slaveholders who explain that the sale was to reunite a family. Like Jacobs, he sometimes describes more than one version of a story, but his goal is the opposite. The slave version is a distanced observation, while the slaveholder version is framed as providing the missing context. Jacobs, on the other hand, often depicts the surface-level version of a story and then fills in the crucial invisible details with slave testimony. She insists on having slaves speak for slave experiences. She dislodges the privilege that white testimony has, while Adams fails to question that privilege. Jacobs demands that the subject speak for her- or himself, while Adams relies on the oppressor to tell the story.

13. Jacobs critiques the incomplete pictures of slavery offered by Mrs. Flint and Adams

as decontextualized images that remove all evidence of racial power, similar to the notion of "disaggregation" articulated by Crenshaw and Peller in "Reel Time/Real Justice."

14. Revised Statutes of North Carolina 111:50. Many states nervously attempted to draw lines specifying when the African blood was diluted enough to permit a legal voice. In Texas, for example, the testimony restriction applied to descendants of blacks only up to the third generation (Stroud 44). Consequently, if an "octaroon" parent and his or her whiter child witnessed the same criminal act, the older witness might be disqualified from uttering a word in the courtroom while the offspring's testimony might be able to convict a white perpetrator.

15. 1 Revised Virginia Code 422, qtd. in Stroud, *A Sketch of the Laws Relating to Slavery* 44 (emphasis his). Other statutes used similar language. In an 1852 Kentucky statute, Native American testimony also was restricted: "A slave, negro, or Indian shall be a competent witness in a case of the commonwealth for or against a slave, negro, or Indian, or in a civil case to which only negroes or Indians are parties, but in no other case" (Kentucky Revised Statutes 107:1). For analysis of this law in postbellum Kentucky, see Higginbotham, *The Matter of Color* 77–80.

16. The previous section of the code permits white citizens to make a complaint against an owner who neglects the clothing or feeding of slaves ("on behalf of such slave"), but there too such person may "exculpate or clear himself from the charge, by his or her own oath" (Public Laws, sec. 38).

17. As early as 1773, slaves organized to submit a petition to the legislative bodies in Massachusetts. The tone was humble, asking only for "such relief as is consistent with your wisdom, justice and goodness," though the petitioners also declared: "We have no property! we have no wives! we have no children! we have no city! no country!" (qtd. in Higginbotham, *The Matter of Color* 86). Governor Hutchinson (who a year earlier signed the Attestation for Phillis Wheatley discussed in chapter 2) never replied to the "Petition of Slaves in Boston." If Goodell found no formal petitions to cite, he might have included any number of pleas to the government published in slave narratives and abolitionist newspapers.

18. Douglass was introduced as a novelty, "a piece of southern '*property*,'" astounding the audience that "*it* could speak." As one of the first fugitives on the circuit, "I had the advantage of being a '*brand new fact*.'" He himself *is* a fact, and many wanted his testimony to stick to the facts, plain and simple: "'Let us have the facts,' said the people. So also said Friend George Foster, who always wished to pin me down to my simple narrative." Another prominent abolitionist, William Collins, more explicitly separated the factual work provided by the slave and the intellectual work performed by white abolitionists: "'Give us the facts,' said Collins, 'we will take care of the philosophy.'" Douglass also reports being told how to deliver his testimony—with "a *little* of the plantation manner of speech" (all quotes from *My Bondage* 220). Douglass explains how abolitionists feared that audiences would not believe that he had been a slave because he was too literate and articulate, and they urged him to speak like they thought a former slave should. While Truth was a different sort of orator, deploying vernacular variety in ways Douglass did not, his analysis still suggests the attitudes that informed the rhetorical decisions of Truth's transcribers.

19. We see the African American men and their struggle through Shaw's eyes, and his character is developed through his voice-over letters and his relationships with other

characters. The African American soldiers, including free blacks, former slaves, and fugitive slaves, have no such depth and background to their characters. This pattern continues in films about twentieth-century struggles: *Mississippi Burning* (in which, to the surprise of many viewers, white FBI agents were civil rights heroes), *Long Walk Home, Cry Freedom, The Power of One,* and *A World Apart,* to name a few. Spike Lee's *Malcolm X* is one of the few films from Hollywood to resist completely any pressure to tell the story through the eyes of a benevolent white character.

20. Scholars (and activists), especially of dominant groups, have a responsibility to cite a variety of voices and to be conscious if they or their sources omit certain voices, most compellingly the voices of the group being discussed. For a discussion of how such erasures appear in civil rights scholarship, see Richard Delgado's essay "The Imperial Scholar," in which he discovers "an inner circle of about a dozen white, male writers who comment on, take polite issue with, extol, criticize, and expand on each other's ideas. It is something like an elaborate minuet" (47). Often, erasures of testimony appear in seemingly trivial sources of information. In the *Columbia Dictionary of Quotations* (as part of the Microsoft Bookshelf '95 CD-ROM), the subject "Slavery" yields twenty-two quotations, yet only one is from a black source, American blues singer Billie Holiday. Somehow, the editors felt that Winston Churchill and Oscar Wilde had more relevant things to say about slavery than Frederick Douglass or Angela Davis. A CD-ROM of quotations certainly is not a scholarly work, but in some ways its everyday quality (it is more immediately accessible than, say, Higginbotham's study of colonial slave law) is part of its insidiousness. In any case, it seems to reveal another legacy of restrictions on black testimony.

21. Describing circumstances from the white citizens' perspective, McLaurin includes data such as the fact that "slaveowners held twice as many horses and sheep as did non-slaveholders, and three times as many cattle" (7). After quoting a boastful letter from a white citizen of the town, McLaurin states, "Then in the 1850s we infer that the people of Fulton were extremely pleased with and proud of their accomplishments" (13). He does not specify that "people" evidently means *white* people here.

22. Pollard opens *Black Diamonds* with a reprint of a *New Orleans Delta* review that finds his work unprejudiced and tolerant. The review locates its praise in the context of general suspicion of works that mix politics and literature, especially in the wake of *Uncle Tom's Cabin:* "In general we are strongly averse to mixing up special questions in ethics or in politics with what is called polite literature" (vii). Pollard's work is different: "The author appears to be a thorough Southerner in education, opinion, sympathy, and attachment; yet, his letters are *remarkably free from sectional prejudice and acerbity,* and, in truth, contain sketches that are amongst the most *catholic, and tolerant, and genial,* we ever had occasion to peruse" (viii, original emphasis).

23. Stowe also rejected taking Jacobs's daughter to England, a trip Jacobs would have paid for, claiming the British would spoil the girl. As Jacobs wrote to Post: "She was afraid that if her situation as a Slave should be known it would subject her to much petting and patronizing which would be more pleasing to a young Girl than useful and the English was very apt to do it and she was very much opposed to it with this class of people" (qtd. in Jacobs 235). Jacobs later used more open sarcasm: "Think dear Amy that a visit to Stafford House would spoil me as Mrs Stowe thinks petting is more than my race can bear well what a pity we poor blacks cant have the firmness and stability of character that you white people have" (xix).

24. See Foster, "Harriet Jacobs's *Incidents* and the 'Careless Daughters' (and Sons) Who Read It," for analysis of how critics fixate on issues of authority, authenticity, and editorial control when addressing the works of African American women in the nineteenth century. In examining implications of framing, I do not argue that Jacobs was a passive object of editorial control; rather, she was active in packaging her own story in powerful ways.

25. The original title was *Linda; or, Incidents in the Life of a Slave Girl.* While "Linda" appeared on the cover of the original edition, only the subtitle appeared on the title page (Foster, "Resisting *Incidents*" 66–68).

26. See Blassingame, *The Slave Community,* for example, whose rejection of the narrative's authenticity was linked in part to gendered assumptions about what was realistic content in a slave narrative.

27. Respectable citizens often vouched for the character of slave writers in such narratives. Douglass had white abolitionists William Lloyd Garrison and Wendell Phillips introduce his 1845 narrative, though he chose the African American "Dr. James M'Cune Smith" for his 1855 introduction.

28. Jacobs uses dialect here, illustrating Fred's constructed simplicity and illiteracy and highlighting her own literate voice by contrast. "'Lord bress you, chile,' he replied. 'You nebber gibs me a lesson dat I don't pray to God to help me to understan' what I spells.' . . . There are thousands, who, like good uncle Fred, are thirsting for the water of life; but the law forbids it" (73).

29. In addition to writing, the 1740 Public Laws of South Carolina punished other forms of communication: "It is absolutely necessary to the safety of this Province, that all due care be taken to restrain the wanderings and meetings of negroes and other slaves . . . and their using and carrying wooden swords, and other mischievous and dangerous weapons, or using or keeping of drums, horns, or other loud instruments, which may call together or give sign or notice to one another of their wicked designs and purposes" (695:36). In "Talking Books," Gates and McKay emphasize that the post-Stono code made "two forms of literacy punishable by law: the mastery of letters, and the mastery of the drum" (xxix). Because they can "give sign," writing and drumming are no less "dangerous weapons" than are swords.

30. Truth's friend Laura Haviland tells the story of Milla Granson, the Louisiana slave (mentioned previously in this chapter) who ran a "midnight school" to teach fellow slaves to read: "It was opened at eleven or twelve o'clock at night, and closed at two o'clock a.m. . . . Her number of scholars was twelve at a time, and when she had taught these to read and write she dismissed them, and again took her apostolic number and brought them up to the extent of her ability, until she had graduated hundreds. A number of them wrote their own passes and started for Canada" (qtd. in Lerner 32–33).

31. Jacobs often demonstrates how the law helps whites defraud blacks. Behavior that ought to be illegal—from breaking contracts to committing rape—is in fact protected if committed against slaves. One of the first transactions Jacobs describes between slave and white is a monetary exchange between the grandmother and her mistress: "She had laid up three hundred dollars, which her mistress one day begged as a loan, promising to pay her soon. The reader probably knows that no promise or writing given to a slave is legally binding; for, according to Southern laws, a slave, *being* property, can *hold* no property. When my grandmother lent her hard earnings to her mistress, she trusted solely to her honor. The honor of a slaveholder to a slave!" (6). Jacobs educates the reader, pretending we already

know the legal fact at issue. The narrator does not tell us the end of that story until the next chapter, so that her implicit criticism of the "honor of a slaveholder" is not proven immediately. "While my grandmother was thus helping to support me from her hard earnings, the three hundred dollars she had lent her mistress were never repaid. When her mistress died, her son-in-law, Dr. Flint, was appointed executor. When grandmother applied to him for payment, he said the estate was insolvent, and the law prohibited payment. It did not, however, prohibit him from retaining the silver candelabra, which had been purchased with that money. I presume they will be handed down in the family, from generation to generation" (11). Flint hides behind the law, which he gives agency and claims "prohibited" him from repaying the loan. The paragraph opens with the grandmother struggling to help her grandchild despite being robbed by her owner and closes with an image of the descendants of the white robbers benefitting from their ill-gotten gains. The white family benefits at the expense of the black family, and the slippery law authorizes such injustices.

32. Jacobs depicts other slaves devising loopholes and justifies such efforts through her description of white law as "the regulations of robbers" (187). The slave Luke obtains his master's money through subterfuge and the letter of the law (he did not *steal* the money because the pair of pants containing the money was *given* to him). Reiterating how poorly Luke had been treated, the narrator asks: "When a man has his wages stolen from him, year after year, and the laws sanction and enforce the threat, how can he be expected to have more regard to honesty than does the man who robs him?" (193). Jacobs rewrites the story so that instead of theft, Luke simply recovers "a portion of his unpaid wages." She applies the language of criminality to the standard operation of slaveholders, not to the technically illegal act of the slave.

33. In Louisiana, for example, one law passed on this question stated, "No one can emancipate his slave unless the slave has attained the age of *thirty years,* and has behaved well at least for four years preceding his emancipation. . . . [except] *a slave who has saved the life of his master, his master's wife or one of his children, [who] may be emancipated at any age*" (qtd. in Stroud 101, emphasis his).

34. That language is especially evocative in reference to a group deemed inferior by the appearance of their skin. A century later, in *The Peculiar Institution,* Stampp uses the odd image of African Americans as "white men with black skins on" (4).

35. Genesis 9:18–27. The "curse of Ham" was a common defense of slavery. Douglass turns the proslavery use of Ham against slavery: "A very different-looking class of people are springing up at the south, and are now held in slavery, from those originally brought to this country from Africa; and if their increase will do no other good, it will do away the force of the argument, that God cursed Ham, and therefore American slavery is right. If the lineal descendants of Ham are alone to be scripturally enslaved, it is certain that slavery at the south must soon become unscriptural" (*Narrative* 41).

36. Douglass ironically uses skin imagery to represent the sticking power of not race but racism. In an 1846 letter from abroad, he contrasts the aristocracies of England with the racism of America: "Whatever may be said of the aristocracies here, there is none based on the color of a man's skin. This species of aristocracy belongs preeminently to 'the land of the free, and the home of the brave.' I have never found it abroad, in any but Americans. It sticks to them wherever they go. They find it almost as hard to get rid of, as to get rid of their skins" (*My Bondage* 227).

37. Slavery advocates often linked white equality to racial hierarchy. Equality is one of the many benefits of slavery listed by Cobb. In a slave society, all citizens—defined as white—are equal, because they are not slaves: "The mass of laborers not being recognized among citizens, every citizen feels that he belongs to an elevated class. It matters not that he is no slaveholder; he is not of the inferior race. . . . The poorest meets the richest as an equal. . . . There is truthfully republican equality in the ruling class. . . . Citizens imbibe freedom with their mother's milk" (ccxiii). Even if "citizen" is defined as white and male, the image conjured up by Cobb is still a fiction: there were vast inequalities and class differences between the slaveholding elite and the white, nonslaveholding poor.

38. Starling, *The Slave Narrative* 337. That number includes a wide range of texts, from books to court records to interviews. Even if we accept more conservative estimates, Hyde is still erasing a quite substantial genre, from a literary or historical standpoint.

39. If pressed, Hyde perhaps would be able to recall at least Douglass or Booker T. Washington as famous ex-slaves who wrote. I suspect that this obliteration of slave testimony was not viewed by Hyde or anyone in his office as a central point, needing research or even contemplation to back it up. He, or a staff person working on the report, most likely assumed, "Slaves didn't write, right?" and wrote the parenthetical. The very smallness of remark does not lessen the omission; in fact, that is what is particularly striking.

Chapter Six

1. In *An Inquiry,* Cobb makes mulattoes a separate and "superior race," permitting an additional layer of racial hierarchy. He offers absolutist declarations about the characteristics of the races, yet race itself is not absolute, by his own admission. Cobb attempts to construct such absolutes precisely because the categories are so unstable. Such slippages persist in twentieth-century laws that attempt to draw firm lines while also revealing anxiety about the ambiguity of those divisions. Virginia's 1924 Preservation of Racial Integrity Act banned interracial marriage and defined "white" as one with "no trace whatsoever of any blood other than Caucasian," while it permitted in the category white "one-sixteenth American Indian blood" to protect descendants of Pocahontas and John Rolfe. There were multiple contradictions in the law, revealing that racial mixing did occur even as its effects were denied. "The racial boundary was drawn differently for white/Indian and white/Negro mixtures, it changed over time for both, and all of the 'pure' racial categories defined by the law—white, Indian, and Negro—included in their definitions mixed-race individuals. Yet the myth of natural categories was maintained, with all the moral force that the idea of a 'natural order' could confer on such a categorization" (Higginbotham and Kopytoff 1982). The law remained in effect for forty-three years.

2. This emotional ruling is authored by the presiding judge of the Georgia Supreme Court, who is described by Cobb as "THE PROFOUND LAWYER, THE ELOQUENT ADVOCATE, THE IRREPROACHABLE JUDGE, AND THE CHRISTIAN PHILOSOPHER" (vii). Irreproachable Judge Lumpkin can claim dispassionate and "temperate" judgment even as he admits to an excited heart in this case (*Stephen v. State* 220).

3. The Mississippi defendant was discharged, but Lumpkin's ruling in the Georgia case resulted in Stephen's execution: "He must be left to abide the penalty of that awful sentence, which adjudges him to be unworthy to have a place longer among the living" (*Stephen v. State* 242). Capital punishment applied because of the race of both accused and

accuser, for "rape, and an attempt to commit a rape, by a slave or free person of color, upon a free white female, are both capitally punished by the laws of this state" (241–42). See Burnham, "An Impossible Marriage," for a detailed comparison of these two cases.

4. McLaurin's modern retelling *Celia: A Slave*, discussed in the previous chapter, similarly keeps men at the center. McLaurin sums up the complicated story by saying the central issue is the inability of slave men to protect their women. The case involves a young woman who was purchased to be a sexual partner. After several years of rape and having begun a relationship with a fellow slave, she murders their owner and eventually is executed. Yet the author of the book concludes: "Perhaps *the most fundamental issue* is the extent to which slave men were able to protect the slave women to whom they were attached" (139, emphasis added).

5. As in the previous chapter, I distinguish between Jacobs, the author of *Incidents,* and Brent, her constructed first-person narrator. Brent clearly represents Jacobs in this autobiographical work, but Jacobs also deploys this narrator and character in particular ways to help her shape her claims.

6. Jacobs offers an earlier model of a white woman standing in judgment of Brent. Jealous Mrs. Flint sets herself up as prosecutor and judge, interrogating and accusing Brent. She produces a Bible: "'Lay your hand on your heart, kiss this holy book, and swear before God that you tell me the truth.'" Brent swears, and Mrs. Flint continues her judicial performance: "'You have taken God's holy word to testify your innocence,' said she. 'If you have deceived me, beware!'" (33). Brent testifies, producing self-pity but not compassion from Mrs. Flint, who later accuses Dr. Flint "of crime." When her accusation of her husband fails, "she would gladly have had me flogged for my supposed false oath" (34–35). Brent is prosecuted, though the victim, and her testimony counts less than her perpetrator's and can lead to her punishment. Jacobs's readers, perhaps inclined to judge Brent, might be discouraged by this negative model.

7. Even the evil deeds of this unkind master (whose calculations, cruelties, and debaucheries are detailed by Jacobs) are rendered secondary to the more fundamental evil of the institution: "Had it not been for slavery, he would have been a better man, and his wife a happier woman" (51).

8. Brown's *Clotel; or, The President's Daughter* tells a fictionalized story about the enslaved offspring of Thomas Jefferson. The 1853 novel first appeared in England and saw print in the U.S. only after Brown changed Jefferson to an unnamed senator. In 1998, DNA testing on the descendants of Jefferson and of his slave Sally Hemmings offered scientific evidence for what many considered old news: Jefferson, like many slaveholders, fathered slaves.

9. See Higginbotham and Kopytoff ("Racial Purity and Interracial Sex"), who discuss how race, appearance, and status did not always correspond. They point out that the "numbers of fair-skinned slaves increased over time, as the slave population 'lightened'" (1972).

10. Jacobs often analyzes racial identity as a construction, though she does not betray the same anxieties that Stroud reveals. In attacking Northerners who became masters, she states: "They seem to satisfy their consciences with the doctrine that God created the Africans to be slaves. What a libel upon the heavenly Father, who 'made of one blood all nations of men!' And then who are Africans? Who can measure the amount of Anglo-Saxon blood coursing in the veins of American slaves?" (44). This identity issue also points to one of the central crimes of slavery: the rape of slave women by white men. In this series

of questions, the constructed human doctrine is set opposite God's quoted intentions and hence reframed as libelous, itself a legal term. Many U.S. laws did purport to measure the amount of African blood in the veins of Americans, sometimes defining exactly what fraction determined blackness for purposes of legal discrimination. Such a law not only is arbitrary but also indicates the constructed racial hierarchy: a drop of African blood can make one black, but an equal amount of Anglo blood—or a majority of Anglo blood—does not make one white. In "A Critique of 'Our Constitution Is Color-Blind,'" Gotanda discusses consequences of and alternatives to this "rule of hypodescent" (258).

11. Jacobs may not be responding directly to Charlotte Brontë's 1847 novel with this line, but she certainly engages with the conventions of nineteenth-century women's novels throughout her narrative.

12. This rhetorical move evokes Fern's inclusion of her character's stock certificate in the closing pages of *Ruth Hall*. While the context is very different, Fern also displaces marriage as the culmination of a woman's life. Economic freedom and professional success, along with motherhood apart from marriage, are the rewards at the end of this largely autobiographical novel, published six years before *Incidents*. Fern's brother is editor Nathaniel Willis, whose wife, Cornelia Grinnel Willis, is the woman who employs, befriends, and purchases Jacobs.

13. See Spillers, "Mama's Baby, Papa's Maybe," for analysis of naming and the links to race, gender, and power (74). Instead of father to son, the name exchange here flows from white great-grandfather to enslaved great-granddaughter.

14. Slavery advocates often invoked comparisons with whites of the poor laboring classes, arguing that slaves were better off and that slave societies were spared a class of poor whites. See, for example, Adams, *South-Side View* ("pauperism is prevented by slavery" [47]) and Cobb ("slavery is a protection from *pauperism,* the bane for which the wisdom of civilized man has not yet prepared an antidote" [ccxiv]).

15. Antislavery sentiment began early in Massachusetts, but no emancipation act was ever passed. Individual cases for freedom tended to be resolved in favor of the slave. In 1783, the judiciary used the 1780 state constitution to prohibit slavery, two years after Elizabeth Freeman successfully sued for her freedom under that document (Franklin 81 and Kaplan and Kaplan 245, but also see Higginbotham, *The Matter of Color* 91–99).

Chapter Seven

1. A Dutch ship traded twenty kidnapped Africans to colonists in Jamestown in 1619, the same year the House of Burgesses met and a year before the Mayflower landed at Plymouth. Notions of representative government and religious freedom in the "New World" emerged alongside practices of human enslavement.

2. A salient example is when Supreme Court nominee Clarence Thomas, accused of harassing Anita Hill, invoked the language of lynching in his defense: "As a black American, it is a high-tech lynching for uppity blacks who in any way deign to think for themselves, to do for themselves, to have different ideas, and it is a message that unless you kowtow to an old order, this is what will happen to you. You will be lynched, destroyed, caricatured by a committee of the U.S. Senate rather than hung from a tree" (qtd. in *Court of Appeal* 22). Conservative appointee Thomas reconstructs himself as the "uppity" one, and his use of the lynching image erases Hill's identity as an African American. Thomas

was remarkably successful at using the lynching metaphor without being countered effectively by any number of competing narratives. Crenshaw notes in particular the failure to point out "that allegations relating to the sexual abuse of black women have had nothing to do with the history of lynching, a tradition based upon white hysteria regarding black male access to white women" (Crenshaw, "Whose Story" 416). See Ida B. Wells's 1895 *A Red Record* for analysis of lynching and the constructions of race and gender invoked to justify this violence. See Carby, "On the Threshold," for discussion of Wells, and Painter's "Who Was Lynched?" for analysis of Thomas's use of the image.

3. Moynihan, a U.S. senator from 1977 to January 2001, continued to make use of his earlier "findings" throughout his political career. See, for example, his 1986 book *Family and Nation* and even his 1993 fund-raising letter, which quotes his 1965 findings as justification for his new welfare proposals. Legislators and journalists also keep Moynihan's thesis alive. See, for example, *The Vanishing Family: Crisis in Black America,* a 1986 television piece featuring Bill Moyers and labeled by Collins as "the film version" of Moynihan's report.

4. The quotations in *The Negro Family* are mainly from white male researchers and scholars. Very little of the testimony is from African American sources. The section on slavery, for example, focuses almost entirely on the findings of two white researchers (Nathan Glazer and Stanley Elkins), fails to incorporate the work of African American scholars, and fails to cite any words of slave testimony. The only extensive use of the work of an African American scholar is that of sociologist E. Franklin Frazier, who had died four years earlier. Many critics have argued that Moynihan appropriated and misused Frazier's work. For example, in "E. Franklin Frazier and Daniel Patrick Moynihan," Platt argues that in selectively quoting from Frazier's *The Negro in the United States,* Moynihan especially omitted Frazier's emphasis on economics: "It appears there was a calculated effort by Moynihan or his staff to find a well known black scholar to legitimate the Moynihan-Johnson viewpoint. Moynihan's motivations aside, his incomplete and selective use of Frazier's work violated the basic canons of research" (271).

5. One section of data focusing entirely on men features a full-page chart titled "ALMOST FOUR TIMES AS MANY NEGROES AS WHITES FAIL THE ARMED FORCES MENTAL TEST." "The ultimate mark of inadequate preparation for life," declares the report, "is the failure rate on the Armed Forces mental test" (*Negro Family* 40), which is visually represented in the chart. That African American men often fail this test is a particular tragedy, Moynihan argues, since the military would offer them "an utterly masculine world. Given the strains of the disorganized and matrifocal family life in which so many Negro youth come of age, the Armed Forces are a dramatic and desperately needed change: a world away from women" (42).

6. From unnumbered prefatory page. While Moynihan ultimately places blame on black matriarchy, he also uses rhetoric that places agency with the nation and constructs African Americans as passive objects. This preface closes with a quotation from Gunnar Myrdal: **"America is free to choose whether the Negro shall remain her liability or become her opportunity"** (boldface in original). In this configuration, America is the agent and is "free to choose" what kind of Negro it prefers.

7. Even before the section titled "Matriarchy" (one of the longest sections in the short report), some of the most dominant charts highlight the problem with women: "Percent of Women with Husbands Absent," "Almost One Fourth of Nonwhite Families Are Headed by a Woman," "Fertility Rates for Nonwhite Women Are One-Third Higher Than Those

for White Women." Numerous other charts map out the rates of "illegitimacy," a flaw linked here to female behavior.

8. Under the heading "Matriarchy" (a subsection of "The Tangle of Pathology"), a study is quoted as evidence: "Whereas the majority of white families are equalitarian, the largest percentage of Negro families are dominated by the wife" (31). Throughout the report, the pathology of (black) matriarchy is set against the norm of (white) patriarchy. An appropriately stable, patriarchal, yet "equalitarian" ideal is constructed for white America and helps to set off the constructed black family structure as abnormal, aberrant, and unstable. "Equalitarian" is neither defined nor supported, but it makes the hierarchy of patriarchy seem more palatable and makes the inversion of matriarchy seem more deviant, even undemocratic.

9. See Jacobs's references to the "Jim Crow car," riding a segregated train to New York, and facing segregated service in a hotel (162, 176). See also Truth's efforts to desegregate Washington, D.C., streetcars. In *Race Matters,* West refers to "Jim and Jane Crow" to emphasize that women are equally affected by racist policies.

10. Qtd. in Meehan, "Moynihan of the Moynihan Report," 48, from Moynihan's 1966 expansion of his report.

11. "But what is the 'condition' of the mother?" Spillers asks. "Is it the 'condition' of enslavement the writer means, or does he mean the 'mark' and the 'knowledge' of the *mother* upon the child that here translates into the culturally forbidden and impure?" (80). Jacobs's analysis of the law that "the child shall follow the condition of the mother" is discussed in chapter 6.

12. See Raymond, "Women as Wombs," which raises questions about the circumstances of these long-term trials and the effects on the women, particularly in Brazil.

13. See Axelson, "Women as Victims," as well as Sims, *The Story of My Life.*

14. See Jones, *Bad Blood.* Some of the doctors who worked on the experiment still insist that there was nothing unethical about it.

15. Skelton and Weintraub, "Most Support Norplant," A1. When asked about slipping from available to mandatory, Wilson said: "Frankly, we haven't decided." Wilson also has encouraged Norplant insertion for Aid to Families with Dependent Children (AFDC) recipients.

16. The second year Norplant was on the market, twenty measures were introduced in thirteen states calling for Norplant use on women convicted of certain crimes or on public assistance (Barnett 9). It is significant that "criminals" and "welfare mothers" are the two groups of women invoked. Local proposals have also surfaced, such as efforts to bring Norplant into particular schools with high birth rates. In addition to medical risks directly posed by Norplant, another potential danger of promoting Norplant as an "easy" contraceptive option is that it provides birth control without any protections against AIDS and other sexually transmitted diseases.

17. An "incentive" presumes choice but is potentially coercive, especially for women who need money. Also, many states (including California and Wisconsin) have considered proposals to deny additional AFDC benefits to women who have more babies. Perhaps the next step will be to require Norplant or another surgical method for all recipients. Coercive "incentives" have appeared in the private sector as well. Barbara Harris of Orange County, California, founded a private organization called Children Requiring a Caring Kommunity (CRACK). The group offers $200 cash to "drug addicted individuals who

volunteer for long term or permanent birth control." By the group's own statistics, a majority of their "volunteers" are women of color. Almost 40 percent are African American. Women seeking the cash incentive must "choose" permanent or long-term contraception, including Norplant, IUD, or tubal ligation (the program is open to men agreeing to vasectomies, but so far only women have taken part). CRACK's web page includes this explanation for readers, who are presumed to be part of the "us" that is fed up with the birth of crack babies and not part of the "them" having the babies: "Believe it or not, drug addicts are no different than the rest of us in a sense that they are also **motivated by money**" (boldface in original). The group explicitly focuses on the appeal of the cash incentive and does not emphasize drug treatment or other efforts to help the newly contracepted woman. See website at www.cracksterilization.com.

18. Low-income women are more likely to use public hospitals, for example, which are more likely than private doctors to be tied into a state's efforts to prosecute drug users or intervene in pregnancies. See Paltrow, *Overview of ACLU National Survey;* Kolata, "Racial Bias Seen"; and Roberts, *Killing the Black Body.*

19. See Roberts; Gallagher, "Prenatal Invasions and Interventions"; and Terry, "The Body Invaded," for discussion and analysis of particular cases.

20. "Feminists use the term 'maternal-fetal conflict' to describe the way in which law, social policies, and medical practices sometimes treat a pregnant woman's interests in opposition to those of the fetus she is carrying. . . . Some feminist scholars have refuted the maternal-fetal conflict by pointing to its relatively recent origin. . . . But the beating of pregnant slaves reveals that slave masters created just such a conflict between Black women and their unborn children to support their own economic interests" (Roberts 40–41). Citing a former slave's description of how a pregnant woman would be whipped with her stomach placed in a hole in the ground, Roberts writes, "It is the most striking metaphor I know for the evils of policies that seek to protect the fetus while disregarding the humanity of the mother" (41).

21. Roberts provides particularly powerful analysis of how criminal prosecution of crack-addicted mothers "shifts public attention from poverty, racism, and a deficient health care system, implying instead that poor infant health results from the depraved behavior of individual mothers. Poverty—not maternal drug use—is the major threat to the health of Black children in America" (179).

22. *People v. Johnson,* Motion to Modify Sentence, 10 Jan. 1991: 22. Subsequent parenthetical page references are to this transcript, referred to as T3, and to other transcripts from *People v. Johnson:* the Felony Plea, 3 Dec. 1990 (T1), and the Judgment Proceedings, 2 Jan. 1991 (T2).

23. Kerry Patrick, the legislator who introduced Norplant legislation in Kansas, did try to "prove" he was not a racist: "I have hardly lived the life of a racist. I became close friends of a black while attending [law school]. As a result . . . he and I . . . shared an apartment" (Patrick 11A).

24. The Women's Economic Agenda Project reports that some El Salvadoran women who were forced to use Norplant by their government "took pieces of glass and razors and cut it out themselves" (Barnett 9). Roberts cites similar examples in the U.S. (130–31).

25. Similarly downplaying the obstacles to removal, the *Philadelphia Inquirer* editorial stated that women encouraged to use Norplant "can change their minds at any point and *become fertile again*" ("Poverty and Norplant" 18A, emphasis added).

26. The *Inquirer* editorial also mentions government sterilization policies in order to dismiss any similarities. After suggesting cash incentives to encourage low-income women to be implanted, the editorial remarks in parentheses: "(This is not Indira Gandhi offering portable radios to women who agree to be sterilized)" ("Poverty and Norplant" 18A).

27. See Reilly, *The Surgical Solution,* for discussion of *Buck v. Bell* (1927) and *Skinner v. Oklahoma* (1942). Between 1907 and 1960, more than 60,000 people were sterilized in the U.S. without consent (2). Several states still permit "eugenic sterilization" in some form (148). In the case of a Nebraska woman who sued after she was committed to a state home and required to be sterilized to leave, the court wrote, in language similar to Broadman's: "The order does not require her sterilization. It does provide, in accordance with the statute, that she shall not be released unless she is sterilized. *The choice is hers*" (Reilly, *The Surgical Solution* 149, original emphasis).

28. See Roberts as well as Aptheker, "Sterilization, Experimentation, and Imperialism."

29. For example, the ways in which Johnson's crime and criminal status are defined affect the constructed "facts" about her. When Broadman asks Johnson for a reminder of her last conviction, she replies, "It was for credit card forgery," stating the offense. "That's being a thief in my mind," Broadman responds, "and here we're charged with bad parent" (*People v. Johnson* T1 3). Any number of factors might result in the act of forgery (needing money to feed one's family, for example), but the condition of being a thief is an identity, not a behavior question. Given this transformation, it follows to turn the crime of child abuse into the classification of being a bad parent, a broader denouncement calling for a broader range of penalties. It becomes easier to sentence Johnson to birth control if the focus is shifted from her crime of "Fel 273(d) injury" to her identity as "bad parent." The space for intervention becomes wider.

30. The dynamic here recalls the legal construction of slaves and free blacks without any capacity to make their own choices. *Bailey v. Poindexter* and *Bryan v. Walton* were discussed in chapter 5 and reveal the judicial anxiety around allowing African Americans to have a voice in their own fate.

31. All of the quotations from this study are drawn from Musham, Darr, and Strossner, "A Qualitative Study" (465–70). The study involved focus groups with women who were guaranteed confidentiality, so the women are not identified by name. All the women were low-income, and 60 percent were African American.

32. Thomas's comments are from a 1994 documentary, *Skin Deep,* qtd. in Roberts 104.

33. Again quoting from the *Inquirer* editorial, "The main reason more black children are living in poverty is that the people having the most children are the ones least capable of supporting them" ("Poverty and Norplant" 18A). Like Moynihan, the editorial seeks to tap into the desire to explain poverty through the behavior of the poor. Reproduction does not cause poverty, and such claims obfuscate the role of racism and other social and economic causes. Roberts provides particularly compelling analysis of this dynamic throughout her book.

34. See, for example, the rulings by Judges Lumpkin, Daniel, and Harris discussed in chapter 5.

35. In this particular arena, judicial authority outweighs other forms of authority. A separate document submitted to the court is an affidavit of Philip Darney, M.D., M.Sc.: three pages with a sixteen-page curriculum vitae. This particular witness, testifying on Johnson's behalf, struggles for an authorized voice. All his credentials, however, do not counteract The Court dismissing him as one of the nuclear scientists in World War II.

36. Earlier, Johnson's attorney had offered a supposedly more sympathetic metaphor, comparing the judge's ruling to "this movie that I saw when I was a kid, 'Invaders from Mars,' in which these aliens came down to earth and implanted these devices in the back of persons' necks and used that to control their activity" (T3). Of course, he is trying to make the ruling seem ludicrous by this comparison, but it is still interesting that his comparison also erases gender, as women become "persons" and white male judges become "aliens." Johnson's sentence is based on gender (a man could not fulfill the condition), yet both metaphors take gender out of the picture.

37. See, for example, Davis (particularly "Racism, Birth Control, and Reproductive Rights" in *Women, Race, and Class*), Roberts, Aptheker, and Reilly.

38. The lawmaker proposing the Kansas Norplant regulations provided dollar figures for money saved per "welfare mother" or "crack user" implanted (Patrick 11A). A 1975 eugenic sterilization law in West Virginia was defended as a "tax-saving measure" (Reilly 148).

39. I do not mean to diminish the valid and vital efforts for abortion rights. Until the 1960s and 1970s, birth control and abortion were still illegal in most of the U.S. Today, those choices are technically legal but often inaccessible, as a result of continuing legal restrictions (such as waiting periods or parental consent requirements), financial obstacles (the federal Hyde Amendment, for example, which bans public funding for most abortions), practical obstacles (such as the inability to find a provider in one's neighborhood or even in one's state), and safety concerns (stemming from factors such as abortion opponents who have occupied and even bombed or fired upon family planning clinics).

40. Roberts argues for a notion of reproductive freedom that prioritizes social justice and not just individual autonomy. "The abstract freedom to choose is of meager value without meaningful options from which to choose and the ability to effectuate one's choice" (309). She concludes that although African American women's struggles have been "left out of the official story of reproductive rights," it is precisely their story that "can lead to a more radical vision of reproductive justice" (312). Her analysis and the sheer amount of data that she amasses make a compelling case for rethinking familiar conceptions of reproductive liberty.

bibliography

Acts of South Carolina. An Act Respecting Slaves, Free Negroes, Mulattoes, and Mestizoes, for Inforcing the Punctual Performance of Patrol Duty, and to Impose Certain Restrictions on the Emancipation of Slaves. Dec. 1800. 36–41.

Adams, Nehemiah. *South-Side View of Slavery; or, Three Months at the South, in 1854.* 1854. New York: Negro UP, 1969.

Allen, Robert, and Pamela Allen. *Reluctant Reformers.* Washington, D.C.: Howard UP, 1974.

"American Woman Suffrage Association." *New York Tribune,* 12 May 1870: 2. In Suzanne Pullon Fitch and Roseann M. Mandziuk. *Sojourner Truth as Orator.* 174.

Ammons, Elizabeth. *Conflicting Stories: American Women Writers at the Turn into the Twentieth Century.* New York: Oxford UP, 1992.

Andolsen, Barbara Hilkert. *"Daughters of Jefferson, Daughters of Bootblacks": Racism and American Feminism.* Macon: Mercer UP, 1986.

Aptheker, Herbert. "Sterilization, Experimentation, and Imperialism." *Political Affairs* 53.1 (1974): 38–48.

Axelson, Diana E. "Women as Victims of Medical Experimentation: J. Marion Sims' Surgery on Slave Women, 1845–1850." *Sage* 2.4 (1985): 10–13.

Bailey v. Poindexter. 14 Gratton (Virginia) 132 (1858).

Bardaglio, Peter. *Reconstructing the Household: Families, Sex, and the Law in the Nineteenth-Century South.* Chapel Hill: U North Carolina P, 1995.

Barnett, Andrea. "Norplant: Welfare Reform through Birth Control." *Missoula Independent,* 29 Jan. 1993: 8–9.

Barrett, Lindon. "Self-Knowledge, Law, and African American Autobiography: Lucy A. Delaney's 'From the Darkness Cometh the Light.'" In *The Culture of Autobiography: Constructions of Self-Representation.* Ed. Robert Folkenflik. Stanford: Stanford UP, 1993. 104–24.

Bartlett, Katharine T., and Rosanne Kennedy, eds. *Feminist Legal Theory: Readings in Law and Gender.* Boulder: Westview, 1991.

Bassard, Katherine Clay. "Gender and Genre: Black Women's Autobiography and the Ideology of Literacy." *African American Review* 26.1 (1992): 119–29.

Berlant, Lauren. "The Queen of America Goes to Washington City: Harriet Jacobs, Frances Harper, Anita Hill." *American Literature* 65 (1993): 549.

Berry, Mary Frances. *The Pig Farmer's Daughter and Other Tales of American Justice : Episodes of Racism and Sexism in the Courts from 1865 to the Present.* New York: Knopf, 1999.

Birnbaum, Michele. "Dark Dialects: Scientific and Literary Realism in Joel Chandler Harris's *Uncle Remus* Series." *New Orleans Review* 18.1 (1991): 36–45.

Blassingame, John W. *The Slave Community: Plantation Life in the Ante-Bellum South.* New York: Oxford UP, 1972.

Bradwell v. Illinois. 83 U.S. 130 (1873).

Branan, Karen. "Lani Guinier: The Anatomy of a Betrayal." *Ms.* Sept./Oct. 1993: 50–57.

Braxton, Joanne. "Harriet Jacobs' *Incidents in the Life of a Slave Girl:* The Redefinition of the Slave Narrative Genre." *Massachusetts Review* 27 (1986): 379–87.

Brown, William Wells. *Clotel; or, The President's Daughter: A Narrative of Slave Life in the United States.* 1853. New York: Carol Publishing Group, 1995.

Bryan v. Walton. 14 Georgia 185 (1853).

Burnham, Margaret. "An Impossible Marriage: Slave Law and Family Law." *Law and Inequality: A Journal of Theory and Practice* 5 (1987): 187–225.

"Call Me Mister!" *Sixty Minutes.* CBS. 10 Jan. 1999.

Caraway, Nancie. *Segregated Sisterhood: Racism and the Politics of American Feminism.* Knoxville: U Tennessee P, 1991.

Carby, Hazel. *Reconstructing Womanhood: The Emergence of the Afro-American Woman Novelist.* New York: Oxford UP, 1987.

———. "'On the Threshold of Woman's Era': Lynching, Empire, and Sexuality in Black Feminist Theory." In Henry Louis Gates Jr. *Race, Writing, and Difference.* 301–16.

Catterall, Helen Tunnicliff, ed. *Judicial Cases Concerning American Slavery and the Negro.* 5 vols. New York: Octagon, 1926.

Chase-Riboud, Barbara. *Echo of Lions.* New York: Morrow, 1989.

Cobb, Thomas R. R. *An Inquiry into the Law of Negro Slavery in the United States of America.* 1858. New York: Negro UP, 1968.

Cole, Johnnetta. "Militant Black Women in Early U.S. History." *Black Scholar* April 1978: 38–44.

Collins, Kathleen. "Shadow and Substance: Sojourner Truth." *History of Photography* 7.3 (1983): 183–205.

Collins, Patricia Hill. *Black Feminist Thought: Knowledge, Consciousness, and the Politics of Empowerment.* New York: Routledge, 1991.

———. "A Comparison of Two Works on Black Family Life." *Signs* 14.4 (1989): 875–84.

"Colloquy: Racism in the Wake of the Los Angeles Riots." *Denver University Law Review* 70.2 (1993): 187–312.

The Concise History of Woman Suffrage: Selections from the Classic Works of Stanton, Anthony, Gage, and Harper. Ed. Mari Jo Buhle and Paul Buhle. Urbana: U Illinois P, 1978.

Conneau, Theophilus. *A Slaver's Log Book or 20 Years' Residence in Africa.* 1854. Englewood Cliffs, N.J.: Prentice-Hall, 1976.

Court of Appeal: The Black Community Speaks Out on the Racial and Sexual Politics of Thomas vs. Hill. Ed. Robert Chrisman and Robert Allen. New York: Ballantine, 1992.

Cover, Robert M. *Justice Accused: Antislavery and the Judicial Process.* New Haven: Yale UP, 1975.

Crenshaw, Kimberlé. "A Black Feminist Critique of Antidiscrimination Law and Politics." In *The Politics of Law: A Progressive Critique*. Ed. David Kairys. New York: Pantheon, 1990. 195–218.

———. "Demarginalizing the Intersection of Race and Sex: A Black Feminist Critique of Antidiscrimination Doctrine, Feminist Theory, and Antiracist Politics." *University of Chicago Legal Forum* 1989: 139–67.

———. "Whose Story Is It, Anyway? Feminist and Antiracist Appropriations of Anita Hill." In *Race-ing Justice, En-Gendering Power: Essays on Anita Hill, Clarence Thomas, and the Construction of Social Reality.* Ed. Toni Morrison. New York: Pantheon, 1992. 402–40.

Crenshaw, Kimberlé, et al., eds. *Critical Race Theory: The Key Writings That Formed the Movement.* New York: New Press, 1995.

Crenshaw, Kimberlé, and Gary Peller. "Reel Time/Real Justice." *Denver University Law Review* 70.2 (1993): 283–96.

Davis, Angela Y. *Women, Culture, and Politics.* New York: Random House, 1989.

———. *Women, Race, and Class.* New York: Vintage Books, 1983.

Davis, Charles T., and Henry Louis Gates Jr. *The Slave's Narrative.* New York: Oxford UP, 1985.

Davis, Peggy Cooper. *Neglected Stories: The Constitution and Family Values.* New York: Hill and Wang, 1998.

Deck, Alice. "Whose Book Is This? Authorial Versus Editorial Control of Harriet Brent Jacobs' *Incidents.*" *Women's Studies International Forum* 10 (1987): 33–40.

Delaney, Lucy. *From the Darkness Cometh the Light; or, Struggles for Freedom.* 1891. In *Six Women's Slave Narratives.* Ed. Henry Louis Gates Jr. New York: Oxford UP, 1988.

Delgado, Richard. "The Imperial Scholar." In Kimberlé Crenshaw et al., eds. *Critical Race Theory.* 46–57.

Dilanni, Denise. *Deadly Deception.* Videocassette. Films for the Humanities and Sciences, 1993.

Douglass, Frederick. *My Bondage and My Freedom.* 1855. Urbana: U Illinois P, 1987.

———. *The Narrative of the Life of Frederick Douglass, an American Slave, Written by Himself.* 1845. Boston: Bedford Books, 1993.

———. "What to the Slave Is the Fourth of July?" In Frederick Douglass. *My Bondage and My Freedom.* 284–87.

Du Bois, W. E. B. *The Souls of Black Folk.* 1903. New York: Bantam, 1989.

Elkins, Stanley. *Slavery: A Problem in American Institutional and Intellectual Life.* New York: Universal Library, 1963.

Emerson, Ralph Waldo. "The Fugitive Slave Law." In *The Complete Works of Ralph Waldo Emerson.* Ed. Edward Waldo Emerson. Centenary Edition. Boston: Houghton Mifflin, 1903–4.

Fauset, Arthur Huff. *Sojourner Truth: God's Faithful Pilgrim.* Chapel Hill: U North Carolina P, 1938.

Fetrow, Fred M. *Robert Hayden.* Boston: Twayne Publishers, 1984.

Fehrenbacher, Don E. *Slavery, Law, and Politics: The Dred Scott Case in Historical Perspective.* New York: Oxford UP, 1981.

Fern, Fanny. *Ruth Hall and Other Writings.* 1855. Ed. Joyce W. Warren. New Brunswick, N.J.: Rutgers UP, 1986.

Finkelman, Paul. *The Law of Freedom and Bondage: A Casebook.* New York: Oceana, 1986.
———. "*Prigg v. Pennsylvania* and Northern State Courts: Anti-Slavery Use of a Pro-Slavery Decision." *Civil War History* 25 (1979): 5–35.
"First Annual Meeting of the American Equal Rights Association." *National Anti-Slavery Standard,* 1 June 1867: 3. In Suzanne Pullon Fitch and Roseann M. Mandziuk. *Sojourner Truth as Orator.* 127–28.
Fitch, Suzanne Pullon, and Roseann M. Mandziuk. *Sojourner Truth as Orator: Wit, Story, and Song.* Westport, Conn.: Greenwood Press, 1997.
Fitzhugh, George. *Sociology for the South; or, The Failure of Free Society.* New York: Franklin, 1854.
Foote, Julia. *A Brand Plucked from the Fire: An Autobiographical Sketch.* 1879. In *Sisters of the Spirit.* Ed. William L. Andrews. Bloomington: Indiana UP, 1986.
Foster, Frances Smith. "Harriet Jacobs's *Incidents* and the 'Careless Daughters' (and Sons) Who Read It." In *The (Other) American Traditions: Nineteenth-Century Women Writers.* Ed. Joyce Warren. New Brunswick, N.J.: Rutgers UP, 1993. 92–107.
———. "Resisting *Incidents.*" In *Harriet Jacobs and Incidents in the Life of a Slave Girl.* Ed. Deborah M. Garfield and Rafia Zafar. New York: Cambridge UP, 1996. 57–75.
———. "Ultimate Victims: Black Women in Slave Narratives." *Journal of American Culture* 1 (1978): 845–54.
———. *Witnessing Slavery: The Development of Ante-bellum Slave Narratives.* Westport, Conn.: Greenwood Press, 1979.
———. *Written by Herself: Literary Production by African American Women, 1746–1892.* Bloomington: Indiana UP, 1993.
Franklin, John Hope. *From Slavery to Freedom: A History of African Americans.* New York: Alfred A. Knopf, 1994.
Frazier, E. Franklin. *The Negro in the United States.* New York: Macmillan, 1949.
Fredrickson, George M. *The Black Image in the White Mind: The Debate on Afro-American Character and Destiny, 1817–1914.* Hanover, N.H.: Wesleyan UP, 1971.
Gage, Frances. "Sojourner Truth." *National Anti-Slavery Standard,* 2 May 1863: 4.
Gallagher, Janet. "Prenatal Invasions and Interventions: What's Wrong with Fetal Rights." *Harvard Women's Law Journal* 10 (1987): 9–58.
Gates, Henry Louis Jr. "Writing 'Race' and the Difference It Makes." In Henry Louis Gates Jr., ed. *Race, Writing and Difference.* 1–20.
———, ed. *Race, Writing, and Difference.* Chicago: U Chicago P, 1985.
Gates, Henry Louis Jr., and Nellie McKay. "Talking Books." Preface to *The Norton Anthology of African American Literature.* New York: Norton, 1997. xxvii–xli.
George (a Slave) v. State. 37 Mississippi 316 (1859).
Gilbert, Sandra, and Susan Gubar, eds. *The Norton Anthology of Literature by Women: The Tradition in English.* New York: Norton, 1996.
Ginsburg, Carl. *Race and Media: The Enduring Life of the Moynihan Report.* New York: Institute for Media Analysis, 1989.
Glazer, Nathan, and Daniel Patrick Moynihan. *Beyond the Melting Pot: The Negroes, Puerto Ricans, Jews, Italians, and Irish of New York City.* Cambridge: MIT, 1970.
Goodell, William. *The American Slave Code in Theory and Practice: Its Distinctive Features Shown by Its Statutes, Judicial Decisions, and Illustrative Facts.* 1853. New York: Negro UP, 1968.

Gotanda, Neil. "A Critique of 'Our Constitution Is Color-Blind.'" In Kimberlé Crenshaw et al., eds. *Critical Race Theory.* 257–75.

Greenberg, Kenneth S., ed. *The Confessions of Nat Turner and Related Documents.* 1831. Boston: Bedford Books, 1996.

Grossberg, Michael. *Governing the Hearth: Law and Family in Nineteenth-Century America.* Chapel Hill: U North Carolina P, 1985.

Gutman, Herbert. *Slavery and the Numbers Game: A Critique of Time on the Cross.* Chicago: U Illinois P, 1975.

Gwin, Minrose. *Black and White Women in the Old South: The Peculiar Sisterhood in American Literature.* Knoxville: U Tennessee P, 1985.

Hamilton, Virginia. *Anthony Burns: The Defeat and Triumph of a Fugitive Slave.* New York: Knopf, 1988.

Hammon, Jupiter. "An Address to Miss Phillis Wheatly." In Sidney Kaplan and Emma Nograndy Kaplan. *The Black Presence in the Era of the American Revolution.* 195.

Haraway, Donna. "Ecce Homo, Ain't (Ar'n't) I a Woman, and Inappropriate/d Others: The Human in a Post-Humanist Landscape." In *Feminists Theorize the Political.* Ed. Judith Butler and Joan W. Scott. New York: Routledge, 1992. 86–100.

Harlowe, Marie. "Sojourner Truth: The First Sit-In." *Negro History Bulletin* 29.4 (1966): 173.

Harris, Angela P. "Race and Essentialism in Feminist Legal Theory." In Katharine T. Bartlett and Rosanne Kennedy, eds. *Feminist Legal Theory: Readings in Law and Gender.* 235–62.

Hatcher, John. *From the Auroral Darkness: The Life and Poetry of Robert Hayden.* Oxford: George Ronald, 1984

Hayden, Robert. *Collected Poems.* Ed. Frederick Glaysher. New York: Liveright, 1985.

Henderson, Mae Gwendolyn. "Speaking in Tongues: Dialogics, Dialectics, and the Black Woman Writer's Literary Tradition." In *Feminists Theorize the Political.* Ed. Judith Butler and Joan W. Scott. New York: Routledge, 1992. 144–66.

Higginbotham, A. Leon, Jr. *The Matter of Color: Race and the American Legal Process: The Colonial Period.* New York: Oxford UP, 1978.

———. *Shades of Freedom: Racial Politics and the Presumptions of the American Legal Process.* New York: Oxford UP, 1996.

Higginbotham, A. Leon, Jr., and Barbara K. Kopytoff. "Racial Purity and Interracial Sex in the Law of Colonial and Antebellum Virginia." *Georgetown Law Journal* 77 (1989): 1967–2029.

Hine, Darlene Clark, ed. *Black Women in American History: From Colonial Times through the Nineteenth Century.* Brooklyn, N.Y.: Carlson, 1990.

Hill, Robert, et al. *Research on the African-American Family: A Holistic Perspective.* Westport, Conn.: Auburn, 1993.

hooks, bell. *Ain't I a Woman: Black Women and Feminism.* Boston: South End, 1981.

———. "Feminist Scholarship: Ethical Issues." In *Talking Back: Thinking Feminist, Thinking Black.* Boston: South End Press, 1989. 42–48.

———. "Reflections on Race and Sex." In *Yearning: Race, Gender, and Cultural Politics.* Boston: South End Press, 1990. 57–64.

Hull, Gloria T., Patricia Bell Scott, and Barbara Smith, eds. *All the Women Are White, All the Blacks Are Men, but Some of Us Are Brave: Black Women's Studies.* Old Westbury, N.Y.: Feminist Press, 1982.

Hyde, Henry. *The Collegiate Speech Protection Act Briefing Paper.* Washington, D.C., 1991.

Ingraham, Edward. Letter to George Livermore. 11 Jan. 1850. Library of Congress, Washington, D.C.

Jacobs, Harriet A. *Incidents in the Life of a Slave Girl, Written by Herself.* 1861. Ed. Jean Fagan Yellin. Cambridge: Harvard UP, 1987.

James, Henry. *William Wetmore Story and His Friends.* 2 vols. Boston: Houghton Mifflin, 1903.

Jaynes, Gregory. "Suit on Race Recalls Lines Drawn Under Slavery." *New York Times,* 30 Sept. 1982: B16.

Jed, Stephanie. "Sixteenth-Century Scholars as Agents of Conquest: New World Objects and the Politics of F-acts." Paper delivered to the Semiotic Society of America. October 1991.

Johnsen, Dawn E. "The Creation of Fetal Rights: Conflicts with Women's Constitutional Rights to Liberty, Privacy, and Equal Protection." *Yale Law Journal* 95 (1986): 599–625.

Johnson, James Hugo. *Race Relations in Virginia and Miscegenation in the South, 1776–1860.* Amherst: U Massachusetts P, 1970.

Jones, James. *Bad Blood.* New York: Free Press, 1981.

Jordan, June. "The Difficult Miracle of Black Poetry in America; or, Something like a Sonnet for Phillis Wheatley." *Massachusetts Review* summer 1986: 252–62.

Kaplan, Sidney, and Emma Nograndy Kaplan. *The Black Presence in the Era of the American Revolution.* Amherst: U Massachusetts P, 1989.

Kerber, Linda. "Separate Spheres, Female Worlds, Woman's Place: The Rhetoric of Women's History." *Journal of American History* 75.6 (1988): 9–39.

Kohrs, Karlyn. "Style and Content in the Rhetoric of Early Afro-American Feminists." *Quarterly Journal of Speech* 72 (1986): 444.

Kolata, Gina. "Racial Bias Seen in Prosecuting Pregnant Addicts." *New York Times,* 20 July 1990: A13.

Kolder, Veronika, Janet Gallagher, and M. T. Parson. "Court-Ordered Obstetrical Interventions." *New England Journal of Medicine* 316 (1987): 1192–96.

Kondracke, Morton. "The Two Black Americas: A Regress Report." *New Republic,* 6 Feb. 1989: 18.

Kulman, Linda. "The Storm over a Statue." *US News and World Report,* 30 June 1997: 11.

Lauter, Paul, et al., eds. *The Heath Anthology of American Literature.* Vol. 1. Lexington, Ky.: Heath, 1990.

Laws of New York. An Act Relative to Slaves and Servants. 31 Mar. 1817. Chap. 137: 136–44.

Lebedun, Jean. "Harriet Beecher Stowe's Interest in Sojourner Truth, Black Feminist." *American Literature* 13 (1974): 359–63.

Lebsock, Suzanne. "Free Black Women and the Question of Matriarchy: Petersburg, Virginia, 1784–1820." *Feminist Studies* 8 (1982): 277–98.

"Lecture by Sojourner Truth." *New York Tribune,* 8 Nov. 1853: 6. In Suzanne Pullon Fitch and Roseann M. Mandziuk. *Sojourner Truth as Orator.* 155–56.

Lerner, Gerda, ed. *Black Women in White America: A Documentary History.* New York: Vintage, 1992.

Levernier, James A. "Wheatley's 'On Being Brought from Africa to America.'" *Explicator* 40.1 (fall 1981): 25–26.

Lombardo, Paul. "Miscegenation, Eugenics, and Racism: Historical Footnotes to *Loving v. Virginia.*" *UC Davis Law Review* 21 (1988): 421–52.

Lorde, Audre. "Age, Race, Class, and Sex: Women Redefining Difference." In *Sister Outsider: Essays and Speeches by Audre Lorde.* Freedom, Calif.: Crossing Press Feminist Series, 1984. 114–23.

Love, Dorothy. *A Salute to Historic Black Women.* Chicago: Empak, 1984.

Mabee, Carleton. "Sojourner Truth and President Lincoln." *New England Quarterly* 61.4 (1988): 519–29.

Mabee, Carleton, with Susan Mabee Newhouse. *Sojourner Truth: Slave, Prophet, Legend.* New York: New York UP, 1993.

McCall, Laura. "'The Reign of Brute Force Is Now Over': A Content Analysis of *Godey's Lady's Book,* 1830–1860." *Journal of the Early Republic* 9.3 (1989): 217–36.

McCash, William. *Thomas R. R. Cobb: The Making of a Southern Nationalist.* Macon: Mercer UP, 1983.

McKitrick, Eric L., ed. *Slavery Defended: The Views of the Old South.* Englewood Cliffs, N.J.: Prentice-Hall, 1963.

McLaurin, Melton A. *Celia, a Slave: A True Story.* New York: Avon, 1991.

McMillen, Liz. "A Slave Girl's Authentic Life." *Chronicle of Higher Education,* 8 Dec. 1993: A9, A15.

Maier, Pauline. "A Marketplace of Human Souls." Review of *American Slavery, 1619–1877,* by Peter Kolchin. *New York Times Book Review,* 5 Sept. 1993: 9–10.

Matsuda, Mari. "Looking to the Bottom: Critical Legal Studies and Reparations." In Kimberlé Crenshaw et al., eds. *Critical Race Theory.* 63–79.

———. *Where Is Your Body? and Other Essays on Race, Gender and the Law.* Boston: Beacon Press, 1996.

Meehan, Thomas. "Moynihan of the Moynihan Report." *New York Times Magazine,* 31 July 1966: 48.

Melville, Herman. *Benito Cereno.* In *The Piazza Tales and Other Prose Pieces, 1839–1860.* Ed. Harrison Hayford, Alma A. MacDougall, and G. Thomas Tanselle. Chicago: Northwestern UP, 1987. 46–117.

Minow, Martha. *Making All the Difference: Inclusion, Exclusion, and American Law.* Ithaca, N.Y.: Cornell UP, 1990.

Mitchell v. Wells. 37 Mississippi 235 (1859).

Montgomery, Janey Weinhold. *A Comparative Analysis of the Rhetoric of Two Negro Women Orators—Sojourner Truth and Frances E. Watkins Harper.* Hays: Fort Hays Kansas State College, 1968.

Moynihan, Daniel Patrick. *Family and Nation: The Godkin Lectures.* San Diego: Harcourt Brace Jovanovich, 1986.

———. Fund-raising letter. Oct. 1993.

Musham, Catherine, Eva G. Darr, and Mary L. Strossner. "A Qualitative Study of the Perceptions of Dissatisfied Norplant Users." *Journal of Family Practice* 40 (1995): 465–70.

Native American Women's Health Education Resource Center. "Native American Women Uncover Norplant Abuses." *Ms.* Sept./Oct. 1993: 69.

The Negro Family: The Case for National Action. United States Department of Labor. Office of Policy Planning and Research. Washington, D.C.: GPO, 1965.

Nelson, Dana D. "Naked Nature: Science and the Substantiation of Scientific Masculinity in 19th-Century America." Paper delivered at the Modern Language Association conference, 29 Dec. 1993.

——. *The Word in Black and White: Reading "Race" in American Literature.* New York: Oxford UP, 1992.

Nichols, William W. "Slave Narratives: Dismissed Evidence in the Writings of Southern History." *Phylon* 32.4 (1971): 403–9.

Northup, Solomon. *Twelve Years a Slave.* 1853. Ed. Sue Eakin and Joseph Logsdon. Baton Rouge: Louisiana State UP, 1975.

Painter, Nell Irvin. *Sojourner Truth: A Life, a Symbol.* New York: Norton, 1996.

——. "Sojourner Truth in Life and Memory: Writing the Biography of an American Exotic." *Gender and History* 2.1 (1990): 3–16.

——. "Who Was Lynched?" *Nation,* 11 Nov. 1991: 577.

Paltrow, Linda. *Overview of ACLU National Survey.* 30 Oct. 1990. Distributed by ACLU.

Patrick, Kerry. "Poor Women Benefit by Linking Norplant, Welfare Aid." *Wichita Eagle,* 4 Mar. 1991: 11A.

Pauli, Hertha. *Her Name Was Sojourner Truth.* New York: Avon Books, 1962.

People v. Johnson. Felony Plea. California Superior Court, 3 Dec. 1990.

People v. Johnson. Judgment Proceedings. California Superior Court, 2 Jan. 1991.

People v. Johnson. Motion to Modify Sentence. California Superior Court, 10 Jan. 1991.

Platt, Tony. "E. Franklin Frazier and Daniel Patrick Moynihan: Setting the Record Straight." *Contemporary Crises* 11 (1987): 265–77.

Pollard, Edward A. *Black Diamonds Gathered in the Darkey Homes of the South.* 1859. New York: Negro UP, 1968.

"Poverty and Norplant: Can Contraception Reduce the Underclass?" Editorial. *Philadelphia Inquirer,* 12 Dec. 1990: 18A.

Priest, Josiah. *Bible Defence of Slavery; or, The Origin, History, and Fortunes of the Negro Race.* Glasgow, Ky.: Rev. W. S. Brown, 1853.

Pryse, Marjorie, and Hortense Spillers, eds. *Conjuring: Black Women, Fiction, and Literary Tradition.* Bloomington: Indiana UP, 1985.

Public Laws of South Carolina. An Act for the Better Ordering and Governing Negroes and Other Slaves in This Province. 10 May 1740. Chap. 5: Sec. 37. 163–75.

Raymond, Janice. "Women as Wombs: International Traffic in Reproduction." *Ms.* 1.6 (1991): 28–33.

Reilly, Philip. *The Surgical Solution: A History of Involuntary Sterilization in the United States.* Baltimore: Johns Hopkins UP, 1991.

The Revised Statutes of North Carolina, Passed by the General Assembly at the Session of 1836–37. Raleigh: Turner and Hughes, 1837.

Riggs, Marlon. *Ethnic Notions.* Videocassette. California Newsreel, 1987.

Ripley, C. Peter, ed. *The Black Abolitionist Papers.* Chapel Hill: U North Carolina P, 1991.

Roberts, Dorothy. *Killing the Black Body: Race, Reproduction, and the Meaning of Liberty.* New York: Vintage, 1997.

Rosenberg, Rosalind. *Beyond Separate Spheres: Intellectual Roots of Modern Feminism.* New Haven: Yale UP, 1982.

Russell, Michele. "Slave Codes and Liner Notes." In Gloria T. Hull, Patricia Bell Scott, and Barbara Smith, eds. *All the Women Are White.* 129–41.

Ryan, William. *Blaming the Victim.* New York: Vintage Books, 1976.

Sale, Maggie Montesinos. *The Slumbering Volcano: American Slave Revolts and the Production of Rebellious Masculinity.* Durham, N.C.: Duke UP, 1997.

Sanchez-Eppler, Karen. *Touching Liberty: Abolition, Feminism, and the Politics of the Body.* Berkeley: U California P, 1993.

Schafer, Judith. "'Open and Notorious Concubinage': The Emancipation of Slave Mistresses by Will and the Supreme Court in Antebellum Louisiana." *Louisiana History* 28 (1987): 165–82.

Scott v. Sandford. 60 U.S. 393 (1857).

Sims, J. Marion. *The Story of My Life.* 1884. New York: Da Capo Press, 1968.

Skelton, George, and Daniel Weintraub. "Most Support Norplant for Teens, Drug Addicts." *Los Angeles Times,* 27 May 1991: A1.

"Slavery." *Columbia Dictionary of Quotations.* CD-ROM. New York: Columbia UP, 1993.

Smith, Dorothy. *Texts, Facts, and Femininity: Exploring the Relations of Ruling.* New York: Routledge, 1990.

Smith, Venture. *A Narrative of the Life and Adventures of Venture, a Native of Africa.* 1798. In *Early Negro Writing: 1760–1837.* Ed. Dorothy Porter. Baltimore: Black Classic Press, 1995. 538–58.

Smothers, Ronald. "Principal Causes Furor on Mixed-Race Couples." *New York Times,* 16 March 1994: A10.

Spelman, Elizabeth V. *Inessential Woman: Problems of Exclusion in Feminist Thought.* Boston: Beacon Press, 1988.

Spielberg, Steven, dir. *Amistad.* Motion picture. Dreamworks, 1997.

Spillers, Hortense. "Mama's Baby, Papa's Maybe: An American Grammar Book." *Diacritics* 13:3 (1987): 65–81.

Stampp, Kenneth. *The Peculiar Institution: Slavery in the Ante-Bellum South.* New York: Knopf, 1972.

Stanton, Elizabeth Cady, Susan B. Anthony, and Matilda Joslyn Gage, eds. *History of Woman Suffrage.* Vols. 1–3. 1882. New York: Arno and the New York Times, 1969.

Starling, Marion Wilson. *The Slave Narrative: Its Place in American History.* Boston: G. K. Hall, 1981.

Stepto, Robert. *From Behind the Veil: A Study of Afro-American Narrative.* Urbana: U of Illinois P, 1979.

Sterling, Dorothy. *We Are Your Sisters: Black Women in the Nineteenth Century.* New York: Norton, 1984.

Stetson, Erlene, and Linda David. *Glorying in Tribulation: The Lifework of Sojourner Truth.* East Lansing: Michigan State UP, 1994.

Steven (a Slave) v. State. 11 Georgia 225 (1852).

Stewart, Jeffrey. Introduction to *Narrative of Sojourner Truth,* by Sojourner Truth and Olive Gilbert. xxxiii–xlvii.

Stone, Lucy, and Henry B. Blackwell. "Marriage of Lucy Stone under Protest." In *Feminism: The Essential Historical Writings.* Ed. Miriam Schneir. New York: Vintage Books, 1972. 104–5.

Stowe, Harriet Beecher. "Sojourner Truth, the Libyan Sibyl." *Atlantic Monthly* April 1863: 473–81.

———. *A Key to Uncle Tom's Cabin.* 1853. Port Washington, N.Y.: Kennikat Press, 1968.

———. *Uncle Tom's Cabin; or, Life among the Lowly.* 1852. New York: Penguin, 1988.

Stroud, George M. *A Sketch of the Laws Relating to Slavery.* 1856. New York: Negro Universities Press, 1968.

Stuckey, Sterling. *Going Through the Storm: The Influence of African American Art in History.* New York: Oxford UP, 1994.

Styron, William. *Confessions of Nat Turner.* New York: Random House, 1967.

Sundquist, Eric. *To Wake the Nations.* Cambridge: Harvard UP, 1993.

Taub, Nadine, and Elizabeth M. Schneider. "Women's Subordination and the Role of Law." In *The Politics of Law: A Progressive Critique.* Ed. David Kairys. New York: Pantheon Books, 1990. 151–76.

Terborg-Penn, Rosalyn. *African American Women in the Struggle for the Vote, 1850–1920.* Bloomington: Indiana UP: 1998.

———. *Afro-Americans in the Struggle for Woman Suffrage.* Ph.D. diss. Howard U, 1977. Ann Arbor: UMI, 1978. 78–5447.

———. "Discrimination Against Afro-American Women in the Woman's Movement, 1830–1920." In *The Afro-American Woman: Struggles and Images.* Ed. Sharon Harley and Rosalyn Terborg-Penn. Port Washington, N.Y.: Kennikat Press, 1978.

Terry, Jennifer. "The Body Invaded: Medical Surveillance of Women as Reproducers." *Socialist Review* July/Sept. 1989: 13–44.

Thomas, Brook. *Cross-Examinations of Law and Literature: Cooper, Hawthorne, Stowe, and Melville.* Cambridge: Cambridge UP, 1988.

Thoreau, Henry David. *Reform Papers.* Ed. Wendell Glick. Princeton: Princeton UP, 1973.

Truth, Sojourner, and Olive Gilbert. *Narrative of Sojourner Truth; A Bondswoman of Olden Time, with a History of Her Labors and Correspondences Drawn from Her "Book of Life."* 1878. Reprinted with an introduction by Jeffrey Stewart. New York: Oxford UP, 1991.

Tushnet, Mark. *The American Law of Slavery, 1810–1860: Considerations of Humanity and Interest.* Princeton: Princeton UP, 1981.

United States v. Amistad. 40 U.S. 518 (1841).

U.S. v. Vaughn. Washington, D.C., Superior Court, 1988.

Vale, Gilbert. *Fanaticism; Its Sources and Influence, Illustrated by the Simple Narrative of Isabella, in the case of Matthias, Mr. and Mrs. B. Folger, Mr. Pierson, Mr. Mills, Catherine, Isabella, &c. &c.* New York: Published by G. Vale, 1835.

The Vanishing Family: Crisis in Black America. Dir. Ruth Streeter. Reporter Bill Moyers. Videocassette. Carousel Film and Video, 1986.

Virgil. *The Aeneid.* Trans. Robert Fitzgerald. New York: Vintage, 1981.

Walker, Alice. "In Search of Our Mothers' Gardens." In *In Search of Our Mothers' Gardens: Womanist Prose.* New York: Harcourt Brace, 1983. 231–43.

Walker, Barbara. *The Woman's Dictionary of Symbols and Sacred Objects.* San Francisco: Harper, 1988.

Walker, David. *Appeal, in Four Articles, Together with a Preamble, to the Coloured Citizens of the World, but in Particular, and Very Expressly, to Those of the United States of America.* 1929. New York: Hill and Wang, 1995.

Washington, Margaret, ed. *Narrative of Sojourner Truth.* New York: Vintage Books, 1993.

Washington, Mary Helen. *Invented Lives: Narratives of Black Women, 1860–1960.* Garden City, N.Y.: Anchor, 1987.

Wells Barnett, Ida B. *Crusade for Justice: The Autobiography of Ida B. Wells.* Ed. Alfreda Duster. Chicago: U Chicago P, 1970.

————. *A Red Record: Tabulated Statistics and Alleged Causes of Lynchings in the United States.* 1895. In *Southern Horrors and Other Writings: The Anti-Lynching Campaign of Ida B. Wells, 1892–1900.* Ed. Jacqueline Jones Royster. Boston: Bedford Books, 1997. 73–157.

Welter, Barbara. "The Cult of True Womanhood, 1820–1860." *American Quarterly* 18.3 (1966): 151–74.

Wertz, Richard W., and Dorothy C. Wertz. *Lying-In: A History of Childbirth in America.* New Haven: Yale UP, 1989.

West, Cornel. *Race Matters.* Boston: Beacon Press, 1993.

Wheatley, Phillis. *The Collected Works of Phillis Wheatley.* Ed. John Shields. New York: Oxford UP, 1988.

White, Deborah Gray. *Ar'n't I a Woman? Female Slaves in the Plantation South.* New York: Norton, 1985.

Whittier, John Greenleaf. *The Complete Poetical Works of Whittier.* Boston: Houghton Mifflin, 1894.

Williams, Patricia. *The Alchemy of Race and Rights.* Cambridge: Harvard UP, 1991.

"Woman's Rights Convention." *New York Daily Times,* 8 Sept. 1853: 1. In Suzanne Pullon Fitch and Roseann M. Mandziuk. *Sojourner Truth as Orator.* 113–14.

"Women's Rights Convention." *Anti-Slavery Bugle* [Salem, OH] 21 June 1851: 4. In Suzanne Pullon Fitch and Roseann M. Mandziuk. *Sojourner Truth as Orator.* 107–8.

Wood, Peter H. "Nat Turner: The Unknown Slave as Visionary Leader." In *Black Leaders of the Nineteenth Century.* Chicago: U Illinois P, 1988. 21–40.

Woodward, C. Vann. *The Strange Career of Jim Crow.* New York: Oxford UP, 1966.

Yellin, Jean Fagan. *Women and Sisters: The Antislavery Feminists in American Culture.* New Haven: Yale UP, 1989.

Yellin, Jean Fagan, and Cynthia D. Bond, eds. *The Pen Is Ours: A Listing of Writings by and about African-American Women Before 1910.* New York: Oxford UP, 1991.

Zilversmit, Arthur. *The First Emancipation: The Abolition of Slavery in the North.* Chicago: U Chicago P, 1967.

index